ISBN 978-0-243-88975-4
PIBN 10804857

This book is a reproduction of an important historical work. Forgotten Books uses
state-of-the-art technology to digitally reconstruct the work, preserving the original format
whilst repairing imperfections present in the aged copy. In rare cases, an imperfection in
the original, such as a blemish or missing page, may be replicated in our edition. We do,
however, repair the vast majority of imperfections successfully; any imperfections that
remain are intentionally left to preserve the state of such historical works.

1 MONTH OF
FREE
READING

at
www.ForgottenBooks.com

By purchasing this book you are eligible for one month membership to ForgottenBooks.com, giving you unlimited access to our entire collection of over 700,000 titles via our web site and mobile apps.

To claim your free month visit:
www.forgottenbooks.com/free804857

English
Français
Deutsche
Italiano
Español
Português

www.forgottenbooks.com

Mythology Photography **Fiction**
Fishing Christianity **Art** Cooking
Essays Buddhism Freemasonry
Medicine **Biology** Music **Ancient**
Egypt Evolution Carpentry Physics
Dance Geology **Mathematics** Fitness
Shakespeare **Folklore** Yoga Marketing
Confidence Immortality Biographies
Poetry **Psychology** Witchcraft
Electronics Chemistry History **Law**
Accounting **Philosophy** Anthropology
Alchemy Drama Quantum Mechanics
Atheism Sexual Health **Ancient History**
Entrepreneurship Languages Sport
Paleontology Needlework Islam
Metaphysics Investment Archaeology
Parenting Statistics Criminology
Motivational

DISCOURSE I.

GENESIS II. 1—3.

" *Thus the heavens and the earth were finished, and all the host of them. And on the seventh day God ended his work which he had made; and he rested on the seventh day from all his work which he had made. And God blessed the seventh day, and sanctified it; because that in it he had rested from all his work which God created and made.*"

SEVERAL successive meetings have been recently held in this city, by a number of ministers of the gospel and other Christians, for the purpose of conversing on the subject of the profanation of the Sabbath, and of consulting as to the most eligible means of counteracting the progress of this growing evil. I shall not trouble you with any detail of the various proposals suggested, and partially or wholly adopted, on these occasions. The one only needs to be mentioned, in fulfilment of which I now address you. It was resolved, that the ministers of Christ, of all denominations, in the city and neighbourhood, should be requested to call the attention of their respective congregations to the subject simultaneously; so as, if possible, by the very fact of their bearing a concurrent testimony respecting it, by previous agreement, upon the same day,

B

a general impulse might be given to the public mind, and a feeling excited, congenial with their own, at once of regret for the spreading mischief, and of solicitude for the proper application of the needful remedies. What these should be, belongs to a future part of the discussion, which I shall not now anticipate. For it is not my intention to confine myself to a single discourse, and that discourse restricted to the one topic of Sabbath profanation. I mean to enter pretty largely, in a series of Sermons, into the general subject of the obligation and observance of the weekly sabbatical rest. It would be preposterous, to go at once to the consideration of the mode of observing the day, till we have satisfactorily ascertained the scriptural authority for observing it at all. This authority I do not wish to assume; because it has been disputed; and because I have never been fully satisfied with the grounds on which the obligation, under the Christian economy, has usually been made to rest. Not that these grounds are either untenable, or insufficient; but that, in my apprehension, there are additional grounds, still stronger and more direct, which, though they have been adverted to by some advocates of the Christian Sabbath, have been overlooked by others, and have by none had that degree of weight attached to them, to which they seem to be entitled.

In saying this, I should wish to be understood as referring both to the obligation of the day, and to the manner of its observance. On both points, it is of essential importance to ascertain scriptural principles. Our rebukes of Sabbath-profanation can come with comparatively feeble power and partial effect upon the conscience, when we have left unsettled questions and unsatisfied doubts and surmises in the mind, with regard to the obligation of observance :—and even when we may be supposed to have settled the obligation on sufficient grounds; we may find it exceedingly difficult to draw a correct line between observance and profanation in various departments of our admonitions to duty and cautions against sin,—and shall be in danger of leaving, on the one hand, sources of superstitious and gloomy fearfulness, and, on the other, jesuitical excuses for laxity of disposition, and convenient outlets for consciences that are beset by worldly temptations, —unless we can, either from direct precepts or from approved examples, establish some general principle or principles, capable of extensive and easy application to particular cases.

It is a point of fact disputed by none, that the seventhday Sabbath was observed by the Jewish people, under the ancient economy; and by none who believe that economy to have been divine is it doubted, that amongst them it was not a self-authorized celebration, but an institute of Jehovah. One great question, therefore, is— Was it peculiar to that people, or was it, in its origin and obligation, common to mankind? Did the observance commence with the divine legation of Moses, or did it commence at the time referred to in our text? Did the obligation terminate with the Mosaic economy, or did it remain in force under the Christian? And, if we should ascertain it to have begun at creation, and to have continued under Christianity, what authority have we for observing, as our sabbatical rest, the first day of the week, instead of the seventh? These are questions, to which a satisfactory answer is indispensable, before we proceed to the subsequent inquiry, " How is the Sabbath to be sanctified?" that we may be properly assured in our own minds, whether, in keeping sacred the first day of the week, we are really doing the will of God, or whether we are performing an act of mere will-worship, and, without the sanction of his authority, retaining a part of the yoke of bondage, the burdensome ritual of an abolished dispensation.

When I ask the question, *Was the Sabbath a merely Jewish Institution, or was it a moral duty of universal and permanent obligation?*—some of my hearers may naturally enough be startled at the inquiry, and think it a very strange one. " A merely Jewish Institution!" they will say—" how can that be? who can possibly entertain such a fancy, when, in the words which you have just read as the ground of your discourse, we have so simple and explicit a statement of the day having been divinely set apart at the time of the creation of the world?" For the surprise which might thus be expressed, there exists, in my judgment, very good reason. The conclusion drawn from the language of the text—(if that may be called a conclusion from it, which is rather its direct and explicit declaration)—is the conclusion, not of ignorance or inconsideration, but, in spite of the high authority I am about to cite to the contrary, that of sound understanding and common sense. To those of my hearers in whose minds the text has appeared, as well it might, decisive of the question, it is necessary to mention, that in the opinion of some writers, later and more remote, and especially of one scripture moralist, whose judgment is, in many respects, entitled to deference, the seventh day was *not* set apart for sacred observance at the time of the creation;—that there was no such divine institute till the departure of the Israelites from Egypt, two thousand five hundred years afterwards; and that the historian, himself an Israelite, in giving the inspired account of the creation, takes notice of the Sabbath only incidentally and by anticipation, that account, with which the institution was subsequently associated, having naturally enough suggested it to his mind! —This is the opinion of the justly celebrated Dr. Paley.* " As the seventh day," says he, "was erected into a sabbath on account of God's resting upon that day from the work of creation; it was natural enough in the historian, when he had related the history of the creation and of God's ceasing from it on the seventh day, to add, ' And God blessed the Sabbath day and sanctified it, because that on it he had rested from all his work which the Lord God created and made,'—although the blessing and sanctification, i. e. the religious distinction and appropriation of the day, was not actually made for many ages afterwards. The words do not assert that God *then* blessed and sanctified the seventh day, but that he blessed and sanctified it *for that reason :* and if any ask why the Sabbath or sanctification of the seventh day was *then* mentioned, if it was not *then* appointed, the answer is at hand ; the order of connexion, not of time, introduced the men-

* I select Dr. Paley, not only on account of his deserved eminence as a writer, in the theological and moral literature of our country, but because, on this as on other subjects, he brings his argument into short compass, and states it with brevity and precision.—Whether he convinces you or not, he never leaves you at a loss to understand him.

tion of the Sabbath in the history of the subject which it was ordained to commemorate."*

Here, then, is the point to the settlement of which our attention must, in the first instance, be directed;—namely, whether or not the seventh day was actually set apart as a day of religious rest at the time when it is first mentioned, in immediate connexion with the finishing of the work of creation. This, according to Dr. Paley's own admission, is the turning point of the controversy respecting the universality and perpetuity of the obligation. It is fully granted by this eminent writer, that if the Sabbath was instituted immediately after the creation, it must be regarded as a command given to the progenitors of our race, and so obligatory on all the race alike, in all succeeding generations. " If the divine command" (such are the terms of his admission) " was actually delivered at the creation, it was addressed, no doubt, to the whole human species alike, and continues, unless repealed by some subsequent revelation, binding upon all who come to the knowledge of it. If the command was published for the first time in the wilderness, then it was directed to the Jewish people alone ; and something farther, either in the subject or circumstances of the command, will be necessary to show that it was designed for any other." " The former opinion precludes all debate about the extent of the obligation : the latter admits, and, *prima facie*, induces a belief, that the sabbath ought to be considered as part of the peculiar law of the Jewish policy."

* Paley's Moral and Political Philosophy, Sect. on Sabbatical Institutions.

It is comfortable, when a controversy is thus brought to a point, of which the determination is admitted to leave no room for further discussion; when the ground is thus narrowed, and the consequence of satisfactory proof acknowledged to be sure. And I have said thus much, to show you, that the point we are about to consider is of essential importance to our coming to a just conclusion on the great general question.

Look again, then, in the first place, to the terms of our text,—the passage which contains the first mention of the Sabbath:—"Thus the heavens and the earth were finished, and all the host of them. And on the seventh day God ended his work which he had made; and he rested on the seventh day from all his work which he had made. And God blessed the seventh day, and sanctified it; because that in it he had rested from all his work which God created and made."

There is at present no dispute about the meaning of the words used by the historian. It is, on both sides, admitted, that by the seventh day being "*sanctified*," is meant its being *set apart to religious purposes*, as *sacred or holy;* the same sense in which the word is often used afterwards, in the writings of Moses, in application to things and seasons, as well as to persons. The sole question is, whether the day was thus set apart *at that time*. I am most thoroughly convinced that it was, and astonished that to any mind it should ever have appeared otherwise; and I am now to state the grounds of this conviction. Amongst these, I cannot but notice,

1. In the first place, the *plain and simple language of the passage itself*. I need not read it again. Only bear in

appears indisputable, that "MAN" must here be understood generically,—that is, of the human race. The words,
naturally and irresistibly, lead our minds to the time of
his being "made,"—the time of creation. The Sabbath
was not first created, and man created to observe it : but
man was first created, and the Sabbath was instituted for
his benefit. Even if the first part of the antithesis had
stood alone—" The Sabbath was made for man,"; the inference would have been natural, that man did not mean
the Jews merely, but mankind ; when the other part is
added—" Not man for the Sabbath," it becomes unavoidable :—the association is clearly established, by the authority of Christ himself, of the institution of the Sabbath
with the creation of man ; and the Sabbath itself is thus
ascertained to have been an ordinance appointed for the
first progenitors of our race, and for all their progeny.

3. I found a third argument on the language of the
inspired author of the Epistle to the Hebrews, chap. iv.
3—5, " For we which have believed do enter into rest : as
he said, As I have sworn in my wrath, if they shall enter
into my rest ; although the works were finished from the
foundation of the world. For he spake in a certain place
of the seventh day on this wise, And God did rest the
seventh day from all his works. And in this place again,
If they shall enter into my rest." We shall have occasion
to illustrate the whole of this passage at some length in a
future discourse. The principle on which it bears upon
our present argument is very obvious. The words which
have been quoted, clearly imply that the seventh-day rest
had been " entered into" *from the beginning.* Without
this, the continuity and force of the Apostle's reasoning

are gone. The mere finishing of Jehovah's work, and *his own* resting from it, would have been nothing to his purpose; because it might still have left the rest to be entered into *by his people* afterwards. Now, when the Apostle quotes the words of God—"I sware in my wrath they shall not enter into my rest," he does not, in distinguishing this from the sabbatical rest, say—"Although, before this oath of interdiction and exclusion was uttered, the rest of the seventh day *had been instituted in the wilderness for the observance of Israel;*" but, "although the works were finished from the creation of the world"—intimating most clearly, both in language and argument, that *that* rest had been "entered into" from the time of the finishing of creation.

4. I argue the same thing, in the fourth place, from the admitted origin of the division of time into weeks of seven days. It is difficult, if not impossible, to trace this division to any other origin. The phases of the moon, indeed, or her four quarters, as we are accustomed to term them, have been plausibly alleged as affording a sufficiently natural account of it; but a lunar month does not correspond with four times seven days—exceeding the four weeks by a full day and a half. Yet this hebdomadal division of time has existed among all nations, in north, south, east, and west, from the earliest periods to which history and tradition reach; and it is a curious fact, that, amidst all the forgetfulness of God, and the fearful degeneracy and corruption of mankind and of divine institutions, in this our world, hints of the sacredness of the seventh day occur in very ancient heathen poets, and remnants of the practice of its observance are found to have

all along existed amongst the different tribes of the human family.—Now, our argument is this. If this division of time had the origin thus assigned to it, the *reason* of it must, of course, have been originally known, namely, the fact of the Creator's having made the world in six days, and rested on the seventh.—God's "resting" means two things,—his *cessation* from his work, and his *complacency* in it. These two things are expressed in the language of Moses elsewhere, Exod. xxxi. 17. "For in six days the Lord made heaven and earth; and on the seventh day he *rested, and was refreshed.*" To no one who is even superficially versant in the Holy Scriptures, can it be necessary to say, that such terms as these, when applied to Deity, are not meant to convey any such ideas as those of repose from fatigue, and the recruiting of exhausted strength. The first words, indeed, of the narrative of creation should be enough to silence the profanity of the scoffer, and to command into awe the leer of his scornful countenance—" God said, Let there be light ; and there was light." The Book which opens with such an exhibition of the divine omnipotence, —containing so striking an exemplification of the senti- ment, that of lofty conceptions the simplest expression is the most sublime,—is not to be interpreted as, only a few sentences after, sinking the Almighty from the lofty ma- jesty in which it had thus enthroned him, by representing him as the subject of weariness and exhaustion. If there be one quality, indeed, by which the inspired account of creation is more distinguished than by others, it is its divine simplicity, the entire absence of every thing like effort or labour, on the part of the " Mighty Maker," in bringing into being the various portions of the stupendous

universe. He " speaks, and it is done ; he commands, and
it stands fast :"—" The everlasting God, the Lord, the
Creator of the ends of the earth, fainteth not, neither is
weary: there is no searching of his understanding." It
is true that creation occupied a certain portion of time :
but not because omnipotence required it. The same word
that commanded into existence the successive parts could,
with equal ease, by one *fiat*, have commanded the whole.
But there was a design in its being ordered otherwise ;
and the design related to man. It was, to give commencement to such a division of time amongst the inhabitants of
the new-formed world, as should connect the finished work
of creation with a commemorative day. Between the
divine eternity (let it be recollected) and the divisions of
time, there can subsist no possible relation. When the
eternal God, therefore, is represented as " resting" in connexion with *a day*,—a limited portion of time,—the representation must, of necessity, have reference to his creatures, and to that order which he intended should be observed amongst them. This is clear. To speak of days
in the eternity of the Godhead, is a sheer absurdity. From
this it follows, (and here returns the point of our argument,) that if God's resting on the seventh day was known
by men, *the reason of it must also have been known*. But
to what does this amount ? Why to this : that the very
existence of the division of time into weeks, or periods of
seven days, necessarily implies the knowledge, on the
part of men, of the divine intention with regard to a Sabbath. Days belong to creatures, not to the Creator ; and,
for my own part, I am altogether unable to imagine, how
the circumstance of God's resting from his work on the

seventh day could possibly be known, without the purpose being also known that this day was to be a day of sacred rest, and religious observance to men. The mere *cessation* from the work of creation could, of course, occupy no time whatever; and the representation of Deity, as resting for a seventh revolution of time, equal to each of the six preceding revolutions, could be nothing more than an impressive mode of intimating to his creatures his intention and his will, respecting their conduct in reference to that day. And if so, the Sabbath must have been known and observed from the beginning.

5. The same thing is apparent, fifthly, from the very terms in which the first mention is made of the Sabbath, by the historian of the Exodus,—the terms which, according to Dr. Paley, record its first institution. Look to the passage—Exod. xvi. 16—30. The historian is speaking of the Manna; and having described its appearance, and the inquisitive surprise of the people on seeing it, he thus proceeds:—" This is the thing which the Lord hath commanded. Gather of it every man according to his eating, an omer for every man, according to the number of your persons; take ye every man for them which are in his tents. And the children of Israel did so, and gathered, some more, some less. And when they did mete it with an omer, he that gathered much had nothing over, and he that gathered little had no lack: they gathered every man according to his eating. And Moses said, Let no man leave of it till the morning. Notwithstanding, they hearkened not unto Moses; but some of them left of it until the morning, and it bred worms, and stank: and Moses was wroth with them. And they gathered it every morning,

every man according to his eating: and when the sun waxed hot, it melted. And it came to pass, that on the sixth day they gathered twice as much bread, two omers for one man: and all the rulers of the congregation came and told Moses. And he said unto them, This is that which the Lord hath said, To-morrow is the rest of the holy Sabbath unto the Lord: bake that which ye will bake to-day, and seethe that ye will seethe; and that which remaineth over lay up for you, to be kept until the morning. And they laid it up till the morning, as Moses bade; and it did not stink, neither was there any worm therein. And Moses said, Eat that to-day; for to-day is a sabbath unto the Lord: to-day ye shall not find it in the field. Six days ye shall gather it; but on the seventh day, which is the Sabbath, in it there shall be none. And it came to pass, that there went out some of the people on the seventh day for to gather, and they found none. And the Lord said unto Moses, How long refuse ye to keep my commandments and my laws? See, for that the Lord hath given you the Sabbath, therefore he giveth you on the sixth day the bread of two days: abide ye every man in his place; let no man go out of his place on the seventh day. So the people rested on the seventh day."

Having read the passage, I would put the question to any man of ordinary understanding and candid simplicity, whether he can imagine this to be the manner in which a religious observance, entirely new, quite unknown before, would have been first legally instituted? Whether is it likest the formality of legislation, or the incidental mention of an institution previously known? Nay, more. In the twenty-second verse, it is said—" And it came to pass that on the sixth day they gathered twice as much bread, two omers for one man; and all the rulers of the congregation came, and told Moses." This circumstance merits special notice. What did the rulers report to Moses? One of two things. Either they told the fact of this double gathering on the sixth day, as a thing which they themselves had not anticipated, and which they feared might be a violation of the order respecting the quantity to be collected daily;—or they reported it as an act of obedience, on the part of the people, to a previous intimation,—telling Moses that they had done as had been commanded. On the former supposition, it will follow, that the people had pursued this course on the sixth day *of their own accord*, anticipating the sabbatical rest of the seventh. On the latter supposition, Moses had made known, to the rulers and to the people, the intimation which had been made by Jehovah to himself. What, then, were the terms of that intimation? It is contained in the fifth verse of the chapter:—" and it shall come to pass, that on the sixth day they shall prepare that which they bring in; and it shall be twice as much as they gather daily." On either of the two suppositions, the inference is clear. If Moses had not yet communicated this divine intimation to the people, and the people gathered their double portion on the sixth day *of their own accord*, it follows that the rest of the seventh day was known and familiar *to them*. If, on the contrary, the communication had been made to them by Moses, and they acted in conformity to it, still the terms in which the intimation is made by Jehovah to Moses himself, imply, with equal clearness, that the seventh day rest was known and familiar *to him*. For God makes.

the intimation, that a double quantity of the Manna should fall, and gives the order that a double quantity should be gathered and prepared, without assigning for these things any reason whatever; which, on the supposition of no sabbatical observance of the seventh day having previously existed, and no distinction between that day and other days,—is utterly unaccountable: whereas, on the contrary supposition, that of its previous celebration, all is natural, and precisely as we should have expected it to be.—When the fact of the people's gathering double on the sixth day was reported by the rulers to Moses, he gave his approving sanction (as on either of the preceding suppositions he must of course have done) to this part of their conduct; and he added the command, that, having done right in *gathering* double, they should further respect the "rest of the holy Sabbath," by *making ready* on the sixth day what might be required for the consumption of the seventh. When he says—" This is that which the Lord hath said; To-morrow is the rest of the holy Sabbath unto the Lord; bake that which ye will bake to-day, and seethe that ye will seethe ;" it is evident, that the thing commanded is not contained in the words, " To-morrow is the rest of the holy Sabbath unto the Lord;" but that these words are the affirmation of a known fact, and that this known fact is assigned as the *reason* of the thing commanded—" bake that ye will bake to-day, and seethe that ye will seethe." For my own part, I can fancy nothing more unreasonable, than to interpret this passage as the original institution of the seventh-day rest,—the law of the Sabbath. If I had said to any one of you yesterday,—" I intend to-morrow to set out on a journey from home,"—you would, with propriety, have said to me in reply, " To-morrow is the Sabbath :" and your language would have proceeded on the assumption that the fact was known and familiar to my mind as well as to yours; but that, from some cause or other at the moment, I had forgotten the time at which I was speaking. So when Moses says, " To-morrow is the Sabbath," he proceeds upon the assumption of a pre-existing and familiar fact, as much as you would do in the answer I have supposed you to make to my proposal,—a fact familiar to himself, and familiar to the people.

It is alleged, I am aware, that there is no intimation in the narrative of this being " the revival of an old forgotten institution." Granted. But what is the legitimate inference? Is the conclusion an unreasonable one, that it was *not* a forgotten Institution? An Institution may continue for a length of time to be only partially observed, or even not observed at all, when its regular observance is prevented by the necessity of the case, and yet not be forgotten. On the supposition, therefore, that the peculiar condition of the children of Israel, during the servitude of Egypt, had interfered with the regular celebration of the sabbatical rest,* it does not follow that it was gone from their remembrance. Conceiving the language of the passage, in the Book of Exodus, to be altogether unlike what

* This, however, although circumstances may be considered as giving it much probability, is not, in all its extent at least, a certainty. " The antiquity of the Sabbath," says Bishop Horsley, " was a thing so well understood among the Jews themselves, that some of their Rabbins had the vanity to pretend that an exact adherence to the observation of this day, under the severities of the Egyptian servitude, was the merit by which their ancestors procured a miraculous deliverance."

must have been used respecting a new and utterly unknown institution, I look upon it as containing satisfactory evidence of the contrary; that however partially and irregularly observed; it had not been forgotten.

The incident recorded in that passage, I need not remind you, preceded the giving of the law from Sinai. I have now, then, to notice, in further corroboration of the previous existence of the Sabbath—

6. In the sixth place; *the terms of that law itself.* You will find them, Exod. xx. 8—11. " Remember the sabbath-day, to keep it holy. Six days shalt thou labour, and do all thy work. But the seventh day is the sabbath of the Lord thy God: in it thou shalt not do any work, thou, nor thy son, nor thy daughter, thy man-servant, nor thy maid-servant, nor thy cattle, nor thy stranger that is within thy gates: For in six days the Lord made heaven and earth, the sea, and all that in them is, and rested the seventh day: wherefore the Lord blessed the sabbath-day, and hallowed it."—It will not be disputed, that the language, "Remember the sabbath-day, to keep it holy," is language which assumes, or presupposes its existence. I grant, that if by any one who hears me the *original institution* of the Sabbath can be considered as contained in the sixteenth chapter of the same Book, on which we have been commenting, then this style may be consistently enough explained. But if the words in that passage "To-morrow is the rest of the holy Sabbath unto the Lord," cannot, on any natural principle, be interpreted as the first enactment of the law of the Sabbath; then the terms of the fourth commandment must refer to a more ancient time of institution: and there is no other to which

it can refer but the time of creation—the time in our
text. That it has this reference, and can have no other, is
rendered most strikingly manifest by the terms of the
reason assigned in this commandment for its observance:
—" for in six days the Lord made heaven and earth, the
sea and all that in them is, and rested the seventh day;
wherefore the Lord blessed the sabbath-day and hallowed it.".
It has commonly been said, that "blessed" and "hallowed," being verbs in the past tense, must refer to past
time and previous institution; and that if this had been
the first institution, the verbs would have been in the
present tense—" wherefore the Lord *blesseth* the seventh
day, and *halloweth* it." Dr. Paley would reply—" It is
not pretended that the fourth commandment contains the
first institution of the Sabbath; its institution took place
before, at the time of the manna." And, although we
might think the reference unreasonable to so recent a date,
we could not deny that it was past time, and would
therefore warrant the use of verbs in the past tense.—
But the conclusion that the reference is to a more remote
period is, in my mind, irresistible, on another ground.—
In the reason of observance—" wherefore the Lord blessed
the seventh day and hallowed it," there is, most evidently,
a reference to the terms of some previous record of the
institution of the Sabbath. Now, when was the seventh
day blessed and hallowed? Where are such terms employed? In the narrative of the manna, when the institution is supposed to have taken place, we have nothing
of the kind. Where, then, in the preceding history, are
these *words of institution* (for so they may with the strictest propriety be called) to be found? The answer is, they

are in our text. We have them here ; and we have them nowhere else. If the terms in the fourth commandment do not refer to those of our text, we know of nothing else to which they can refer. And if they do, then our text must necessarily be understood as a historical statement of what took place at the time, not as a mere anticipation of what was long after to take place in the wilderness. The two things are quite incompatible. If, when quoted in the fourth commandment, they refer to what was past; they cannot, when used in the text, be anticipative of what was to come. The quotation in the fourth commandment may justly be considered as containing an affirmation, that when these words—" the Lord blessed the seventh day, and sanctified it," were used in the history, the Sabbath was instituted. But the words are used only here ; and here then, on divine authority, we have the institution and true date of the Sabbath.—I know not whether I have made my ideas clearly understood, but to my own mind this view of the matter is irresistibly conclusive.

Thus it appears that while, on the one hand, the language of our text in the Book of Genesis cannot, without unnatural straining, be interpreted of an institution to take place in far-remote futurity ; neither, on the other, can the language in the Book of Exodus be interpreted, without similar straining, of a new and previously unknown institution.

There are, however, some alleged difficulties in the way, which are deserving of particular notice.

It is objected to the supposition of the Sabbath having existed from the beginning, that *little or no notice of it is to be found in the inspired account of the antediluvian and patriarchal ages.*—It would be uncandid to deny that this is a singular fact, and an apparently strong objection. The following remarks will mitigate its force, and show it to be at least inconclusive.

1. In the Mosaic history, *weeks* are spoken of as amongst the ordinary well-known divisions of time. Now, if the observations formerly made be well founded, in proof, from this division of time, of the original knowledge of the Sabbath, and of the reason of its institution, there is surely more than a probability that it continued to be known among the worshippers of the true God.

Of the division of time into periods of seven days, one of the most interesting exemplifications occurs in the history of Noah. When this second father of our race sent forth the raven from the Ark, why tarried he *seven* days before he sent forth the dove?—and when this messenger returned, why other seven days, before he sent her forth the second time? and other seven again, when she came back with the symbol of peace, ere he gave her her third and final dismission?—Why seven, rather than six, or eight, or ten?—Why, but because the interval was a week? And the supposition is as pleasing as it is probable, that these winged scouts were sent out on the Sabbath, the day of holy rest, on which, from the little company in the Ark, the only living remnant of a desolated world, the worship of praise and prayer ascended to the God of judgment and of mercy; when they bowed to his awful vengeance, and cast themselves on his gracious and mighty protection.*

* In the account given by the historian, of the respective characters

· 2. The following circumstances are also to be weighed:— That the history is distinguished by succinctness and brevity:—that, on the supposition of the Sabbath having

and offerings of Cain and Abel, an expression is used, which, by some critics, if not with certainty, yet with considerable probability, has been explained of the weekly sabbatical worship. The account is contained in Gen. iv. 3—5. "And in process of time it came to pass, that Cain brought of the fruit of the ground an offering unto the Lord. And Abel, he also brought of the firstlings of his flock, and of the fat thereof. And the Lord had respect unto Abel, and to his offering. But unto Cain, and to his offering, he had not respect. And Cain was very wroth, and his countenance fell." The original phrase, translated "*in process of time*," is rendered on the margin more literally, "*in the end of days*." Our translation implies the lapse of some considerable portion of time in the life of man, at the close of which both the brothers brought their respective oblations. Yet this cannot well mean, in the present case, the period of their growth from infancy to maturity, or manhood; both because it is unnatural to suppose this happening, as to both, the older and the younger, at one time, and because, in the preceding verses, they are spoken of according to their distinctive secular occupations, and consequently as *already* in youth or manhood. Yet it is obvious, that the two brothers "brought" their offerings at *one time* to *one place;* and that the testimony of divine approbation was given to that of Abel in Cain's presence, and, in all probability, in presence of others also; and, indeed, that if the worship of God was to be duly kept up at all, a fixed and statedly returning time for it was indispensable. There appears, therefore, considerable force in the conclusion, that by the phrase "in the end of days," the seventh day, or the last day of what may be called the *creation week*, is meant by the historian;—and the likelihood of this is increased, by the appropriateness which the expression derives from its coming, in the narrative, so immediately after the account of the memorable succession of days employed in creation, and of the consecration of the seventh, the day of cessation and rest.—It is likely too, that the "*day*" mentioned in Job i. 6, when "the sons of God came to present themselves before the Lord," was the Sabbath.—But I do not wish to rest much on such passages, of which the meaning is doubtful.

been well known as an ancient institution, observed from
the beginning, and familiar to those for whom he wrote,
an historian, who was studious of brevity, who recorded
only the more remarkable events and transactions, and
even these succinctly, might, without any great difficulty,
be conceived to carry on his narrative without finding
occasion for any particular mention of it: and that
granting the omission to be ever so strange; if it proves
any thing to the objector's purpose, it will be found to
prove too much,—namely, the non-observance of the Sabbath for the period of at least four hundred years *after the
admitted institution of it at Sinai :* for no mention of it, nor
any allusion to it, occurs in the Books of Joshua
Judges, any more than in that of Genesis : and the argument might be strengthened from the extremely rare
incidental notice of the day for even a greater number
centuries thereafter.   The silence, therefore, of the
rative is not, in either case, admissible as proof of
non-existence of the institution; the correspondence,
this respect, of the history which follows the giving of
law with that which precedes it, neutralising entirely
force of the objection.*

---

* The reply to the objection might be strengthened by parallel cases
For a period of 1500 years, from the birth of Seth till the deluge, no
mention is made of *sacrifice.*—And for a similar period of 1,500 years,
namely, from the entrance of the Israelites into Canaan till the birth
of Christ, although in the phraseology of the historians and prophets
there may be an occasional and chiefly figurative use of the term, there
is no mention whatever of the fact of *circumcision* as an existing rite.
Yet during these periods, there is no ground for question, both these
institutions, sacrifice in the former and circumcision in the latter, were
in regular course of observance.

Another objection has been derived from certain modes of expression in different parts of Scripture, which are thought to indicate the peculiarity of the Sabbath as a Jewish institution. For example, in Nehem. ix. 14, God is said to have "*made known* unto Israel his holy Sabbath." "Nehemiah," says Dr. Paley, "recounts the promulgation of the sabbatic law amongst the transactions of the wilderness; which supplies another considerable argument in aid of our opinion." The whole force of this argument lies in the expression "*made known;*" which is conceived to refer to the discovery and injunction of what was unknown and unobserved before. But the inference is unwarrantable.—The word so rendered is not used with such definite strictness. In Psalm ciii. 7, the Psalmist says, "He *made known* his ways unto Moses, his acts unto the children of Israel." Was Moses the first to whom any of the ways and acts of Jehovah were made known? Assuredly not, on the authority of Moses himself. There might be a fuller and more permanent discovery of them made, when to Israel "were committed the oracles of God;" but "at sundry times and in divers manners," to preceding fathers and prophets, had God made himself and his "acts and ways" known. Dr. Paley considers Nehemiah as having reference, when he speaks of the Sabbath being "made known," not to the fourth commandment, (although the words stand in immediate connexion with the descent on Sinai and the giving of the law,) but to the narrative in the Book of Exodus, where the Sabbath is previously mentioned. Now we have already seen, that the terms of that narrative are such as to convey, so decidedly, the impression of the Sabbath having previously existed, and to be so utterly extraordinary and unprecedented if considered as the terms of a first enactment; that, so far from admitting the expression used by Nehemiah as a proof of the justness of Dr. Paley's interpretation of the narrative, we should regard the narrative as a proof that the expression of Nehemiah is not to be strictly and definitely understood of something quite unknown before, but ought to be taken in its looser acceptation.——In the same passage of Nehemiah, moreover, the *moral* as well as other precepts of the law are represented as " given" and " commanded" to the Israelites.   But the moral precepts of God's will were not, assuredly, then given for the first time: for, in that case, there must have been no moral law before the time of Moses, and consequently no sin; in direct opposition to the apostle Paul's reasoning in Rom. v. 13, 14, where, from the fact of the prevalence of *death* before the time of Moses, he infers the existence of *sin*, and consequently of *a law*, from the beginning; with the view of convincing the Jews, that there was a law antecedent to the Mosaic;—a law, the transgression of which had introduced and perpetuated sin and death, and in the damnatory sentence of which they as well as others were involved.

The principle of these remarks will also apply to another passage of a similar description,—namely, Ezek. xx. 10, 11, 12; in which " the Sabbath is spoken of as *given;*" and " what else," says Dr. Paley, " can this mean than its being *first instituted* in the wilderness ?"   The answer is, that, both in that passage; and in the one formerly quoted from Nehemiah, the same term is applied to God's statutes and judgments, and precepts, and laws, generally, as well as to his Sabbaths; from which it would follow, contrary to manifest truth, that none of them had, in any way, been "given" before.—If an example is desired of the term *given* being used in application to what had a previous existence, we have a decisive one at hand. It occurs in John vii. 22. "Moses therefore *gave unto you* circumcision (not that it is of Moses, but of the fathers) and ye on the Sabbath-day circumcise a man." Here circumcision is represented as *given* to the Jews by Moses, while, in the very same sentence, it is mentioned as having been "of the fathers." What becomes, then, of Paley's question, "What else can *given* mean than *first instituted?*" Might we not say of the Sabbath, with the same propriety as of circumcision—" Moses therefore gave unto you the Sabbath—not that it is of Moses, but of the fathers," and of the fathers even from the beginning? It is clear from this example, that such terms are too strictly interpreted, when they are made with certainty to signify *original institution.* Previously existing institutes and laws might, with no violation of propriety, be spoken of as "made known" and as "given," to a particular people, when, with special solemnity, with peculiar sanctions, and in a systematic and imbodied form, they were delivered from heaven to that people, and when the possession of them in this form became the distinction of that people from others.

Lastly, it is argued that in Exod. xxxi. 16, 17, and some other passages, the Sabbath is spoken of as given to be " *a sign* between Jehovah and the children of Israel :" —on which Dr. Paley observes,—" it does not seem easy to understand, how the Sabbath could be a sign between

God and the people of Israel, unless the observance of it was peculiar to that people, and designed to be so."—But in Deut. vi. 8, the same term is applied to the decalogue, and to the laws and words of God given by Moses to Israel; even to those moral precepts, of which the principle and sum is "Thou shalt love the Lord thy God with all thy heart, and with all thy soul, and with all thy might;" and which they were enjoined to have "in their heart, and to teach diligently unto their children, talking of them when they sat in the house, and when they walked by the way, when they lay down, and when they rose up." Of these precepts, meaning especially the summary of moral duty in the ten commandments, it is said—"Thou shalt bind them *for a sign* upon thine hand." Whatever formed a distinction between the Israelites and other nations was a sign. The giving of the law and the possession of it were such a sign. "He showed his word unto Jacob, his statutes and judgments to Israel; he hath not dealt so with any nation." This was their great and divinely conferred distinction. But surely it would sound strangely to say, that the law which is summed up in love to God and love to man, could not be a sign to the people of Israel, "unless the obligation of it was peculiar to that people, and designed to be so."—All the laws and institutions of God, moreover, and the Sabbath among the rest, were a sign between Jehovah and Israel, as forming, on both sides, *a test:*—they were a test of *their obedience to him,* and of *his faithfulness to them.*—It is somewhat singular, that, even when the Sabbath is spoken of as being a sign between God and Israel, the reason given for its observance is one which contains in it nothing at all peculiar to that people; nothing respecting their deliverance from Egypt, or any of the other signal interpositions of Jehovah in their favour,—although these, as we shall afterwards see, are subsequently superadded as grounds of its celebration,—but simply the original reason, assigned in our text:—" The children of Israel shall keep the Sabbath, to observe the Sabbath throughout their generations, for a perpetual covenant: it is a sign between me and the children of Israel for ever: for in six days the Lord made heaven and earth, and on the seventh day he rested and was refreshed." Exod. xxxi. 16, 17.

Here we must close for the present. In next discourse we shall consider the moral nature and the permanent obligation of the Sabbath, as one of the precepts of the Decalogue.

DISCOURSE II.

EXODUS xx. 8—11.

" Remember the Sabbath-day, to keep it holy. Six days shalt thou labour, and do all thy work: But the seventh day is the Sabbath of the Lord thy God: in it thou shalt not do any work, thou, nor thy son, nor thy daughter, thy man-servant, nor thy maid-servant, nor thy cattle, nor thy stranger that is within thy gates: For in six days the Lord made heaven and earth, the sea, and all that in them is, and rested the seventh day: wherefore the Lord blessed the Sabbath-day, and hallowed it."

In closing the former discourse, we promised to consider in this, the moral nature and permanent obligation of the Sabbath, as one of the precepts of the Decalogue. To this subject we now proceed.

There are some writers, who have attempted to set aside all argument for the permanence of the Sabbath drawn from the fourth commandment, by denying altogether the continued obligation of the law of the two tables, under the Christian economy. The grounds of this denial, then, demand our first and serious attention. The question is important, not only as it relates to the point before us, but more generally. If it be as these writers contend,—if the precepts of the Decalogue remain not in force,—if, although formerly a law to Israel, they are not now a law to us,—: there were comparatively little interest in the investigation of their import, and little benefit to be derived from it. Curiosity, in that case, would be the sole principle and motive of our inquiry. It would be a topic of mere antiquarian speculation; or, at the best, it would only yield us a lesson of the wisdom of God, in giving a law adapted to the circumstances and character of a particular people. We shall, however, I trust, find satisfactory evidence on which to rest our conviction, that we have in them a deeper and more direct concern.

The law of the ten commandments, you are all aware, was delivered to Israel at Mount Sinai, soon after their leaving Egypt; and it was given in circumstances, and with accompaniments, of impressive solemnity, and appalling terror. The scene is thus described by the inspired historian—Exod. xix. 16—24. "And it came to pass, on the third day, in the morning, that there were thunders and lightnings, and a thick cloud upon the mount, and the voice of the trumpet exceeding loud; so that all the people that was in the camp trembled. And Moses brought forth the people out of the camp to meet with God; and they stood at the nether part of the mount. And mount Sinai was altogether on a smoke, because the Lord descended upon it in fire; and the smoke thereof ascended as the smoke of a furnace, and the whole mount quaked greatly. And when the voice of the trumpet sounded long, and waxed louder and louder, Moses spake, and God answered him by a voice. And the Lord came down upon mount Sinai, on the top of the mount: and the Lord called Moses up to the top of the mount; and Moses went up. And the Lord said unto Moses, Go down, charge the people, lest they break through unto the Lord to gaze, and many of them perish. And let the priests also, which come near to the Lord, sanctify themselves, lest the Lord break forth upon them. And Moses said unto the Lord, the people cannot come up to mount Sinai: for thou chargest us, saying, Set bounds about the mount, and sanctify it. And the Lord said unto him, Away, get thee down, and thou shalt come up, thou, and Aaron with thee: but let not the priests and the people break through to come up to the Lord, lest he break forth upon them."—With reference to this scene, the writer of the Epistle to the Hebrews says, " So terrible was the sight, that Moses said, I exceedingly fear and quake."

Amidst these circumstances of dread sublimity, Jehovah uttered the ten commandments, " with his own voice, out of the midst of the fire, and of the thick darkness ;" and he afterwards wrote them on two tables of stone, and delivered them to Moses, to be preserved to future generations, in memorial of the covenant between himself and the people of Israel. The tables were called " the tables of the covenant ;" and they are expressly and repeatedly said to have been " written by the finger of God." We ought surely, therefore, to approach the consideration of these precepts with a portion of the awe with which they were originally received. Of this awe, the account is related in the following terms by Moses, in recapitulating to the people the leading facts of Jehovah's dealings with them :—" These words the Lord spake unto all your assembly in the mount, out of the midst of the fire, of the cloud, and of the thick darkness, with a great voice ; and he added no more : and he wrote them on two tables of stone, and delivered them unto me. And it came to pass, when ye heard the voice out of the midst of the darkness, (for the mountain did burn with fire,) that ye came near unto me, even all the heads of your tribes, and your elders ; and ye said, Behold the Lord our God hath showed us his glory, and his great‑ ness, and we have heard his voice out of the midst of the fire : we have seen this day that God doth talk with man, and he liveth. Now, therefore, why should we die ? for this great fire will consume us. If we hear the voice of the Lord our God any more, then we shall die. For who is there of all flesh that hath heard the voice of the living God speaking out of the midst of the fire, as we have, and lived ? Go thou near, and hear all that the Lord our God shall say ; and speak thou unto us all that the Lord our God shall speak unto thee, and we will hear it, and do it. And the Lord heard the voice of your words, when ye spake unto me ; and the Lord said unto me, I have heard the voice of the words of this people, which they have spoken unto thee : they have well said all that they have spoken. Oh that there were such an heart in them, that they would fear me, and keep all my commandments always, that it might be well with them, and with their children for ever !"—From the *terror*, indeed, with which the scene affected the Israelites, we are happily free ; for we have now the full and clear discovery of the " minis‑ tration of righteousness," to counteract the overwhelming influence of " the ministration of condemnation and death." The contemplation of the " mount of the Lord, on which the Lamb was provided for a burnt-offering," allays the terrors of the " mount that might be touched, and that burned with fire." The "voice of love and mercy" that "sounds from Calvary," charms away the dread of the thunders of Sinai. But still, to such a display of the divine purity, and majesty, and avenging righteousness, it becomes us to approach with solemn awe. For, although Calvary teaches a lesson of grace, which could not be learned from Sinai, yet it teaches, at the same time, and that even more impressively, the lesson of God's immaculate holiness, and unbending rectitude and truth:— " Wherefore we, receiving a kingdom which cannot be moved, let us have grace, whereby we may serve God acceptably, with reverence and godly fear: for even our God is a consuming fire." *

It is not to be denied, that in some of the statements and reasonings of the apostle Paul, one of the principal difficulties arises from the more comprehensive and the more restricted acceptations in which, on different occasions, he uses the term "LAW." A general consideration of this subject, however important, would lead us into too wide a digression. We must restrict our present discussion entirely to the Decalogue,—the law of the two tables,—the ten commandments. That these commandments were remarkably distinguished, first by their being uttered from Sinai by the voice of God, and afterwards by their being written with his finger on the tables of stone, is matter of fact, which cannot be questioned. It *has* been questioned, however, whether this distinction was not more accidental than designed. It has been conceived to have arisen rather from circumstances which happened to occur at the time, than from divine intention on account of any peculiar

* Heb. xii. 28, 29.

excellence or comprehensiveness in the precepts themselves. The origin of the distinction, according to one very acute and intelligent writer,* was the circumstance of Jehovah's having been interrupted by the fears of the people, which brought them to Moses, with the earnest entreaty, that God might not thus speak unto them any more. He imagines, that, but for this, other parts of the law would have been delivered in the same way, and that the distinction was thus circumstantial only, and accidental. It does not appear to me, that this view of the matter accords well with the terms of the narrative, as already quoted—" These words the Lord spake unto all your assembly, in the Mount, out of the midst of the fire, of the cloud, and of the thick darkness, with a great voice; AND HE ADDED NO MORE." This mode of expression appears to me clearly to indicate, that at the close of the ten commandments, there was a cessation of the voice by which they were uttered. Each of the ten must, of course, have been separated from the succeeding one, by an intervening pause. But after the tenth, there was evidently something more,—a cessation of the voice,—indicating, that these commandments contained the substance of the law, or of the people's part of the divine covenant. This receives striking confirmation from the language of Moses, in the preceding chapter of Deuteronomy, verses 12, 13. "And the Lord spake unto you out of the midst of the fire: ye heard the voice of the words, but saw no similitude; only ye heard a voice. And he declared unto you

* Mr. Hallet, in his work entitled, A Free and Impartial Study of the Holy Scriptures recommended: being Notes on some peculiar texts, with Discourses and Observations on various subjects. Disc. iii.

his covenant, which he commanded you to perform, even ten commandments; and he wrote them upon two tables of stone." Nothing can well be more explicit than this, "he declared unto you his covenant, which he commanded you to perform, even ten commandments." No wonder, then, that on the utterance of the tenth, the voice ceased, and "he added no more." His "covenant had been declared, which he commanded them to perform." It was not a mere specimen of his law, which had chanced to be distinguished from the rest in the way mentioned; it was a summary of its moral requirements.

The evidence being so unsatisfactory, of the accidental nature of the distinction between these commandments and others, there is, of course, equally little ground for the further allegation, that the sole reason of these Commandments being committed to the tables of stone, was the fact of their having been thus accidentally distinguished; this fact alone being supposed to have given them their peculiar eminence, as a select specimen of the precepts of the God of Israel; and the honour of being recorded in stone having been added, in consequence of the previous accidental honour of having been exclusively uttered by the divine voice. It appears to me sufficiently clear, that they were both uttered from heaven, and inscribed on stone, as being precepts of primary and comprehensive importance, containing the great essential articles of the people's obedience; and that, on this account, they are denominated so repeatedly "the covenant," and the tables containing them, the "tables of the covenant."

Yet on these grounds, and others to which the discussion will immediately lead, it has been argued, that the Decalogue is not more of permanent and universal obligation, than any other parts of the Mosaic institutes; that its obligation was limited to the Jews, and came to a close with the Old Testament dispensation; and that it forms no part of the law of Christian duty. In support of this conclusion, apostolic authority has been adduced. Paul, it has been alleged, evidently declares the law of the ten commandments abrogated, when he writes of it, in the following terms [2 Cor. iii. 7, 8, 11.] "But if the ministration of death, written and engraven in stones, was glorious, so that the children of Israel could not stedfastly behold the face of Moses for the glory of his countenance; which glory was to be done away; how shall not the ministration of the Spirit be rather glorious? For if that which is done away was glorious, much more that which remaineth is glorious." It ought, however, to be carefully observed, that the subject of which the apostle is treating, when he thus writes, is the superior spirituality of the new covenant dispensation to that of the old. The distinction which he makes between the one and the other, is that between writing on stone, and writing on the heart. And what is it, then, that is written on the heart? What if we shall find, that it is the very law which, of old, was written on stone? To decide this, let us look to the prophetic description of the new covenant, as contrasted with the old. Jer. xxxi. 31—34. "Behold the days come, saith the Lord, that I will make a new covenant with the house of Israel, and with the house of Judah; not according to the covenant that I made with their fathers, in the day that I took them by the hand, to bring them out of the land of Egypt; (which my covenant they brake, although I was an husband unto them, saith the Lord;) But this shall be the covenant that I will make with the house of Israel; after those days, saith the Lord, I will put my law in their inward parts, and write it in their hearts; and will be their God, and they shall be my people. And they shall teach no more every man his neighbour, and every man his brother, saying, Know the Lord: for they shall all know me, from the least of them unto the greatest of them, saith the Lord: for I will forgive their iniquity, and I will remember their sin no more."—It is with the first of these new covenant promises we have at present to do—" I will put my law in their inward parts, and write it in their hearts." It will not surely be questioned, that in the terms of this promise, there is an allusion to the writing of the law, under the former covenant, *upon stone.* The contrast, therefore, in the prophet, is the same as that in the apostle. The very law that was, of old, written on the tables of stone is, under the new dispensation, written on the fleshy tables of the heart. I ask, then, is this abrogation? Is the transference of the law from stone to the heart the disannulling of it? And if not, must not the apostle, when he speaks of that which was written and engraven in stones being " done away," be understood as referring, not to the moral substance of the law, but to the comparative *externality* of that economy under which it was " written and engraven on stones?" Surely that law was not abolished, which, in the full spirituality of its import, was written by " the Spirit of the living God," upon the renewed heart. This certainly was retaining the substance, and parting only with what was outward and transitory. The tables of stone are broken and thrown away, when the law, which they contained, comes to be restored to its original place, the heart of man. And the very comparison, which we have been noticing, involves in it a satisfactory proof, that the law of the two tables does contain a summary of the essential principles of religion and morality in general. As the law which, under the New Covenant, is written on the heart, it can contain no less.

I would farther ask, what is a law? Is it the mere form of words, in which a duty is enjoined, or a sin prohibited? Is it not, rather, the injunction of the duty, and the prohibition of the sin, under whatever form of words they are conveyed? The same duties may be commanded, and the same sins forbidden, in different terms, and yet the law itself remain unchanged. A question, therefore, naturally suggests itself, namely, Does the law of Christ, as given in the New Testament, correspond in its requirements to the law of the two tables? If it does; then, even on the supposition of the terms being different in which the requirements are expressed,—to say that the precepts of the latter are abrogated, and are no longer binding on Christians, will be to say no more than that the form of words is set aside, while the law itself continues the same. It is the *matter* of duty, and not the *expression*, that constitutes the law. We can readily conceive the legal codes of two nations to be very different in their forms of expression, and yet substantially, and even to the minutest item, to contain the same enactments. Should we not, in such a case, say of the two countries, that they were governed by the same laws?

The same sentiment, namely, that it is the essential

elements of duty, and not any forms of words in which these elements may be imbodied, that constitute the law, may be further confirmed and illustrated, by considering what was the state of things *before* the giving of the law to Israel. Sin is scripturally defined "the transgression of law;" and, while it is the maxim both of inspiration and of common sense, that " where no law is, there is no transgression," it is not less clear, that where there is no transgression, there can be no punitive infliction. On these principles, as we formerly saw, the apostle Paul argues, that, since there was *death* before the giving of the law, there must have been *sin ;* and that, consequently, there must have been a law before that given by Moses, of which sin was the transgression :—a law which was the common rule of obligation to the human race, and of which men universally, Gentiles and Jews alike, were the violators, and, as such, under a common damnatory sentence. The moral obligations of Jews and Gentiles, considered as fellow-members of the human family, must ever have been the same; and the apostle's argument with the Jews requires us to believe, that the moral law, as given by Moses, was substantially (that is in all its essential principles and requirements) the same with what had existed from the beginning, of which sin was the transgression, and death the sanction. Indeed, in the moral government of God over his creatures, we cannot imagine the existence of two laws. The relations of God to men, and of men to God, have always been the same; and the same obligations on the part of the creature have arisen out of them. And, as the grand design of God, in separating to himself the seed of Abraham, was, to keep alive in the world the true knowledge of himself,—of his character, of his will, and of his purposes of saving mercy; we have the very same reason for thinking, that the moral law given by Moses had been his law to man from the beginning, as we have for thinking that the character which he gives of himself had been his character from the beginning; or that the salvation pointed to by the ceremonial institutions of Judaism was the "common salvation," revealed to our first parents, for themselves and for their progeny, without distinction, in the first promise. If the moral law, as given by Moses, was any thing different from what had all along been the divine code of morals to man, then do we desiderate the accomplishment of one at least of the ends of the separation of Israel,—the exhibition, namely, to the surrounding nations of the will of the one living and true God, as the moral governor of the world. Nay we may say, I think, without presumption, that if it were otherwise, there would be a singular defect in revelation. There is a close and interesting relation between the law and the gospel. It is the transgression of the former that has necessitated the gracious provisions of the latter. Would it not, then, be a strange thing, that we should have no authoritative discovery of the will of God as to human duty, the transgression of which has given rise to the grace of God in human salvation? It is, assuredly, as transgressors of law, that Gentiles as well as Jews are under condemnation. The denunciation, Gal. iii. 10, " Cursed is every one that continueth not in all things which are written in the book of the law to do them," includes the one as well as the other. For although the Gentiles have not, as the Jews had, the *written* law, the apostle clearly identifies the principles and requirements of the law of nature with those of the law of revelation; (however imperfectly, in consequence of natural corruption, those principles and requirements might be understood,) when he says—Rom. ii. 13—15, " For not the hearers of the law are just before God, but the doers of the law shall be justified: For when the Gentiles, which have not the law, do by nature the things contained in the law, these, having not the law, are a law unto themselves; which show the work of the law written in their hearts, their conscience also bearing witness, and their thoughts the mean while accusing or else excusing one another." We have nothing to do, in our present argument, with the leading design of these words, when taken in connexion with what precedes;—which is, to affirm and establish the great general principle in God's judicial administration, that responsibility is according to privilege. But there are two things to be learned from them, which are directly and decisively to our purpose. The first is, that the law which the Jews had, and the Gentiles had not, is the law given by Moses; and consequently, that the distinction usually made, in explaining the word " law" as on different occasions used by the apostle, between the *moral* law and the *ceremonial*, is not an arbitrary but a fair and legitimate one: for, that it is of the moral and not of the ceremonial precepts of Moses that Paul here speaks, it would be a waste of words, and an insult to your understandings, to set about proving; and yet in his argument, without adverting to the ceremonial institutes at all, he calls those precepts simply " the law." The second is, that the dictates of the divine will, in natural conscience, (except in as far as they are perverted by circumstances of temptation, operating upon the various forms of corruption) are the same as the dictates of his will in the written law. On no principle but this, is it possible to understand the affirmation, that when the Gentiles " do by nature things contained in the law," they " show the work of the law written in their hearts." They were, in fact, then, under the same law; only they had it not in its written form : they had it with the obscurity and imperfection of natural reason, compared with the clearness and fulness of direct divine revelation. But still it was the same law. This much the apostle most explicitly intimates. It was the same law, then, which was written on the heart of man originally; of which the dictates, more or less partial and corrupted, remain in the conscience of man still; which was promulgated by Jehovah to Israel, in its complete uncorrupted form, and with full attestation of its authority; which, having been originally written on the heart, was then recorded in stone; and which, under a later and more spiritual economy, was again, as we have seen, to be transferred from the stone to the heart. The truth is, that in all ages and countries, and under every dispensation of divine discovery, the law of God, as the rule of moral duty to man, must, of necessity, be the same; subject, it may be, under the divine prescription, to such occasional and temporary modifications as do not encroach upon its great principles, but essentially without change. The law which was given at Sinai, had been the law from the beginning, and shall be the law unto the end. Christ and Moses, as we shall see more fully immediately, are in this respect one.

It has, to my mind, much the appearance of quirk and evasion to allege,—and yet it has been alleged with all seriousness by men of sound judgment and acute discrimination,—that it is not *as given to the Jews* that the precepts of the Mosaic law are binding upon Christians. This is very true; but it is a mere truism; it has the sound of an argument, but no more. For, to what does it amount? Only to this; that it is not as given to one man, that a command is binding upon another. The law of God is not obligatory upon you, when considered as enjoined upon me. As given to the Jews, it was, of course, binding upon the Jews only. This is too self-evident to be worthy of formal statement. The sole question ought to be, whether the ten commandments, uttered from Sinai by the voice of God, and by his finger written on the tables of stone, do, or do not, contain a summary of the leading articles of moral duty. If they do, they were binding before, they have been binding since, and they must be binding to the end. They have never been binding, however, either before or since, because they were given to the Jews; but they were given to the Jews, because they were the principles, universally and perpetually obligatory, of moral rectitude.

The idea of the ten commandments containing such a summary, has been treated by the writer formerly adverted to, and by some others, with a sarcastic ridicule, which might, perhaps, have been as wisely spared. We have already seen how flimsy the foundation is, for the theory of that writer, by which the pre-eminence of these precepts above others is resolved into a mere contingency. Had the principle of that theory been correct, it would have followed, that any other ten of the precepts of the Mosaic law, did we only suppose, them to have been uttered first,—that is, to have preceded the alleged interruption of the divine voice by the fears of the people,— would have answered the same end, and would have suited equally well for being committed to the tables of stone, and denominated, "the words of the covenant." But we are instantly and strongly sensible that this is as far as possible from being the case. In point of fact, these ten commandments have been almost universally allowed to contain a comprehensive syllabus of principles; of the great articles of religious and moral duty; duty to God, and duty to men. And not, I am satisfied, without more than plausible reason. Let us glance at them for a moment. The former of the two tables (as we are accustomed to divide them) contains four precepts, which regulate our duty to God. Of these, the first enjoins the *exclusive appropriation* of religious veneration, homage, and service, to the one God: the second prescribes the *spirituality* of the divine worship, assuming the spirituality of its object, as incapable of being represented by any external similitude: the third commands the *sacredness* of the name of Jehovah, and of every thing with which that name is associated: and the fourth ordains the *constancy* and *regularity* of God's worship, and of the solemn commemoration of the doings of his hands. Now these precepts are unquestionably most comprehensive. If we worship and serve the one God only; if we worship and serve him according to his spiritual nature; if we hold in habitual and practical reverence his name and character; and if we bear in constant devout remembrance and com-

memoration the wonders of his wisdom, power, and goodness,—there will be little deficient in either our inward
feelings, or our outward duties, to our Maker.—And the
second table is hardly less comprehensive in its arrangement and general principles, as a manual of our duties to
one another. It begins with the first of earthly relations,
and the obligations arising out of it, as the foundation and
origin of all the rest, and the germ and pattern of the
duties belonging respectively to them : then follow, con-
secutively, the ordained sacredness of *life*, of *chastity*, of
property, of *reputation*, and of *every thing pertaining to our
neighbour;* the last commandment, at the same time, intimating, as a kind of key to the rest, that they were all
to be interpreted as the laws of him who " searches the
reins and hearts," and as regulating the thoughts and
desires, as well as the words and actions. Now, surely,
if we are duly regardful, in thought, in word, and in
deed, of our neighbour's life, of his purity, of his property,
of his character, and of every thing that pertains to him,
never wishing him evil, never grudging him good;—he
will have little cause to complain of any thing wanting,
either in the frame of our mind, or in the course of our
conduct.—The two tables of stone, with the law of the ten
commandments graven upon them, were, by divine direction, to be deposited in the ark, or little chest of shittim-
wood, overlaid with gold, ordered to be made for its
reception ; and the ark, thus containing " the testimony,"
and thence called " the ark of the testimony," was to be
the resting-place of the mercy-seat, between the cherubim,
from which Jehovah was graciously to commune with his
people, through their priestly representative. The mercy-

seat was a beautiful type of Christ, through whom it is
that Jehovah is propitious to sinners; and the circumstance of the mercy-seat being placed upon the ark of the
testimony, was strikingly significant of the consistency of
the grace of the gospel with the claims of the law,—of the
exercise of mercy through the blood of the covenant with
the unabated demands of legal righteousness. And this
view of the typical arrangement of the Holy of Holies,
may itself serve as an additional proof of the comprehensiveness of the law of the two tables.

There are, it may be observed, two summaries of the
divine law of moral duty. There is a summary, consisting
of its great comprehensive spiritual principles; and there
is a summary of leading articles of practical virtue, or out-
lines of the influence of these great principles upon the
conduct.

The first of these two summaries may be found as it
came from the lips of the Redeemer himself, in Matth.
xxii. 34—40. "But when the Pharisees had heard that
he had put the Sadducees to silence, they were gathered
together. Then one of them, which was a lawyer, asked
him a question, tempting him, and saying, Master, which
is the great commandment in the law? Jesus said unto
him, Thou shalt love the Lord thy God with all thy heart,
and with all thy soul, and with all thy mind. This is the
first and great commandment. And the second is like
unto it, Thou shalt love thy neighbour as thyself. On
these two commandments hang all the law and the prophets."—The second summary is the one on which we
have just been commenting,—contained in the ten commandments.

It is further worthy of observation, that, between these two summaries, there is a beautiful correspondence. The four precepts of the first table of the law are the practical counterpart of the first of the two great principles, the love of God:—the six precepts of the second table are, in like manner, the practical counterpart of the second of these principles, the love of our neighbour. And the very manner in which the comprehensiveness of love is sometimes illustrated in the New Testament, seems to show, that the law of the two tables was regarded by the apostles as still the summary of its duties, and as still binding on the people of God. How strikingly is this the case in Rom. xiii. 8—10. " Owe no man any thing, but to love one another: for he that loveth another hath fulfilled the law. For this, Thou shalt not commit adultery, Thou shalt not kill, Thou shalt not steal, Thou shalt not bear false witness, Thou shalt not covet; and if there be any other commandment, it is briefly comprehended in this saying, namely, Thou shalt love thy neighbour as thyself. Love worketh no ill to his neighbour: therefore love is the fulfilling of the law." Here are five out of the six precepts of the second table of the Decalogue (and we have the sixth elsewhere, Eph. vi. 1—3.) adduced as the practical detail of the Christian law of love to our neighbour. Had the apostle been speaking of love to God, have not we in this an evidence, that he would have cited the four precepts of the first table as fulfilled in that higher principle? And is this the language of one who regarded the obligation of these precepts as having ceased? Let it be remembered, that both the two summaries, which we have mentioned, belonged to the law *as given by Moses;*

and there is just as much authority for saying, that the obligation of love to God and love to our neighbour has ceased, as for saying, that the obligation of the ten commandments has ceased. If the two are still binding, so are the ten. "

In ridiculing this comprehensive principle of interpretation, Mr. Hallet avails himself especially of the fifth commandment; and, it must be confessed, with no little appearance of reason.—" It seems very surprising to me," says he, " to hear wise and learned men talk as if the fifth commandment required all the duties that are incumbent on men in the various relations of life. ' Honour thy father and mother' is as plain an expression as any expression in a law of general use needs to be. But how dark have men made it, when they have interpreted it as meaning, Honour the king, the priest, and other superiors ! Who would have suspected, that in a law delivered for the use of children, the words father and mother should mean king, priest, prophet, &c. ? But, supposing it possible to interpret father and mother of all superiors, is it not still more surprising to hear them interpreted as signifying equals, and even inferiors ? Is it not strange, that ' Honour thy father and mother' should be a command to parents to educate their children in the fear of God, and to brothers and sisters to love one another ?"——I was once very much inclined to join with Mr. Hallet in considering this as an arbitrary and extravagant principle of interpretation :— but, although I am not even yet prepared to vindicate, in all their extent, the terms of explanation used by the Westminster divines, yet the following remarks may at least show, that there is less of arbitrary extravagance in their

D

interpretation, and less ground, consequently, for the ridicule thrown upon it, than might at first view appear.

1. We have authority,—the very highest authority, for adopting a principle of interpretation which includes more than is directly expressed by the precise letter of the law. So that, in the mere circumstance of exceeding the strictly literal meaning, we are not chargeable with what is in itself illegitimate and unauthorized. Thus our Lord, in the sermon on the mount, explains the sixth commandment, "Thou shalt not kill," as prohibitory, not merely of the act of murder, but of the inward passion of causeless or excessive anger, and of the words of contumelious reviling; and no terms can be more correctly expressive of the latitude of interpretation thus justified, than those of the Westminster divines, when they represent the sixth commandment as forbidding, not only the taking away of life, but "*whatsoever tendeth thereunto.*" The seventh commandment, in like manner, 'Thou shalt not commit adultery," is, according to this divine interpreter, violated by every lascivious look, by every unchaste desire. These and other parts of that discourse contain a distinct warrant for extending the principle of interpretation beyond the simple letter of the precept. And it is sufficiently evident, that our Lord is not there to be understood as putting upon the law a new interpretation of his own, but only as affirming its original and legitimate meaning, in opposition to the partial, corrupt, anti-spiritual glosses of the Jewish expounders.

2. It is certainly deserving of notice, how appropriately the second table begins. It is with the duties we owe *to parents*. These follow immediately after our duties to

God have been disposed of;—parents being the first of all fellow-creatures to whom, after God, we owe love, honour, and obedience. And the law of the two tables being necessarily, (from its nature, as a brief abstract,) restricted to leading principles, this precept may be fairly assumed to imply more than it directly expresses.

3. The heart that is in a right state in regard to this first and highest of earthly obligations, may be justly said to have in it what I may call a *germinating principle* of all the other relative duties. Not only does the very structure of the precept assume the authority of parents, and implicitly presuppose duties on their part to their children; But the very fulfilment, in a right manner, of the duties of children prepares and fits for the subsequent discharge of the duties of parents. They who, from principle and affection, have truly honoured their father and mother, will love, and cherish, and protect, and do good to, their own children. The one set of duties are an excellent preparative for the other. He who knows experimentally the heart of a child will be able, even in the exercise of parental authority itself, to apply the golden rule—" Whatsoever ye would that men should do to you, do ye also to them likewise."—A right state of feeling, too, towards parents, amongst the members of the same family, will infallibly be accompanied with a right state of feeling towards one another. It can hardly be, that brothers and sisters should have the same congenial sentiments towards the objects of their common affection, and yet hate, despise and ill-treat one another.

4. In this first of earthly relations, the *general principles of authority and submission* may be properly considered as

comprehended. It is natural that *this* relation, being the foundation and origin of all others, should, in a brief summary, where it was neither intended nor possible to enter into minute specification, should be selected for this purpose. When the mind is properly trained to filial subordination, it is prepared for legitimate subordination of all other kinds; and the duly principled exercise of parental authority will fit for every other description of divinely instituted rule. The precept thus contains, as I have said, a germinating principle; so that the heart that is truly, and on proper grounds, right here, will not be far wrong in any of the other relations of life. The nursery is the elementary training school for them all.

5. These general remarks seem to receive countenance and confirmation from the very frequent *analogical reference* to *this* relation, in speaking of the nature and claims of others Thus, of superiors in age it is said—" Rebuke not an old man, but entreat him as a father:"—Princes of peculiarly excellent and patriotic character are the fathers of their people :—Men of eminent usefulness and high estimation in the church are, on the same principle, fathers—" My father, my father !" exclaimed Elisha to the departing Elijah—" the chariots of Israel, and the horsemen thereof :"—thus too, servants regard and address kind and affectionate masters—2 Kings v. 13:—the pupils of the prophets were, in old times, denominated their sons :—and the converts of a minister of Christ are, in the phraseology of the New Testament, his spiritual children—" Though ye have ten thousand instructors in Christ, yet have ye not many fathers ; for in Christ Jesus I have begotten you through the gospel."

On such grounds as these, the comprehensive principle of interpretation may, to a considerable extent, be vindicated, and rescued from harsh censure and hasty ridicule. Too much may have been represented as actually included and directly inculcated in the precept : but, as one of a few leading principles, intended to bring the moral duties within the limits of a very brief statement, and by their influence to train and discipline the mind for all the more minute details, it will be found, in the place which it occupies, to bear the marks of divine wisdom.

There is a declaration of our Lord, in his sermon on the mount, which bears directly on the subject before us of the continued obligation of the moral law, and which must not be passed without due notice. He says, Matth. v. 17, 18, " Think not that I am come to destroy the law or the prophets : I am not come to destroy, but to fulfil. For verily I say unto you, till heaven and earth pass, one jot or one tittle shall in no wise pass from the law, till all be fulfilled." In the connexion in which these words stand, they appear to me conclusive of the present question. Let us seriously attend to them.

The general sentiment of the words appears to be, that there was a perfect harmony between what the Messiah had come to accomplish, and all that had gone before ; that there was no contradiction, no incongruity. The remark applies to the whole of the preceding revelation. Of that revelation no part whatever was to be frustrated, or made void, by his coming and work. All, on the contrary, instead of being " destroyed," or subverted, was to be " fulfilled," or ratified ;—every part, according to its peculiar nature and end. Every declaration of God should be proved true; every prediction should find its accomplishment; every promise, and every threatening, should be verified; every type should meet with its corresponding reality, every shadow find its substance, every institution its appropriate object; and the whole of the ancient revelation should have its divine authority established, and should continue in full force, as an integral part of the communications of God's mind and will to men, retaining to the end, in conjunction with the New Testament, the character given of it by the apostle, in opposition to all that is apocryphal and human—" From a child thou hast known the Holy Scriptures, which are able to make thee wise unto salvation, through faith which is in Christ Jesus. All Scripture is given by inspiration of God, and is profitable for doctrine, for reproof, for correction, and for instruction in righteousness; that the man of God may be perfect, thoroughly furnished unto every good work." 2 Tim. iii. 15—17.

It is with "the law," not with "the prophets," that we have at present to do. Respecting it Jesus affirms, that he came not to destroy, but to fulfil,—and to fulfil, even to the minutest "jot or tittle." Now, there is one part of the law, to which, at first view, this declaration may appear hardly applicable; that part, I mean, which is usually called the ceremonial law. Was not the whole system, it will naturally be asked, of that typical and shadowy ritual to be "done away in Christ," to be finally and for ever set aside? I answer, most assuredly. At the time when our Lord uttered the words, it had "waxed old, and was ready to vanish away." The entire Jewish dispensation was, about to be abrogated, and to give place to a new, more spiritual, and permanent state of things.—But, true as this is, there is an important sense, in which even the ceremonial law did not fail. That cannot, with any propriety, be said to fail, which fully answers every end proposed in it by him who appointed it. Such was the case here. By the coming and work of Jesus, the end or design, of the ancient ritual was made distinctly manifest; and it was made manifest by being fulfilled. Every part of it attained its object. Not one jot or tittle could be said, in this respect, to fail. Not the most minute rite, or circumstance of a rite, in the entire system of ceremonial observance, failed of having its meaning explained and its purpose accomplished.—In this way the divine authority of that system was established. It was shown to be of God, and in every part of it to be worthy of its Author. Its excellence lay, not in itself, but in its reference to what it prefigured,—in its end, and in its appropriateness to that end. In itself, it consisted of weak and beggarly elements; but still they were the elements of what was transcendently excellent and glorious. In itself, "it had no glory by reason of the glory that excelleth;" but of that very glory it might be truly said to have partaken, inasmuch as it contained its emblematical representations,—the symbolical pre-intimations of " that which was to come."—This part of the law, then, had its fulfilment. Its end was answered; and its divinely perfect adaptation to that end was made beautifully apparent. It was " the bringing in of a better hope ;" and the full revelation of that better hope gave honour and lustre to that which represented and introduced it. The ceremo-

nial law was never so truly "magnified and made honourable," as when it was fulfilled and set aside. When "the
Sun of righteousness" arose, he shed back a brilliant light
on all that had gone before, illuminating its obscurity, and
imparting to it a glory unseen till then.—Thus, it will far
from being any part of the design of Christ's mission and
work to do dishonour to any one of the previous institutions of God. On the contrary, every divine end, in every
divine ordinance, was clearly shown and fully answered;
" not one jot or tittle failed ; all was fulfilled."

From the connexion, however, in which our Lord's
words stand, it will hardly admit of question, that he has
a special reference in them to the *moral* rather than the
ceremonial law. All that follows, containing explanations
and comments on precepts strictly moral, is an evidence of
this :—and the two immediately subsequent verses appear
peculiarly decisive of it: verses 19, 20, " Whosoever,
therefore, shall break one of the least of these commandments, and shall teach men so, he shall be called the least in
the kingdom of heaven: but whosoever shall do and teach
them, the same shall be called great in the kingdom of
heaven. For I say unto you, that except your righteousness shall exceed the righteousness of the scribes and
Pharisees, ye shall in no case enter into the kingdom of
heaven."—Is it not very clear from these words, that the
commandments of which the Saviour speaks are commandments which were to continue in force in " the kingdom
of heaven," or the New Testament church ? If not, how
could the breach and the non-inculcation of them on the
one hand, and the observance and teaching of them on the
other, be the standard of estimation and honour in that

kingdom? Now we know, both from the authority of the divine word, and from corresponding fact, that this is not the case with the institutions of the ceremonial law; —and neither is it the case with the peculiar civil polity of the Jews. Of what commandments, then, can our Lord be conceived to speak, if not of the precepts of the moral law?—To suppose him to speak of the ceremonial law, and to affirm that the man should be of no repute in the kingdom of heaven, who himself neglected and taught others to neglect, even the least of the outward and typical institutes of Judaism, would be at utter variance with the entire character of the divine scheme,—at variance with both Judaism and Christianity,—with the temporary and preparatory nature of the one, and with the spirituality, universality, and permanence of the other. And no less inconsistent would it be, to apply his words to the institutes of the Jewish civil law; these having been designed for the nation of Israel, and having no possible place under the new constitution of the church of God. Nothing remains, therefore, to which his words *can* be applied, but the moral law;—that law, of which, accordingly, he immediately proceeds to correct the misinterpretations and abuses, and to affirm, in opposition to these the spirituality and extensiveness, in all its requirements.

He came, then, not to subvert, but to fulfil and ratify, *the moral law*: and I need not say, when the connexion of his words is considered, that I mean the moral law, *as given to Israel.* He was to fulfil and ratify it, as well as the ceremonial; but in a different way, a way that accorded, as in the other case, with its nature and end. The end of the ceremonial law did not admit of its being permanent; the end of the moral law did not admit of its being temporary. The ceremonial law answered its end, when it had introduced the new spiritual dispensation; its sacrifices being superseded by that of Christ, and its "diverse washings" by the "ministration of the Spirit." But the moral law has for its end the regulation of the heart and conduct of men; and, that being a permanent end, the rule is permanent for its continued attainment. The ceremonial law did not fail, although it ceased. Its cessation was not its failure; for before it ceased it had served its purpose. But with regard to the moral law, cessation would be failure. Its end would, to a great extent, be frustrated; its purpose cut off in the midst. That purpose remains to be answered, so long as there remains an accountable agent on earth, of whose character it is designed as the director and the test.

In considering, therefore, a little, in what manner the moral law was ratified, fulfilled, prevented from failing, by the work of Christ, we may find farther evidence of its permanent obligation. In illustration of this, let me remark—

1. In the first place, that the highest honour was put upon the law *by his own perfect obedience to all its precepts.*—The law of God had been fearfully dishonoured by the disobedience and rebellion of men. It had been disregarded; it had been trampled under foot. In the hearts of the vast majority its principles had no place, nor its precepts in the practice of their lives. And even in the best of men,—the best of those who had been renewed by the Spirit of God,—there was not one that presented a genuine and faithful transcript of its holy requirements.

But in the heart of "the man Christ Jesus," the leading principles of love to God and love to man, in which, we have seen, it is summed up, were sinlessly perfect,—perfect in degree, perfect in exercise. There was no deficiency, no deviation,—not in one thought, or word, or look, or action. Every chord of that heart was in perfect unison. Every step of that life was on the centre-line of holy virtue. The pure eye of Omniscience, on the strictest scrutiny, discerned nothing there but what it delighted to behold. The character was a full display of what the divine law required,—a display, such as never had been seen on earth, since paradise was lost. It "magnified and made it honourable." When you look at this "man Christ Jesus"—"holy, harmless, undefiled, separate from sinners," you see a perfect combination of every excellence: and yet, what more was this than a living exemplification of the divine law? Never was such honour put upon it; never was its excellence so gloriously shewn, as when, in the obedience of the Son of God, it met with its all-perfect counterpart,—as when He said, and fulfilled the saying, "Lo I come,—I delight to do thy will, O my God; yea, thy law is within my heart."—The bearing of this on our present subject we shall see immediately.

2. He verified his declaration, in the second place, *by enduring the law's penal sanction;—bearing what was due for its violation.*—That his sufferings and death amounted to this,—that they were substitutionally penal, and an exhaustion of the law's curse, is affirmed in many parts of Scripture. "As many as are of the works of the law," says Paul, Gal. iii. 10, 13, "are under the curse—for it is written, Cursed is every one that continueth not in all

things written in the book of the law to do them. Christ hath redeemed us from the curse of the law, being made a curse for us." All the sufferings which Christ endured, together with the accursed death in which they terminated, were in fulfilment of the denunciations of the law against transgression. Its sanction was as sure, as its precepts were righteous. The curse had divine authority in it, as well as the commandments. If the latter do not find their fulfilment, the former must find its execution. The commandment being violated, the curse is incurred; and somewhere or other it must alight,—on the sinner, or on the substitute. Its vials of wrath must be poured out. The law would otherwise be dishonoured; and the authority and glory of the Lawgiver compromised and tarnished. Jesus " magnified the law," by giving a public manifestation of the impossibility of its being transgressed with impunity. The law was covered with glory, when its fearful sanction was owned, and vindicated, and endured, by such a Mediator! Its excellence as a rule of character having been manifested in his sinless life, the righteousness both of its requirements and of its penalty was attested and recorded for ever in his atoning death.

Now, surely the law under which Christ was made, which he perfectly obeyed, whose sanction he endured, from whose curse he delivers, was not a law of merely partial and temporary obligation; confined to the Jews, and to the period of their peculiar economy. If it was, then his atonement could not extend beyond the limits of the law's obligation. It must have been confined to those who were under that law. This appears an inevitable consequence. The curse, from which Christ is

epresented as having delivered those who were under it
y becoming a curse for them, was the curse pronounced
y the law of Moses. It was that law which said, on the
ne hand, " The man that doeth these things shall live by
hem;" and, on the other, " Cursed is every one that con-
irmeth not all the words of this law,"—or, in the apos-
le's equivalent terms, " who continueth not in all things
vritten in the book of the law to do them." This, then,
s the curse from which Christ saves. But if the Jews
mly were under that law, the Jews only could be under
ts curse:—and if the Jews only were under the curse,
he Jews only could be redeemed from the curse. The
aw of Moses, therefore, must be regarded as, in its moral
rinciples and requirements, the law of mankind; includ-
ng under its obligation, and its sanction, men of all coun-
ries, and of all generations. If we would not restrict the
tonement and the deliverance, we must not restrict the
aw. When the apostle repeatedly affirms that " by the
eeds of the law *no flesh living* shall be justified," he is,
rithout question, speaking of the law as given by Moses.
lut if that law was exclusively Jewish, then " no flesh
ving" besides the Jews were under it; and it was very
ain to say that they could not be justified by it, seeing they
ould not be condemned by it. Their condemnation must
ave been on the ground of another law. But of no other
aw is Christ represented as bearing the curse; and there-
ore there can be no provision made by his propitiatory
eath for their deliverance.

3. In the third place, Jesus honoured and established the
aw by his *spiritual interpretation of its meaning*. Men
ave naturally a great aversion to the hold which the law

takes of the heart. They cannot bear its spirituality. Influenced by this dislike, the Jewish interpreters put upon its precepts many false glosses, corresponding with their carnal, worldly desires. They limited and explained away whatever was most offensive, and accommodated the law to the likings of fallen nature. This system of misinterpretation and perversion, our divine Master, in his sermon on the mount, sets himself to oppose. He is not, as we have already hinted, to be understood as putting a new construction of his own upon ancient precepts, accommodating them, by a spiritual interpretation, to New Testament times. Even were this supposed to be the case, it would be far from lessening the force of our argument. It would rather, indeed, increase it. For why introduce this spiritual commentary on the law, as the sense in which it was to be understood in his own kingdom, unless in that kingdom it was to continue in force? But we apprehend it was not so. He rather asserts the primitive meaning of the commandments—their original and permanent import. They were always spiritual. The laws of the Searcher of hearts could never be otherwise. They always required the regulating of the thoughts and desires in conformity with their principles, as well as of the words and actions. Christ does not, as many seem to imagine, improve upon Moses:—he explains and enforces the true sense of the law, as given by Moses, when uncorrupted by Jewish glosses and traditions. In this way, too, he "magnified and made it honourable." Its glory consists in its spirituality. By a contrary style of interpretation, it was dishonoured and degraded. And, so far from concurring in those comments, by which divine precepts were reduced, and modified, and destroyed, Jesus set himself against them; asserting the glory and the entire and permanent obligation of the law, in the full spiritual amount of every one of its requirements. Instead of making void the law, he thus showed himself jealous of every encroachment, and of every corruption, and determined to maintain its unsullied purity and heart-searching perfection.

Let any candid person read those parts of the sermon on the mount, which contain our Lord's comments on the law, and try if he can persuade himself that those precepts, of which, with divine dignity, he reprehends the perversion and affirms the spiritual and comprehensive import, were precepts of a law which, after all his solicitude and pains to expound and settle its meaning, he had himself come to set aside, and of which the partial and temporary obligation was immediately, and for ever, to cease? Can he imagine, while he reads, that the interpretation relates to *past time only*? Can he conceive, that when the Divine Speaker, himself possessing all the authority of legislation, after stating the misinterpretation, subjoins his own solemn dictate, " But I say unto you"— " but I say unto you,"—he has no reference to future obligation, but is speaking of a rule which, at the very time, was on the point of abrogation? For example ;—when he says, " Ye have heard that it hath been said by them of old time, Thou shalt love thy neighbour, and hate thine enemy; but I say unto you, Love your enemies"—it is needless, surely, to remind the reader that " Thou shalt love thy neighbour, and hate thine enemy" was not the law of Moses. The precept, " Thou shalt love thy neighbour," never involved in it a permission to hate an enemy.

It was, on the contrary, the express requisition of that law—"If thou meet thine enemy's ox, or his ass, going astray, thou shalt surely bring it back to him again. If thou seest the ass of him that hateth thee lying under his burden, and wouldst forbear to help him, thou shalt surely help with him." Exod. xxiii. 4, 5. And when, in answer to the question, "Who is my neighbour?" Jesus delivered the parable of the good Samaritan, he inculcated on him who asked the question, and on the Jewish people, no new principle or precept of his own, but what the law of love, as given by Moses, had all along required. Surely, then, nothing can be more unreasonable, than to suppose, that when, in the sermon on the mount, he "spake as one having authority," he merely explained a law, the period of whose obligation was nearly past, without at all intending to lay down any rule for the future! And if he did intend to lay down a rule for the future, what is that rule but the law of Moses spiritually interpreted,—that is, interpreted in its original and divine meaning?

I do not mean to say, that the spiritual interpretation even of a law that had ceased, or was about to cease, would not have been doing honour to the law, and to the lawgiver. It would have been both. The ceremonial law was honoured, by having its true nature and design pointed out, although it was to cease; and so, even on the supposition of its temporary obligation, would the moral law have been honoured, by the authoritative declaration of what the Divine Lawgiver intended it to be, during the limited period of its continuance. But the King of Zion goes farther than this. The law which he spiritually interprets he establishes, for perpetuity, as the law of his own kingdom. The whole of his language intimates this, and especially that in the nineteenth verse—" Whosoever, therefore, shall break one of the least of these commandments, and shall teach men so, the same shall, in the kingdom of heaven, be called the least; but whosoever shall do and teach them, the same shall, in the kingdom of heaven, be called great." I am at a loss, I repeat, for a principle of explanation to these words, if " in the kingdom of heaven," or under his own mediatorial reign, the commandments of which he speaks were not to remain in force, but were only to be regarded as remnants of the past, as Jewish antiquities, as the enactments of a divine, indeed, but abrogated dispensation.

To these considerations I might add, that Jesus honoured and established the law, in his recommending and enforcing obedience to its precepts by new and powerful motives,—even all the motives of the light and love of God contained in his gospel:—and in the communications of his Holy Spirit, for the express purpose of bringing sinners, through the discoveries of that gospel, into conformity with its requirements. But, on these topics, I shall not insist, as they open too wide and general a field, and are not so directly connected with the present argument.—This much, however, I may further say,—that *the nature of the connexion between the law and the gospel* is such, as to afford the very strongest presumptive evidence, that the former, as well as the latter, is universal and permanent. First of all, then, it is the law that necessitates the gospel. It is because the law has been broken,—broken in the very spirit and essence of all its requirements, by the alienation of man's heart from God,—that the grace of the gospel has become necessary. The breach of the law has given rise to the pressing exigency in the condition of man, which the mediation of Christ was designed to provide for. The law itself, as given by God, is never represented as " unto death," but " unto life." It was " ordained unto life;" and its language ever has been, and ever must be—" This do, and thou shalt live." But, in regard to the purpose of obtaining life, it was of old, and it is still, " weak through the flesh,"—perfectly competent to the end in itself, but incompetent through the depravity of man. " If there had been a law given," says Paul, Gal. iii. 21, " which could have given life, verily righteousness should have been by the law :"—that is, if the law of God had been such as that man, the subject of depravity, could have rendered to it the obedience which it requires; or if that law had contained in it any provision of pardon for disobedience; then justification, or acceptance with God, should have been on the ground of that law. But all men being, in spirit and practice, transgressors, this is out of the question. Righteousness cannot come by the law. " The commandment, which was ordained to life, is found," by the conscious sinner, " to be unto death." He feels the necessity of grace, and is shut up to Christ " as the end of the law for righteousness, to every one that believeth." " For (what the law could not do, in that it was weak through the flesh) God, sending his own Son in the likeness of sinful flesh, and for sin, hath condemned sin in the flesh; that the righteousness of the law might be fulfilled in us, who walk not after the flesh, but after the spirit." Rom. viii. 3, 4. Of what law is it that the apostle, in these and many other similar passages, speaks? It must be of a law that was on inspired record; a written law. But there was no written law, no law on inspired record, except the Mosaic. Are we, then, to suppose, that in his argument respecting the necessity of the grace of the gospel, the apostle draws his conclusions from a law that was binding upon the Jews alone, and of which the obligation lasted no longer than till the close of the old and temporary dispensation? If we do suppose this, then must his conclusions be limited. The exigency of the case, arising from the transgression of the law, could exist, as we formerly noticed, only as to those who were under the law. And if we are called to demonstrate the necessity of the grace of the gospel *now*, where are we to take our stand? Where are we to find our demonstrative test? We have no divinely delivered and authenticated law, from the principles and precepts of which we can deduce our conclusion; for the only such law that existed before the gospel never, it seems, comprehended under its sanction more than one people; and, having passed away with the abrogated institutions of that people, now comprehends none whatever of the human race! We have no stand, then, in framing our demonstration, but what we call *the law of nature*; or, the intimations of the divine will gathered from the dictates of conscience in fallen men, with all the ten thousand biassing and blinding influences by which those dictates are perverted and diversified. We have no settled, no divinely authorized standard. Even when we have succeeded in proving the inspiration of the sacred volume, we have still no inspired law, from which we can argue with our fellow-men, in demonstrating how the violated authority of God has rendered the grace of the gospel necessary for them. We can show them in our book the gospel which reveals the ground of pardon; but we cannot show them in our book the law which has condemned them. There is no such law there. There is a Jewish law; but there is no law of universal and perpetual obligation;—there is a law for the seed of Abraham, and for the "time then present," but not a law for mankind, and for all generations. Does not this make a material deficiency, in the authority and consistency of our argument? Our law and our gospel must be derived from different sources of information; the one from reason and conscience only, the other from revelation. It is vain to say, in reply, we have the law of Christ. True; but the law from which we must derive our demonstration of the necessity of the gospel, must of course be a law that existed before the gospel,—not a law given by the Author of the gospel to those who receive his grace. When the apostle, after saying, as before quoted, " If there had been a law given which could have given life, verily righteousness should have been by the law," immediately adds, " But the scripture hath concluded all under sin, that the promise by faith of Jesus Christ might be given to them that believe;" what means he? Surely by "*all*" being " concluded under sin," he means *Jews and Gentiles* alike. But " sin is the transgression of the law." When, therefore, the scripture " concludes all under sin," it concludes all in transgression of the law,—and under the condemning sentence of the law. Now, there can be no reasonable question, that the law of which he had been speaking, and from which he had been reasoning, is the law as contained in the Old Testament Scriptures. That, therefore, must have been the original and universal law, binding on all men, and the test by which the rectitude or the perverseness of the dictates of reason and of natural conscience is to be tried and determined. I cannot but regard this view of the case as highly important. I cannot willingly admit, (what must, however, be the case on the hypothesis in question, of the partial and temporary obligation of the law of Moses) that the apostle's demonstration of the necessity of the grace of the gospel from the fact of the law having been broken, embraces in its conclusion the Jews alone. And as little can I willingly admit, that, in *our* demonstration of this necessity, we can take our position on no higher and surer authority than that of natural conscience; that, though we can show a divinely revealed gospel we cannot show a divinely revealed law,—but, while we appeal to revelation for what we argue *to*, can appeal to reason only for what we argue *from*.

While the law thus shows the necessity of the gospel, and, by convicting the conscience, impresses its value, and recommends its grace to acceptance; the gospel, on the other side, endears the law. "The mercies of God," as made known in the discoveries of the gospel, fill the heart of the believing sinner with overflowing gratitude: Feeling his need of a Saviour, and seeing in Christ a Saviour suited to his need, he is captivated by the grace that has provided such a Saviour, and, under the impulse of that holy love which has displaced the native enmity of his heart, is desirous to "glorify God," as the God of his salvation, "with his body and with his Spirit which are God's." In this state of mind and heart, how will he regard the law? Does he hate it, because it has condemned him? No. He sees and owns it to be "holy, and just, and good." He regards it as a transcript of the moral excellence of its Divine Author; and, in proportion as he delights in God, he delights in his law. Every precept of it, now that he has been freed from the fear which hath torment, and has felt the attractions of divine love, and given his heart up to their influence, comes before his mind as the intimation of the will of one to whom he has become infinitely indebted. The law is the will of Him who has given him the gospel,—of the God of his salvation,—the God who "delighteth in mercy,"—the God who "spared not his own Son but freely gave him up for us all." Every consideration, therefore, in the gospel, which demands and draws forth his gratitude, recommends and endears the law. Having renounced the heaven-insulting presumption of dependance on the law as the condition of life, he yet cannot renounce it as his standard of duty. Of that new life of which the faith of the gospel is the principle, the law becomes the rule. Every violation of any of its precepts is now a trespass, not against authority only, but against love,—the love that "passeth knowledge," brought to light by the gospel. So that, while he "delights in the law of God after the inward man," his chief distress of spirit arises from the "law in his members," that still "wars against the law of his mind," and strives to bring him into subjection to the law of sin. Such is the connexion, and such the reciprocation of influence, between the law and the gospel. The law, by giving the knowledge of sin, and convicting the conscience of guilt, and filling with the fear of wrath, recommends to acceptance the grace of the gospel :—and the grace of the gospel, received in humility and grateful love, recommends to obedience the precepts of the law. The will of the lawgiver is endeared by the grace of the Saviour :—and the believer says, indignantly, "Do we then make void the law through faith? God forbid: yea, we establish the law." The very love which the gospel inspires, is the fulfilling of the law. He who is under its influence will be disposed to say, with a proportional decision of mind and fervour of spirit—"Therefore I esteem all thy commandments concerning all things to be right; and I hate every false way."

With regard, indeed, to the renovating power of the gospel in the spiritually enlightened soul,—what does it amount to? When, in conversion, a sinner is "renewed in the spirit of his mind," and "puts on Christ," what does his character become? What does the gospel do to it? Does it not *bring it into conformity to the law?* What else, what more, what better, can it do? We have already seen, that the first promise of the new or gospel covenant is that God will "put his law in the inward parts, and write it in the heart:"—and while the Spirit of God does this, he does it by the discovery to the mind of the love revealed in the gospel. It is at the foot of the cross that the heart receives this new impress of the divine law; an impress that is subsequently transcribed into the life. I say, what other, or greater, or better change than this can the gospel be supposed to effect? When the apostle says, "The carnal mind is enmity against God," he expresses the sum of human depravity. And what is the proof and manifestation of the enmity?

It lies in what immediately follows—" For it is not subject to the law of God, neither indeed can be." How can a mind at enmity with God be subject to a law of which the principle and essence is love? And what does the gospel, but introduce this principle? " Faith worketh by love." Faith produces love; and love obedience. If enmity is the sum of opposition to the law, love is the sum of conformity to it.—The law, we have said, is a transcript of the moral excellence of the Lawgiver. Is there, then, any difference between the view of that excellence given by the law, and the view of it given by the gospel? I answer, No. There is, substantially, none. There is no discrepancy between the one and the other. The law is said to be " holy, and just, and good." It corresponds in these its attributes with the character of Him who has given it:—He is holy, and just, and good. And what else is the testimony of the gospel? What does Calvary teach us of God, but that he is holy, and just, and good? The difference lies (for a difference there is) in the *kind* of display given of the divine *goodness*. The law is good. It is the preceptive will of a good God. It is fitted to promote the well-being of all who obey it. Every command, and every prohibition, is the command, and is the prohibition of a benevolent being. But for transgressors, the law contains no intimations of goodness. It is all threatening,—all unbending justice. The discovery of goodness to men *as sinners*, belongs not to the law, but to the gospel :—and it there appears under the aspect of *mercy;* mercy being goodness in its relation to the guilty and the miserable. And where this gospel, —the revelation of the mercy of God in Christ,—exerts

s renewing energy on the sinner's heart, what better can
do than rendering him holy, and just, and good? What
etter than bringing him, in spirit and in conduct, into
rogressive conformity to that law, of which this is the
divinely inspired description? And what law, we again
ask, is this? Is it not a law to which we can point, as
authoritatively dictated in the book of God? Is it not
he law of which the heart-searching spirituality was
winced to the apostle's mind and conscience by its clos-
ng precept, "Thou shalt not covet?" And we repeat
our former question—Is this, can this be, a law that
has passed away, and whose obligation never extended
beyond the precincts of the land of Israel? Is it not
rather the law of God *to man?*—that law, whose essential
principles constituted the divine image in which he
was originally created, while their absence is the sum of
his apostasy; sinless conformity to which was the perfection of the heavenly Saviour's character; the inscription of which on the heart is man's restoration to his
Maker's likeness; and which, when the inscription is
perfected, and the remaining traces of sin obliterated,
shall be the glory and the bliss of the paradise above?

I have been induced to dwell the longer on the universality and permanence of the law, because it is an
essential link in our present argument; and because of
its general importance in other connexions. The formal
denial of it has been recently revived by a writer of
eminence in the English Church;* and some other di-

---

* Dr. Whately: Essays on some of the Difficulties in the Writings of
St. Paul. Essay V. On the abolition of the Mosaic law.

vines, of the most evangelical sentiments and approved character, have been disposed, I cannot but think unwittingly, to adopt the same views.

The sentiments of those who admitting, in general, the permanence of the moral law, question, notwithstanding, the moral nature of the fourth commandment, and rank the Sabbath among positive institutions, shall be considered in next discourse.

DISCOURSE III.

Exod. xx. 81—1.

" Remember the sabbath-day, to keep it holy. Six days shalt thou labour, and do all thy work : But the seventh day is the sabbath of the Lord thy God : in it thou shalt not do any work, thou, nor thy son, nor thy daughter, thy man-servant, nor thy maid-servant, nor thy cattle, nor thy stranger that is within thy gates : For in six days the Lord made heaven and earth, the sea, and all that in them is, and rested the seventh day : wherefore the Lord blessed the sabbath-day, and hallowed it."

Having, in last discourse, gone at considerable length into the discussion of the general question respecting the continued obligation of the Decalogue, we shall now take some notice of the sentiment of those who, while they do not question the permanence of the moral law generally, are, notwithstanding, disposed to regard the Sabbath as belonging rather to the class of positive institutions than of moral precepts, and to make it an exception to the general principle.

In commencing my observations on this view of the case, it may be freely admitted, that the Sabbath, considered as the setting apart of a special day for a special purpose, does bear very much of the appearance of a positive institute,—an institute, that is, the observance of which is founded solely in a specific enactment, and is not deducible from the general principles of moral obligation.* That in one respect it *is* of this nature, namely, in as far as regards the prescribed proportion of our time to be devoted to the end in view, we may notice more fully, immediately. But in the mean time I wish to remark, that, even on the supposition of its being entirely positive, the conclusion against its permanence is too hasty. If, indeed, it could be proved, that it belonged to the positive institutions *peculiar to the Mosaic economy,* it might not be so easy to evade the inference. But from the mere admission of its positive nature, the inference is not legitimate. That it *may* be abrogated, is a fair deduction; that it *must,* is more than the admission warrants. The question comes to be one of fact. Has it been divinely instituted? and if it has, has it been divinely repealed? Persons are apt to fancy, that, in order to prove an ancient Institution not to be binding, they have nothing to do but to show it to be of what they call a positive nature. But this is obviously a mistake. An observance which can plead the positive enactments of divine authority, is as really of moral obligation, so long as it continues unrepealed, as if it were one of the eternal and universal prin-

* " Under the name of positive institutions, we comprehend all those impositions and restraints, which, not being suggested to any man by his conscience, and having no necessary and natural connexion with the dictates of that internal monitor, seem to have no importance but what they derive from the will of a superior who prescribes them." Horsley. Serm. xxi.

ciples of right and wrong. Who will presume to inter-
pose his authority, to set aside what the will of Deity
has enacted? No will but his own can abrogate his own
institutions. In the case of the institutions of the Mosaic
ceremonial, we have his revealed will for their abrogation
as well as for their observance. We know from himself
that their use was partial and transient. But we distinctly
deny; and have endeavoured formerly to assign good
reason for the denial, that the Sabbath was at all one of
the peculiarities of that dispensation. And if we have
succeeded in making good our point, that it had its origin
at creation—we have, on Dr. Paley's own admission,
equally succeeded in settling the question of its universal
and permanent obligation. Let its nature be what you
will—moral, or positive, or mixed,—it is a divine institution;—a divine institution, not for the Jews alone, but for
mankind; and for mankind, not during a limited period
only, but to all generations.—The question, therefore, of
its moral or positive nature, is not a question of which the
settlement is indispensable to our argument respecting its permanence:—for, although the establishment of
its moral character might, on the one hand, infer its perpetuity, the proof of its being entirely positive would not,
on the other, infer its cessation.

The question, however, is still important, and intimately connected with our discussion; especially as we
are unwilling to allow the adversary even the seeming
advantage, unreal as it is, from the supposed positive nature of the sabbatical observance. A modern writer of
the English Church, formerly referred to,* says—"The

* Dr. Whately.

fourth commandment is evidently not a moral, but a positive, precept. The dogma of the Assembly of Divines, at Westminster (in their confession of faith), that the observance of the Sabbath is part of the Moral law, is to me utterly unintelligible." This is truly surprising. Surely the very place which the fourth commandment holds in the Decalogue, as one of ten, of which all the other nine are without controversy moral, affords of itself a proof, which, although it may be characterised as only presumptive, is yet of great force, that it also is of the same description. How came it there? How came the Supreme Legislator, the God of order, to introduce into the midst of a code, distinctly and confessedly moral, one precept of a character so diverse from all the rest? This is, *a priori*, highly improbable. Yet, if the precept did bear upon it, decidedly and unequivocally, such a character of diversity, however much we might have wondered at the seeming incongruity, we must, of course, have admitted the fact; and, whether able to account for it or not, have acquiesced in its propriety, as the arrangement of a wisdom superior to ours. But we cannot, by any means, admit, what appears to this writer so manifest. The view given of the commandment, by the Westminster Divines, as "part of the moral law," instead of deserving the designation of an "unintelligible dogma," appears to be not merely defensible, but the only sound and consistent one: and the sole thing that seems unintelligible is, on what principle a mind like that of Dr. Whately should ever have regarded it in such a light.

It will not surely be disputed, that the worship of God, and the cultivation of the principles of piety, or true religion, are duties of a moral nature. What duties can be more so? They belong to the first and highest of all our moral relations,—that in which we stand to our Creator. There is no denying this. The prescribed exercises, and avowed ends, of the institution are, in the very highest sense of the term, moral. But if the worship of God, or the expression of those sentiments and affections towards him which constitute inward devotion, be an incumbent moral duty: it is a duty, for the efficient fulfilment of which some stated seasons are of obvious utility. If, indeed, there is to be such a thing at all as *social* worship, in which men jointly recognise their common origin and dependance, and their obligations to their one Maker and Benefactor, and thus cherish, on the highest ground, their mutual feelings of unity and love,—utility becomes too feeble a term; such stated seasons being evidently of imperious necessity. And the universal practice of mankind, even under the corruptest forms of false religion, seems to ascertain such social worship to be a dictate, either of the law of nature, or of original and traditionary revelation. If devoting a portion of our time to such purposes as the Sabbath is designed to promote, be a moral duty; then does it not, naturally and properly, belong to God to determine and fix the proportion?

The truth is, that the commandment may be considered as of a mixed character. The duty which it enjoins is moral—pre-eminently moral; while the precise proportion of time, authoritatively demanded as sacred to that duty, is positive. For aught we can perceive, God might have created the world in seven days, and rested on the eighth; or in nine days, and rested on the tenth. In the latter case, instead of weeks of seven days, we should have had decades. We do not feel, in making such a supposition, any thing at all incongruous,—any thing in the least degree revolting to our moral principles. If we do, a moment's examination of the feeling will satisfy us, that it arises entirely from the association of sacredness with the actually existing arrangement; and that, had this arrangement been one of decades instead of weeks, the feeling would have been exactly the reverse of what it is; the sacredness being attached to the tenth day, and the uneasy misgiving to the seventh. But the admission of the positive or arbitrary nature of the mere proportion of the time cannot, with any semblance of reason, be considered as nullifying the morality of the precept. There is nothing more of the positive in it than what arises from the necessity of the case. The duty itself is moral. But, in order to the regular and effective fulfilment of the duty, such a fulfilment of it as shall be most conducive to his own glory, and the benefit of his creatures, the infinitely Wise and Good has seen it needful to prescribe a time for it;—not to leave the proportion to the capricious option of every individual, especially in a world where, he foresaw, there would be so powerful a tendency to neglect the duty altogether,—but to set apart and hallow a definite day,—to say, One day in seven shall be devoted to sabbatical rest, and the employments and purposes of devotion. Does the precept become, in consequence of its assuming this definitive form, less moral than if it had been couched in more general terms? Why should a command, which, had it simply enjoined that God should be worshipped, and the devout affections cultivated, (and I might have added those too of humanity and mercy,) would, without hesitation, have been ranked with moral precepts, become unfit for a place amongst them,—so·unfit as that to consider it a part of the moral law should be pronounced "unintelligible,"—merely because it adds to the general injunction of the duty the prescription of the time of doing it ?—Let me illustrate my meaning by the supposition of a parallel case. The law contains precepts of benevolence. Suppose, then, that among its moral commands, there had been one, not simply enjoining practical kindness, but, along with this, specifying the extent of bounty to which that kindness should reach ; requiring, for example, every man to devote *a tenth* of his substance to the support and comfort of his fellow-men ; to the advancement of their temporal and spiritual well-being : would not this have become a duty of distinct moral obligation ? It would not surely have lost its moral nature, because, along with the general principle of benevolence, it regulated the *minimum* of benevolent bestowment.   The analogy between the supposed case, and the case illustrated by it, is close. In either, there is what I have called the fixing of a *minimum*. The only difference is, that the one relates to time, the other to property.   Each says, this much *at least ;* but does not prohibit more : this much of your time for the service of God, and this much of your substance for the good of men ; but as much more of both as a pious or a charitable disposition may prompt.

Let no one allege that my argument goes to establish the moral obligation and permanence of *tithes.* By no means.   There is quite abundant evidence that the tithing system was peculiarly Jewish ; as much so as the various

other prescribed gifts and offerings by which divine minis-
trations, and the ministers who conducted them, were then
to be provided for. Could evidence be produced that,
either for the purposes of piety, or of charity, a tenth was,
by a general law, required of men previously to the Mosaic
economy, and that, under the gospel dispensation, this
rule, like the other moral precepts, is repeated, as retaining its authority, the objection would have been valid ; nor
should we have sought to resist the conclusion to which it
led, of the permanent moral obligation of the tithe. These
are the circumstances in which the law of the Sabbath
stands. We have formerly traced its obligation to the
beginning of the world, and proved its universality ; and
we shall, by and by, see the amount of proof for its
continuance under the gospel. All that we contend for
at present is, that its being the appointment of a set time
for duties admitted in themselves to be moral, does not at
all affect its *morality*, or deprive it of its right to a place
amongst those precepts of the law, of which the moral
nature is universally acknowledged.

It seems to me, I confess, a very strange thing, that,
because this command prescribes the proportions of time
which are to be devoted to secular and to spiritual concerns,
to the labours of the present world, and to the service
of God and preparation for the world to come,—it is
therefore, entitled to rank only with positive enactments. Is there nothing moral in the use of time ? And
can there be nothing moral in a precept that regulates its
distribution ? Is not time, on the contrary, one of those
gifts which we are most in danger of undervaluing, and
consequently of squandering and abusing ? And are we

not, from the earthly tendencies of our nature, in especial danger of appropriating it entirely to worldly occupations and ends? And would not this be most immoral, and most injurious? However little thought of, time, which is a species of universal property, is in reality more precious than any other. According as it is neglected and abused on the one hand, or employed and improved on the other, will it be productive of a corresponding amount of evil or of good,—of glory or of dishonour to God, of benefit or of injury to man. It is the first thing for which we have to account. The responsibility attaches to every hour. Every moment, as it flies along, bears with it to the judgment-seat a charge of evil, or a testimony of good. There is no one thing of more serious consequence than the *moral use of time,*—the application of moral principle to its occupation. And if the Divine Legislator has laid down a general rule for its distribution,—a rule inclusive of our twofold interests, for time and for eternity, can there be any rule which has a clearer title to a place in the moral law? As a precept that merely distinguishes one day from another, it has the aspect of a positive institute:— but as a precept fixing the great general principle for the use of time, and directly designed for the very highest moral and spiritual purposes, it must be assigned to a different class.

But it has been argued, that we are partial in our conclusions; that if we are bound by the fourth commandment as a part of the law of Moses, we must be bound with regard to the *day,* the *mode of observance,* and the *penalty* affixed to its violation.—This is an objection which calls for our serious notice.

With regard, then, to the *penalty*—(for we shall reverse the order in which we have named the particulars)—it may be observed, that the particular punishment annexed, under a peculiar dispensation, to the transgression of any command, does not affect the nature of the command itself. It is adventitious. It is not properly a part of the command. It may be only a temporary appendage to a precept, which in itself is moral, and of permanent obligation. We have formerly shown that the law of the Sabbath was not a peculiar institute of the Mosaic ritual, but was in existence and force from the beginning. Like other moral precepts of the same antiquity, it was introduced into the law given from Sinai. And were we to consider ourselves as bound by the penalty affixed under the Jewish theocracy to the violation of this particular law, let us see to what conclusion this would conduct us.—*Idolatry* was, in like manner, under the Jewish dispensation, punishable, as a capital offence, with death. Now idolatry involved guilt, as a transgression of the first commandment. It will follow, therefore, that we are not bound by the moral prohibition in that commandment, unless we are at the same time bound to the execution of its then annexed penalty.—The same was the case, too, with *stubborn filial disobedience*, which was a trespass against the fifth commandment; with *adultery*, or the violation of the seventh; and with *blasphemy*, the breach of the third. These are confessedly moral precepts. Are we not at all bound, then, by the moral duty which they inculcate, unless we are at the same time bound by the enactment which made death their penalty?—I am aware of the reply. We are bound, it will be said, by the moral principle of such pre-

:epts ; but it is not *as a part of the law of Moses,*—It is not *is given to the Jews.* · We have formerly noticed this distinction, as an inconsiderate and untenable one. An observation or two more may set it in a still clearer light. Why did Jehovah separate the seed of Abraham as his peculiar people ? Was it to make known to them truths and duties which belonged only to themselves, and in which the rest of mankind had no concern ? Certainly not. It was to reveal to them his character, and mind, and will, and future purposes ; that there might be a record, and a practical remembrancer, of what was in danger of being universally forgotten. Now, what should we think of that man's wisdom, who, with regard to any of the great truths revealed by God to the Jewish people, those for example respecting his unity, and his various natural and moral perfections, should say,—These are important truths, no doubt ; but it is not *as made known to the Jews* that we are bound to believe them ! Yet, would not this be much about as reasonable as to say, in regard to the discovery of the divine will made to that people, These are important moral precepts, no doubt ; but it is not *as given to the Jews* that we are bound to obey them ? Why were these truths made known by Jehovah to the Jews, but because they were, and had from the beginning been, essential and immutable truths respecting Himself ;—truths which had been " most surely believed " by man before the entrance of sin,—but of which the awful prevalence of evil had nearly swept the remembrance from the earth ? And is not the same observation applicable to the discovery made of his *will,* as well as to that made·

of his *character?* Why is a code of moral precepts given to the Jews, but as a record of what had been from the first the essential elements of human duty,—the moral law of God to man?—It may legitimately follow, therefore, that we are bound by the moral precept,—although it does not follow that we are bound by the peculiar penalty then annexed to the transgression of it. There is no inconsistency, in regarding the former as of universal obligation, and the latter as peculiarly Jewish. The law respecting the penalty, indeed, arose out of that exclusively Jewish system of government, established and maintained by the immediate presence and interposition of Deity,—the system usually termed the Theocracy. No other people can be bound to conformity to the penal sanctions of the Jewish law, unless it can make out for itself the existence of a similar relation to God. But this does not at all affect the universal obligation of its moral precepts.

With regard to the *duties* of the day, or the *mode of its observance;* we cannot, without anticipation, enter into the subject now. We shall consider it largely hereafter:— and one point which we hope then to establish will be, that the differences between the observance of the Sabbath as enjoined upon the Jews, and the observance of it as obligatory on Christians, are not, by any means, so great as is generally imagined, and as the present objection assumes;—that the peculiar strictness of the Mosaic sabbatism, which has been considered as in harmony with the stern and slavish character of " the ministration of condemnation," has been extravagantly over-rated;—that in fact the great principles by which sabbatical duties are to be regulated were the same under the old as under the new economy.

It is further objected, that if we are to follow the injunction of the fourth commandment, we must be bound to the observance of the particular *day of the week* on which the Jewish Sabbath was celebrated:—that is, we should hold *the seventh day*, and the seventh day alone, sacred.

In answer to this part of the objection, I would begin by observing, that it equally applies to the law of the Sabbath, whether we regard the institution as a part of the Decalogue, or as commencing from the creation. In either case, it was the seventh day that was hallowed by God, and observed by man. The objection, therefore, is of the greater consequence, inasmuch as, which view soever we adopt of the origin of the Sabbath, it would, if valid at all, be alike conclusive against the legitimacy of the first day of the week.—It is of consequence, however, in determining to what the precept binds us, to bear in mind the necessary diversities in the natural divisions of time in different parts of the world. It is obviously impossible that the command, whencesoever we date its obligation in time, can bind us to the observance of the same identical hours which constituted the Sabbath where it was originally instituted. The beginning and end of natural days, and consequently the beginning and end of weeks, necessarily vary according to the latitude and longitude of places; and while in some countries, as amongst the Jews, the day is calculated from sunset to sunset, in others, as amongst ourselves, it is reckoned from midnight to midnight. It is inconceivable, that a precept of this kind should be made to depend, in the essence of its observance, on circumstances such as these, which might render conformity to it in some instances difficult, and in others impracticable. The Sabbath, as a day, cannot, in the nature of things, be celebrated at the same time in all parts of the world. Whether it be the seventh or the first day of the week, it must be the seventh or the first, according to diversities of latitude, and according to established customary modes of computation.—The tendency of these remarks is to show, that, since the essence of the observance required does not depend on the identity of the hours and minutes appropriated to it in different places, neither does it depend on the identity of the day itself.—Let me not be misunderstood. I do not mean, that, provided men set apart a seventh portion of their time, it matters not which day of the week they select for the purpose; that they may accommodate this to their own convenience, every man choosing for himself and keeping his own sabbath,—or even varying the day from week to week, as considerations of personal or domestic seasonableness may direct. Far from it. Such a principle would be utterly at variance with all order, and with the divine purposes in the institution of the Sabbath. What I mean is, that a divinely authorized change of the day, supposing such a change can be proved, is not a change that at all affects the essence of the precept. The observance itself is essentially the same as before: and the general reason of the observance continues also the same; only that there is superinduced an additional ground to that on which it originally rested,—and that additional ground one of such magnitude and interest, as, in the mind of the Legislator himself, to warrant the alteration.

The case stands simply thus :—At the original institution of the Sabbath, one special reason is assigned for its celebration :—" On the seventh day God ended his work which he had made; and he rested on the seventh day from all his work which he had made. And God blessed the Sabbath-day, and sanctified it, because that in it he had rested from all his work which God created and made," Gen. ii. 2, 3. The Sabbath was thus, in its origin, a commemoration of the great work of creation,—a day, to keep men in mind of the origin of all things,—of the power, and wisdom, and goodness of the all-glorious Creator, and of the duty of fearing, and loving, and worshipping, and serving him. This was the grand primary reason of the institution; and this reason has never, by any change, been superseded. But when the law of the Sabbath was long after enjoined upon the Jews,—while the original and primary reason was assigned for the observance, there was an additional consideration urged upon them, as a motive to conscientious steadfastness in this duty. This you will find in Deut. v. 12—15. " Keep the sabbath-day to sanctify it, as the Lord thy God hath commanded thee. Six days shalt thou labour, and do all thy work; but the seventh day is the sabbath of the Lord thy God : in it thou shalt not do any work, thou, nor thy son, nor thy daughter, nor thy man-servant, nor thy maid-servant, nor thine ox, nor thine ass, nor any of thy cattle, nor thy stranger that is within thy gates; that thy man-servant and thy maid-servant may rest as well as thou. And remember that thou wast a servant in the land of

Egypt, and that the Lord thy God brought thee out thence, through a mighty hand, and by a stretched-out arm: therefore the Lord thy God commanded thee to keep the sabbath-day." That the reason here assigned was only an additional one, not to the superseding or exclusion of the first, we have only to consult our text to be satisfied:—for here, in the solemn promulgation of the law from Sinai, the original reason is the one that is specially and alone introduced:—" for in six days the Lord made heaven and earth, and the sea, and all that in them is; wherefore the Lord blessed the sabbath-day, and hallowed it."

This, then, clearly proves, that other considerations inculcating the observance of the Sabbath might be added to the original one. On the same principle on which God added a second, he might add a third. Make the supposition, then, that at the fulness of time, the completion of the work of redemption had been assigned as a new reason for the celebration of the Sabbath, and that the day at the same time had been retained. It is evident, that he who added the deliverance from Egypt as a reason for keeping the Sabbath, might have added also the greater redemption effected by the Son of God. Had this been done, we should have been in the very same circumstances (with the exception of the superior greatness of the additional motive) in which the Jews were, when God's power and goodness in their deliverance from Egypt were added to his power and goodness in creation, as a subject of the sabbatical commemoration. But here lies the difference. The divine excellence of the work of Christ, and the surpassing preciousness of the blessings of his salvation, are such, that they must not, like the temporal deliverance

from Egypt, hold the place of a merely subordinate, se-
condary, additional reason for the celebration of the Sabbath. They must have the first place. First in the divine
estimate of excellence and glory, they must be first in
man's grateful and reverential commemoration. How,
then, shall their superior importance be marked in the
celebration? Why, in order to give them the lead, the
day shall be changed. Creation had the day formerly;
redemption shall have it now. Not, in either case, exclusively. The sabbatical commemoration of creation would
necessarily, from the time of the fall and the first promise,
be associated, in the minds of devout believing worshippers, with the anticipation of the promised redemption;
and the Creator be worshipped as the God of salvation.
And in like manner, on the Christian Sabbath, the God
of grace, the God and Father of our Lord Jesus Christ,
is worshipped, not to the exclusion of his creative power,
and majesty, and goodness, although with special reference to his redeeming mercy. Redemption only takes the
lead, as it is so pre-eminently entitled to do, among the
subjects of celebration; and in this way, the change of the
day no more alters the nature of the duty, than if redemption had only been introduced as an additional reason, and
the former day had been retained. A divinely authorized
change in the time is not divine abrogation. The change
of the day does not essentially change the thing.

I now proceed to observe, what is of essential consequence, that the observance of a Sabbath is the consecration of A DAY—AN ENTIRE DAY,—to God, and to spiritual
exercises and ends,—a day's cessation from secular engage-

ments. If it was a day formerly, it must be a day still. There are those who, in giving up the seventh day, give up a DAY of religious rest altogether. Renouncing all previous obligations, as cancelled, and taking, or professing to take, their lesson of duty from the New Testament alone, they fancy that in it the whole amount of obligation connected with the Sabbath consists in the duty of believers *to meet on that day for worship, in commemoration of the work of their Master.* This is a point of first rate consequence. Let us endeavour to ascertain how it stands.

That it is the duty of believers to meet on the first day of the week, for the worship of God, and the celebration of New Testament ordinances, is generally admitted. It is plain, from the recorded practice of the churches in apostolic times; of which we shall take a little notice immediately. The question now before us is, not whether this be a duty, but whether it be *all* that the day requires; whether the Sabbath be a secular day like others, with the exception that on it Christians are bound to meet together for worship, or whether the whole day be still sacred. Now, although I would not be disposed, on all occasions, to argue from consequences, yet there are cases in which the obviously legitimate consequences of a principle become a strong presumptive proof against its soundness. Now, it is very plain to every reader of the New Testament, that while there is evidence of the believers having been accustomed to meet on that day, there is nothing explicit in the form either of precept or of example, as to the time and the duration of their meetings; whether they met once, or twice, or oftener, and how long they remained together at each meeting. The question then immediately suggests itself—If the day be secular like other days, with only this exception,—then what proportion is secular, and what proportion sacred? How much does the authority of our Master oblige us to appropriate to the public exercises of his service, and how much does he leave us at liberty to devote to the world's engagements? The language of Acts xx. 7. "On the first day of the week, when the disciples came together to break bread, Paul preached to them, and continued his speech until midnight," and, as afterwards appears, "even till break of day,"—most naturally leads our minds to *the evening* as the time of meeting. I am persuaded that, in this case, it was so;—that the remarkable incident recorded, as the consequence of Paul's long preaching, the historian means to say, took place at that particular time of the day, when the disciples came together for the celebration of the Lord's Supper. I do not doubt that they had met before, at other times of the day; but if I were called to prove, in point of fact, that they had done so, I should feel myself at a loss for evidence. Supposing, then, that they met in the evening, is this the example we are to imitate? Some, I believe, have said it is, and have acted accordingly, considering the rest of the day as their own, and evincing the earthly tendency of their minds, by the use they have made of it. And can any who hold the same general principle reasonably find fault? *They* may meet, according to their respective fancies, in the morning, or afternoon, or both: but the others, the partisans of the evening, have quite as good authority for their practice, perhaps better. The truth is, that on such a principle, all is thrown loose: and the amount of observance, undetermined by either law or example, left to the ever-varying dictates of human caprice.

Professors of the faith of Christ would do well to examine closely the principle, or the state of heart, from which such a sentiment springs,—the disposition by which they are induced to argue away the observance of the sabbath, as an entire day of sacred rest and religious exercise. It is true, that we live under a new and more spiritual dispensation. But surely, never was implied argument more unfortunate and self-destructive. Never were premises more fatal to the very conclusion they are brought to support! We live under a spiritual dispensation :—and is the secularizing of the sabbath more befitting a spiritual dispensation than the religious observance of it?—more calculated to promote the divine life in the soul, than the dedication of it to the exercises of devotion and the means of heavenly-mindedness? Is a spiritual dispensation, a dispensation of release from spiritual exercises? Or is there any one divine institution more eminently fitted for the advancement of spirituality of mind, than the day of God when duly observed?—So strong is the impression of this in my mind, both from the obvious reason of the thing, and from the general experience, recorded from many a happy and grateful heart, of the children of God,—that it forms a powerful presumptive argument for the unlikelihood, (I had almost said the impossibility) of its having, under the new economy, been set aside. A spiritual dispensation is not a dispensation, surely, under which the means of spirituality are taken away! And, when I consider the spiritual constitution of the sabbath, and its adaptation to spiritual improvement, and the fearfully anti-spiritual consequences of its cessation, I cannot bring myself to imagine, that such an institution should be ranked by the inspired apostle among the worldly rites of a transitory ceremonial,—the beggarly elements of an introductory and carnal dispensation,—the burdensome observances of a " yoke which neither the Jews of his time nor their fathers were able to bear ;"— that he should characterize it as " against us, and contrary to us, nailed to the cross, and taken out of the way !" O.l is there a child of God that could feel this a privilege ? —a privilege, to be released from the duty of consecrating so large a portion of his time as one day in seven to the service of God, to self-examination, and to the cultivation of fellowship with the world to come ! Is this indeed a part of the " liberty wherewith Christ makes his people free ?" What conceptions must these men have of a spiritual dispensation, and of spiritual liberty, who fancy it a part of these that they have a larger allowance of time for secular and worldly occupations ! Is it spirituality of mind that exults in such a freedom ? Is there not, on the contrary, just ground for more than apprehension, when a man begins to discover and bring forward arguments against the obligation to observe the first day of the week (assuming for the present the change of the day) as an entire day of holy rest and spiritual exercise, that if, before, there was any disposition in him to call it " a delight," the disposition is sadly on the decline ? That a Christian should be solicitous to add as much more of his time, for the cultivation of the principles and affections of godliness, as he can redeem from the necessary engagements of the world, I can readily understand. But that a man, under the full influence of the spirit of evangelical piety, can listen with complacency to reasonings that would deprive him of a portion of his spiritual enjoyment, and abridge the instituted means of his advancement in grace,—" demands a doubt." I could not desire a more convincing proof that a man's heart is " not right with God,"—that there is a secret spiritual declension, a " leaving of the first love," than the discovery of a disposition to insinuate doubts about the obligation of the sabbath, and to do this with a listless *sang-froid*, and without any apparent shrinking or trembling of heart at the conclusion :—nor can I fancy a clearer evidence of a church " having a name to live while it is dead," or a more ominous symptom of its approaching darkness and desolation than the prevalence of such a spirit,—the rise, and progress of a tendency to speculate about the abrogation, or even about the curtailment of the sabbath.

But what evidence, you will now ask,—what evidence have we that the day is changed, and that the first day of the week has, by divine authority, been substituted for the seventh ?—The proofs on this subject have usually been deduced, inferentially, from the example of the first Christians, as that example is gathered from the history and the Epistles of the New Testament. I am more and more satisfied, that there is evidence more direct than this; and in another discourse I hope to be able satisfactorily to exhibit it. I mean, not, however, to question the fairness or the sufficiency of the indirect argument. I think it perfectly conclusive.—That " the practice of the first " churches (under the guidance of the Apostles) as

"recorded in the New Testament, is equivalent, in value
"and authority, to direct precept," is a principle of the
soundness of which I am fully satisfied, as well as that
"we have that which is equivalent to the precept, by
"having the record of the usage."* That "the primi-
"tive churches, during the ministry of the Apostles, ob-
"served the first day of the week, as the day of their
"social worship and most solemn services," has been
established from the New Testament with irresistible
force, especially from two passages. The first is, Acts
xx. 6, 7. " And we sailed away from Philippi after the
days of unleavened bread, and came unto them to Troas
in five days; where we abode seven days. And upon the
first day of the week, when the disciples came together
to break bread, Paul preached unto them, ready to depart
on the morrow, and continued his speech until midnight."
" It would seem, then, that the Apostle was anxious not
" to protract his stay at Troas a single day, after he had
" enjoyed an opportunity of meeting with the assembled
" Church; that the day of their meeting was the first day
" of the week; and that for the arrival of that day, the
" apostle had waited an entire week. Now from all this
" we should infer, that no special or extraordinary meet-
" ing had been called, but that he waited for the day on
" which they were accustomed to assemble."† The other
passage is, 1 Cor. xvi. 1, 2. " Now concerning the collection which is for the saints, as I ordered the churches
of Galatia, so also do ye. On the first day of every week,
let each of you lay somewhat by itself, according as he may

* Burder's Law of the Sabbath, p. 61, 62.   † Ibid. p. 65.

F

have prospered, putting it into the treasury; that when I come, there may be then no collections."* "The wish of "the apostle was, to prevent the necessity of making col- "lections on his arrival. This object could not be secured "unless the brethren not only set apart their respective "contributions, but also collected them together so as to "make one common fund. They could only pour them "into one common treasury, when they were assembled "together in one place. They were directed, therefore, "to make a weekly collection, on that day on which they "were accustomed to meet as a church. The day speci- "fied is the first day of the week. On the first day of the "week, therefore, they were accustomed to meet together "for religious observances."

The inference thus drawn from these passages, and corroborated by various others, as well as by all the ear- liest records of ecclesiastical antiquity, cannot be with- stood. As it stands, however, it goes no further than to the fact of the first day of the week having been the day on which the early Christians were in the practice of holding their assemblies for the celebration of the ordi- nances of Christ. The fact is an important one, and one from which the sanctification of the day, as the day of sab- batical rest under the new dispensation, may, we think,

* Dr. Macknight's translation. There seems to be truth in the Dr.'s objection to the common translation of the words ταξ ἑαυτον ταθεν, θησαυριζων· "let every one of you *lay by him in store*"—namely, that it is inconsistent with the last part of the verse; "that there be no gath- erings when I come:"—for, according to that translation, the collec- tions would still have been to make at the Apostle's coming.—The com- ment of my friend Dr. Burder, which I have introduced in the discourse, is founded on this translation of Dr. Macknight, which, in common with him, I think preferable to that of our received version.

be reasonably deduced. Yet we would fain press the inference itself, if it can legitimately be done, a little further:—because the fact is granted by some of those who, notwithstanding, deny or question the existence of any sabbatical distinction of days under the gospel dispensation. —Thus Dr. Paley, after adducing the usual proofs of the first Christians having been accustomed to assemble for worship on the first day of the week, adds :—" It will be " remembered, that we are contending, by these proofs, " for no other duty upon the first day of the week, than " that of holding and frequenting religious assemblies. A cessation upon that day from labour, beyond the time " of attendance upon public worship, is not intimated in " any passage of the New Testament; nor did Christ or " his apostles deliver, that we know of, any command " to their disciples for a discontinuance, upon that day, " of the common offices of their professions : a reserve, " which none will see reason to wonder at, or to blame as " a defect in the institution, who consider that, in the " primitive condition of Christianity, the observation of a " new sabbath would have been useless, or inconvenient, " or impracticable."*—Others are more decided and scorn- " ful:"—" Warned by the apostle," says a modern Soci- " nian writer, " I presume not to condemn any man for

* The Dr. proceeds to assign his reasons for this. But the question is one, not so much of reasoning as of fact. And he appears to forget, even in the reasons which he does assign, that, to a very considerable extent, the principle of them militates against the duty of holding and frequenting religious assemblies on that day, as well as against the entire consecration of it to spiritual purposes.—*Paley's Mor. and Pol. Phil.* p. 336. *Edin. Ed.* 1816.

" his sabbatical observation of the first day of the week;
" —but, zealous of the liberty with which Christ has made
" us free, and regarding, as the apostle recommends, no
" man's censures for not observing the sabbath-day, I
" have no hesitation in asserting, that under the gospel
" dispensation, ' every day is alike.'   Of public worship
" I am a sincere advocate; and, it having been the uni-
" form practice of the Christian Church to assemble for
" this purpose on the first day of the week, I highly ap-
" prove of the continuance of this laudable and useful
" custom. But that under the Christian dispensation one
" day is more holy than another; or that any employment,
" or any amusement, which is lawful on other days, is
" unlawful on the Sunday, can never be proved, either
" from the Christian scriptures, or from ecclesiastical an-
" tiquity."* We need not be greatly astonished, that one
who could not find in the scriptures the divinity and
atonement of Christ, the depravity of human nature, and
the existence and influences of the Holy Spirit should
have been little at a loss to exclude from them the duty
of sanctifying the Lord's day; and that, even as to the
public worship of that day, he should have made light of
the admitted example of the apostolic churches, commend-
ing it indeed as a " laudable and useful custom," and
condescending to " approve of its continuance," but not
at all allowing in it any obligation of divine authority.
But still, since the fact of the churches assembling on
the first day of the week is thus granted, and yet the sanctity of the day questioned and denied,—we would fain
try how far any of the passages, quoted or referred to,

* Belsham's Review of Wilberforce, p. 159.

admit of any inference beyond the simple fact. We cannot but think they do.

Should I put the question to any of you, What is a week?—you would smile in surprise, and, if you thought is worth while to answer me at all, would reply, A week! why, a period of seven days, to be sure.—Yet the smile might be spared. The reply is to a certain extent correct; but it is deficient. A week is, properly, *six days of labour and one of rest*. This was the original week. It was, if I may venture the expression, God's week. It was the division of time, of which he set the example to man—and we do not, therefore, observe the week aright, unless we do it according to the pattern. Considered merely as a portion of time, a week is seven days:—but, considered as a period of time appointed to men in a particular form, and according to an exemplified appropriation of its parts, it is more;—it is a period of seven days, in which men conform themselves to the divine conduct, in working six days and resting one.

Now, of the passages formerly quoted from the New Testament, to prove the practice of the people of God statedly meeting, in their church capacity, on the first day of the week, there is one which appears to me to bear, legitimately and forcibly, a further inference,—the inference, namely, that the first day of the week was observed as the divinely appointed day of sabbatical rest. The passage is 1 Cor. xvi. 1, 2. "Now concerning the collection which is for the saints, as I ordered the churches of Galatia, so also do ye. On the first day of every week, let each of you lay somewhat by itself, according as he may have prospered, putting it into the treasury;

that when I come, there may be then no collections." Taking this passage in connexion with the ancient and divinely instituted division of time, what does it teach us? We have here *a period of labour*, during which, the supposition is, they might experience, in the providence of God, various degrees of prosperity or success; and we have *a day*, on which a proportion of the results of this success was to be laid aside, and put into the treasury, for a charitable purpose. Is not this very much like the ancient arrangement and practice?—six days of worldly business, "buying and selling, and getting gain,"—and a day on which business was not to be done, nor gain to be made, but on which a portion of what *had been* made was to be allocated to the claims of benevolence and piety? Are not the apostle's words much the same in import as if he had said,—*Upon the day of rest* put into the sacred treasury, according to the measure in which you may have prospered *during the days of labour?* Here, then, we have not only the fact of its having been their practice to meet on the first day of the week, for the worship of God; we have, moreover, the *original week*, the six days of labour, and the one of sacred rest. If this view of the case be correct, (and I am satisfied it is,) it goes to condemn the practice of those who are for observing both sabbaths,— the old and the new. This would make five days of labour, and two of rest, and would thus be in the face of the divine example, in settling the appropriation of time to man.

There is another passage, not formerly cited, from which the inference to the consecration of the whole day appears to be no less legitimate: it is Rev. i. 10. "I was in the

spirit on the Lord's day," That a particular *natural
day* is here meant, I shall take for granted; conceiving
any who may think otherwise, as if it might mean a period
of time, or the gospel day,—unworthy of being reasoned
with. As little doubt, surely, can there exist, *what* day
was meant by the designation. The first day of the week,
beyond all controversy. The designation is most appropriate; this being the day on which "the Lord," after
having "died for the sins" of his people, was "raised
again for their justification,"—the day on which he "saw
the path of life," arising in triumph over his conquered
enemies; the day on which, having "finished his work,
he entered into his rest;"—a day of joy and praise, of
universal jubilee to the church of God, on earth and in
heaven. It is "the Lord's day:" it is HIS—sacred to him,
and to the memory and celebration of his work. He seems
to have intended, by his appearances on this day to his
disciples, after he was risen from the dead, to mark it as
his own, and to intimate to his followers that they should
so regard it, and keep it sacred accordingly. On the day of
his rising, he appeared amongst them when they were
assembled together; and, on that day se'ennight, repeated
the appearance. "The celebration of these two first
Sundays," says Bishop Horsley, "was honoured with our
Lord's own presence. It was, perhaps, to set a mark of
distinction on this day in particular, that the intervening
week passed off, as it should seem, without any repetition
of his visit to the eleven apostles." And, after his ascension, the grand day of the Spirit's effusion, and the glorious commencement of his reign, the pentecostal day, was
the first day of the week! To complete our argument,

the expression ought to be compared with those of the Old Testament, in which the seventh day is spoken of as Jehovah's sabbath: "the seventh day," says our text itself, "is the sabbath of the Lord thy God." And Jehovah frequently denominates it "my sabbath." Let us beware, then, of alienating from the Lord that day which he claims as his own; let us beware of abridging it,—of secularizing its sacred hours,—of applying any of them to our own purposes, and not to the ends for which HE has set it apart. This, in the forcible language of the last of the ancient prophets of Israel, would be to "rob God," depriving Him and his house of what is his due, and bringing upon ourselves the guilt of sacrilege.

There is still another passage, which I consider as containing decisive authority both for the change of the day from the seventh to the first, and for the consecration of the entire day to spiritual rest. I refer to Heb. iv. 9, 10. "There remaineth, therefore, a rest to the people of God: for he that is entered into his rest, he also hath ceased from his own works, as God did from his." But this passage is of too much importance to be disposed of at the close of an address, which has already detained you so long. I shall take it up in a separate discourse: and I hope to convince you that it contains, in most appropriate terms, a direct New Testament statute for the observance of the first day of the week, as the Christian sabbath.

Meantime, I shall have produced a happy practical effect, if aught that has been already advanced shall, in any degree, have confirmed conviction where it previously existed, and have settled it where it was shaken and wavering.

DISCOURSE IV.

HEB. iv. 9, 10.

"There remaineth therefore a rest to the people of God. For he that is entered into his rest, he also hath ceased from his own works, as God did from his."

I AM satisfied that the course of argument pursued in preceding discourses, respecting the origin, the moral nature, and the permanent obligations of the Sabbath, and respecting the change, under the Christian dispensation, from the seventh day to the first, is legitimate and conclusive. Still, however, it may be asked,—and the question is a very natural one,—Is there no deliverance in the New Testament, on a subject so important, of a less inferential and more direct nature? Is there no way in which we can arrive at the conclusion, but a process of induction? Although there were not, we should not at all admit the conclusion itself to be the less valid, or the duty the less imperative. Yet some preceptive injunction of a more express and positive description, may be admitted to be desirable;—and I hope to convince you, that the text now read, to which I alluded in the close of last discourse, contains such an injunction, and is in fact a New Testament statute for the observance of the first day of the week as the Christian Sabbath. Considering, indeed, the difference subsisting, among commentators of eminence, in their views of the passage, it would be presumptuous to say that I should regard it as decisive, even had it stood by itself, unaccompanied by the corroborative evidence of example :—yet I must be allowed to express my surprise, that there should not have been greater harmony amongst expounders as to its true meaning, when taken in connexion with that evidence.*

In entering on our exposition of the passage, it is necessary, in the first instance, to call your special attention to the fact, that, in the original language, the word which is rendered *rest* in the ninth verse—" There remaineth, therefore, *a rest* to the people of God,"—is an entirely different word from that so translated in the other verses of the chapter—both in the preceding and subsequent context.† The marginal rendering is " the keeping of a Sabbath." And that this is the strict and proper import

* The authorities of Calvin, Whitby, Doddridge, Pierce, Maclean, Scott, Stuart, Schleusner, are all against me. There is one, however, who is in himself a host, with whose interpretation the one given in the following discourse is in very near coincidence—Dr. John Owen. I might refer also to Mr. John Glass in his Dissertation (contained in his works) on the three divine rests, as holding the same view of the sabbatism in the ninth verse, that is here given; though I cannot acquiesce in his exposition of some parts of the apostle's reasoning.

† It is Σαββατισμος. The other word, throughout the chapter, is αναπαυσις. The former is properly a Hebrew noun, with a Greek form and termination. The verb from which it is formed, occurs in various places in the Septuagint version :—the noun, only in this passage of the Apostle.

of the term, does not admit of a doubt. It is a noun of regular formation from the verb, which, in the Septuagint translation of the Old Testament, is used for *keeping a Sabbath*, or, (if we may coin a correspondent English word,) *sabbatising*. It is usually interpreted here of the eternal rest,—the rest of heaven, on the principle of regarding that rest in the light of a perpetual Sabbath ;— a final cessation from all the toils and troubles of time, and a never-ending enjoyment of the service and fellowship of God. We dispute not the propriety of this view of the heavenly state. It is, in itself, scriptural, and full of delight. The sole question is, not whether the word admits of this application, but whether this be its application here. My own conviction is, that it is not ; that it has its more literal sense of the keeping of a Sabbath, as a divine institution for the church on earth, commemorative of those events on which the hope of the heavenly rest is founded, and preparatory to that rest in its pure and spiritual joys. I conceive the passage to relate to the change of the day of sabbatical observance from the seventh to the first, and as assigning the reason of that change,—namely, that as the original Sabbath was instituted in commemoration of God's finishing and resting from his work of creation,—so the New Testament Sabbath is assigned to be commemorative of the Lord Jesus Christ's finishing and resting from *his* work—the work of redemption : " There remaineth, therefore, a sabbatism to the people of God ; FOR he that is entered into his rest, he also hath ceased from his own works, as God did from his."

The only other observation necessary respecting the

ms of the text, relates to the word "remaineth." "There remaineth, therefore, a sabbatism' to "the people of God" is very natural for the reader to associate with this word the idea of something which, to all " the people of God" in succession while, on earth, is the object of anticipation and hope,—" remaining " to each at the close of his earthly pilgrimage, and " remaining " to all collectively; when the whole congregation of the redeemed shall have assembled in the upper sanctuary. It should not be forgotten, however, what is the design and structure of this Epistle. The general subject of it is, the succession of the gospel dispensation to that of the law; the manner in which the latter was to be fulfilled and superseded by the former. " The law made nothing perfect." It was " the shade of good things to come." These good things which to come, " *remained* for the people of God," under the economy, when the old should have passed away. This seems to be the sense of the term in our text. I shall not spend time in illustration and proof of the propriety this explanation of it. No one who carefully reads the epistle can doubt that it is equally capable of this acceptation as of the other. This is all I plead for. If the two senses are equally legitimate, the context must determine which of the two is to be preferred. When the apostle says, chap. xi. 39, 40, " These all, having obtained a good report through faith, received not the promise; God having provided some better thing for us, that they without us should not be made perfect;" he speaks of the dispensation of higher and more abundant privilege which was to succeed the Patriarchal and the Mosaic:—and every thing different and superior which it was the design of

God then to introduce, might, with perfect propriety, be said to have "remained for his people" under that dispensation.

There is, I am well aware, an obstacle which, in the minds of many, perhaps of most of my hearers, will lie in the way of the ready acceptance of my present argument. There are few things which more powerfully impede conviction, than a previous habit of mind. With such a habit I have now to contend. It is the habit of having, long and invariably, attached to the terms of my text a different meaning from that which I am affixing to them. Most Christians have never read the verse—" There remaineth, therefore, a rest for the people of God,"—but they have thought of heaven. In prayers, in public discourses, in private conversation, they have heard it, and they have used it, in the same sense. So that " the rest that remaineth for the people of God" has become a fixed and appropriated designation for the place of bliss. The phrase, in this acceptation, is part of the stamped and accredited currency of the language of Zion. And to affix to it another meaning is not only an interference with established usage and the convenience of customary phraseology; it is apt to be felt by the pious mind as a privation of a more serious nature. It is not the loss of a phrase merely; it is the disturbance of the mind's settled associations. It is the dispersion of those sweetly-soothing thoughts of heaven, which the phrase has been wont to suggest. The text has been a pillow to the weary head in the hours of care and sorrow; a pillow, on which many a pleasing vision of the land of rest has cheered the disconsolate spirit. But let the children of God bethink themselves. A change in the meaning of a saint is not a change in the nature of heaven. That it is a "rest re- maining for the people of God" is still a Bible truth; and, if they must have a particular text to which their minds may attach the contemplations and hopes that have clustered around this, they cannot be at a loss, while there stands in the word of God the delightful assurance, "Blessed are the dead that die in the Lord—THEY REST FROM THEIR LABOURS." Let them bethink themselves further. Truth should be their sole object; their only question, respecting any part of the divine word, What is the mind of the Spirit? It is their duty, therefore, to divest their minds of all biassing prepossessions, and to come to the passage before us, as if it were for the first time. And surely every child of God will agree with me in thinking, that if the passage is fairly and legitimately made out to be a New Testament statute for the sabbatism of the first day of the week, it is no trivial end that is answered. There is nothing lost; for heaven remains the same:—there is much gained; for a divine sanction is found to an important duty and a precious privilege.

It is of importance to a right understanding of the text, and of the argument founded upon it, to ascertain with correctness the relation in which it stands to the verses that precede it. The ninth verse, " There remaineth, therefore, a rest to the people of God," is usually consid- ered as the point which the previous train of reasoning is directly intended to prove. Now, were this the case, I freely confess that I should find some difficulty in making my ground good. It is an admitted rule in reasoning, that there should not be any thing in the conclusion be-

yond, or different from what is in the premises. . . Were
the ninth verse, then, the point to be proved, and the
word there translated rest, meant something quite different from the word so translated in the preceding context,
the argument would unquestionably be liable to the objection, which has accordingly been urged against it,[*] that
there is something in the conclusion which is not in the
premises. It does not appear to me, however, that the
proposition in the ninth verse is properly the point to be
proved by what precedes; but that it is rather an inference or conclusion drawn from the point there established.
I do not mean by this, that it is not the point which the
writer had chiefly in his view; but only that he draws it
in the form of a deduction from something else which he
had already proved. From verse 3d to verse 8th, there is
an argument: and the simple question is, whether the
ninth verse be the proposition which that argument is designed to prove; or whether the proposition proved by it
be not rather that which is stated in the beginning of verse
3d, " We who have believed do enter into rest." This
latter appears to me the true state of the case; and then,
from the establishment of that proposition, verse 9th is an
immediate deduction. The writer, it is true, might have
his eye in a special manner directed to the inference which
he meant to draw:—but still, an inference deduced from
the proof of any point is an essentially different thing from
the point proved.

Taking this, then, as our principle of interpretation, let
us consider a little the proposition with which he sets out,

---

[*] See Pierce and Maclean on the passage.

the manner in which he proves it, and then, (what we have at present especially to do with) the inference deduced from it.—The proposition to be proved is in the beginning of the third verse—" For we who have believed do enter into rest." By this I understand the heavenly or everlasting rest. This might be shown by a review of the preceding context. From chap. iii. 6, onwards, the writer's object evidently is to warn against apostasy, and to encourage to perseverance in the profession of the faith. This object he pursues in part by bringing before them an example of the consequences of unbelief, appropriate to their case as Hebrews,—the example, namely, of the race that "came out of Egypt by Moses," whose unbelieving rebellion excluded them from Canaan, and doomed them to die in the wilderness by the sentence of Him who " sware in his wrath, they shall not enter into my rest." On this example he dwells to the close of the preceding chapter:—and, having drawn it to a conclusion in these words—" So we see that *they* could not enter in because of unbelief"—he pointedly applies it in the beginning of chap. iv. " Let *us*, therefore, fear, lest, a promise being left us of entering into his rest, any of you should seem to come short of it." The promise meant in these words can be no other than the promise of the eternal inheritance, prefigured by that which was earthly and temporal.—" For unto us," he adds in the second verse, " was the gospel preached as well as unto them,"—or, more literally, " for we have good tidings declared to us, as well as they." It is true that the good tidings declared to them had immediate relation to the land of promise, the earthly Canaan. But still, their unbelief amounted to the rejection of the ditine promises generally, as contained in the covenant with Abraham. It was unbelief of the gospel, in its then state of discovery; when truths and promises were conveyed by types and figures, and what is spiritual, heavenly, and everlasting was couched under what was earthly, temporal, and transitory. The tidings were to them in vain; and it was their unbelief that lost them the promised blessings—"the word preached did not profit them, not being mixed with faith in them that heard it." Then, in immediate connexion with this statement of the cause of their forfeiting the benefit of the promise, namely their want of faith, there follows the proposition—"For we which have believed do enter into rest;" or rather, "into the rest"—that is, the rest referred to in the first verse, as still in promise. The proposition, then, is, that even now, under the gospel dispensation, there is a rest into which we enter, and enter by faith,—obtaining it through the belief of the testimony and promise of God.

This is the proposition which he goes on to establish. The proof is addressed, in a special manner, to Hebrews, and with the appearance of difficulty, it is really as simple as it is short. Verses 3—8. "For we which have believed do enter into rest, as he said, As I have sworn in my wrath, if they shall enter into my rest: although the works were finished from the foundation of the world. For he spake in a certain place of the seventh day on this wise; And God did rest the seventh day from all his works. And in this place again, If they shall enter into my rest. Seeing therefore it remaineth that some must enter therein; and they to whom it was first preached entered not in because of unbelief;—again, he limiteth a certain day, saying in David, To-day, after so long a time; as it is said, To-day, if ye will hear his voice, harden not your hearts. For if Joshua had given them rest, then would he not afterward have spoken of another day."—In illustration of this argument, let it be noticed,

1. In the first place:—There are in the passage *three rests*;—the seventh day rest, of cessation and complacency, from the work of creation; the rest of Canaan, into which, by divine aid, Joshua conducted the Israelites; and the everlasting rest, or final repose and blessedness of heaven,

2. Secondly:—When Jehovah, with a divine oath, declared respecting the race that had come out of Egypt by Moses,—"they shall not enter into *my rest*,"—he could not, by possibility, mean the first of these three rests, the rest of the seventh day, or the creation rest,—inasmuch as that rest had been entered into by the people of God from the beginning,—even from the time when " the works were finished from the foundation of the world." I say, it had been entered into *by the people of God*. This, as I hinted in a former discourse, is the only view of the case that could be of any avail in the apostle's argument. On the supposition of that rest being confined to Jehovah himself, and of no instituted observance of it having had place amongst men for twenty-five centuries after, it would have been nothing to his purpose:—for, although the works were finished from the foundation of the world, if Jehovah only had rested, the rest of the seventh day would still have remained to be " entered into" on the part of his people. It is true, indeed, that even on the hypothesis of the sabbath having been first instituted in the wilderness, the institution was previous

to the oath of exclusion from Canaan. But this is not the ground on which the apostle argues. When he concludes that the rest meant in that oath of exclusion could not be the seventh day rest, the conclusion is drawn, not from the fact of the seventh day rest having previously commenced in the wilderness, but from the fact of the "works having been finished," and the divine rest from them having consequently been participated by his people, "from the foundation of the world."—The rest meant, then, in the oath of exclusion, "they shall not enter into my rest," is the rest into which God had promised to conduct his people in Canaan. And he calls it "my rest," not only because he had provided it, and pledged his truth and power for its bestowment, saying, "My presence shall go with thee, and I will give thee rest,"—but also, because there He was himself to fix his dwelling-place,—the same "presence" which was to "go with" Moses and Israel, and to "give them rest," engaging at the same time to settle amongst them, and to protect and bless them. "The Lord hath chosen Zion: he hath desired it for his habitation: this is my rest for ever; here will I dwell, for I have desired it."

3. Thirdly:—In the ninety-fifth Psalm there occurs a solemn admonition to the Jews of David's time, to beware of imitating the unbelief and hardness of heart exemplified by the generation that fell in the wilderness. It is in these words:—" For we are his people, and the sheep of his hand. To-day, if ye will hear his voice, harden not your heart, as in the provocation, and as in the day of temptation in the wilderness: When your fathers tempted me, proved me, and saw my work. Forty years long was I grieved with this generation, and said, It is a

people that do err in their heart, and they have not known my ways: Unto whom I sware in 'my wrath,' that they should not enter into my rest."* The apostle interprets this language as implying, or more than implying, that the Jews of that period might also exclude themselves from God's promised rest, and fail of entering in because of unbelief. But the rest into which it was possible for them to fail of entering, could not be the rest of the earthly Canaan; for that rest they and their fathers had long actually possessed. From this, therefore, it appeared, that in God's promise of rest there was included a rest ulterior to that of the earthly Canaan. This inference the apostle draws, with much simplicity and point, in the eighth verse. "For if Joshua had given them rest"—that is, if the divine promise of rest had been verified to the full amount of its intended import by the settlement of Israel under the conduct of Joshua, in the land of Canaan,—then would he not afterward have spoken of another day? of another day, in which the rest was still to be entered into, and in which there should still be the possibility and the danger of forfeiting and coming short of it.—But He (the Holy Ghost namely) did speak, of another day —of a period long subsequent to " Joshua's giving them rest," when his people by name and profession are still exhorted on the one hand, to " hear his voice," and so to obtain the promised rest, and still admonished on the other, that if they refused to hear they must incur the sentence of exclusion. It necessarily follows, that in the promise of God's covenant there is another rest than that of Canaan ;—which can only be the rest of the heavenly

* Psalm xcv. 7—11.

country typified by that of the earthly inheritance. And this is the rest into which "*we who have believed do enter.*" It is, like that which typified it, obtained by faith, and forfeited by unbelief.

The argument from David's language in Psalm xcv. is the very same, in relevancy and conclusiveness, whether it be considered as addressed to the Jews of his own time, or as prophetical, and relating to a still subsequent period —to the time of the Messiah, the season of his reign, the gospel day. That the word *day* in the passage quoted, as on various other occasions, denotes a *period of time* of indefinite duration, is clear, from another part of Paul's writings, 2 Cor. vi. 2, where, after admonishing those to whom he writes, to beware of "receiving the grace of God" revealed by the gospel "in vain," he subjoins, parenthetically, for their encouragement—"For he saith, 'I have heard thee in a time accepted, and in the day of salvation have I succoured thee :' behold now is the accepted time; behold now is the day of salvation." The "accepted *time*," and "the *day* of salvation," are the same period—the period, namely, of the gospel dispensation. The understanding of the words in the ninety-fifth Psalm prophetically, while it can hardly be said to add any thing to the validity of the apostle's argument, imparts to it an additional appropriateness, by giving it a more direct application to those whom he addresses,—to the Jews of his own time.

Let it not be objected to our applying the expression, "We who have believed, *do enter* into rest," to the everlasting or heavenly rest, that the verb is in the present tense, and must therefore relate to what has place now, in the present life. It is no unusual thing for the present tense of the verb to comprehend a period of indefinite duration, distinguished by a special character, and so to be applied to the past, the present, and the future of that period,—denoting rather the certainty of the connexion between it and that which is affirmed as taking place in it. When our Lord says, John xviii. 36, " Now is my kindom not from hence," he expresses the character of his reign, not merely at the time when he uttered the words, (for then, indeed, the reign so characterized had not properly commenced,) but during the whole future period of its duration. On the same principle, " We who have believed, do enter into rest," means simply, that under the present dispensation, there is a rest into which believers do successively enter.

Such, then, is the simple proof of the proposition in the beginning of verse 3d, " We who have believed do enter into rest:" It may be thus summed up:—God sware, respecting the race that came out of Egypt by Moses, "they shall not enter into *my rest.*" That rest could not be the creation rest; for the creation rest had been entered into from the beginning. It was the promised rest of Canaan. But long after the time when Joshua had conducted Israel into the rest of Canaan, David, by the Holy Ghost, admonishes the Jews, either of his own time, or prophetically of a time to come, to beware of the example of those " who entered not in because of unbelief," intimating that unbelief should incur to themselves a similar forfeiture. Now, this forfeiture could not be of the rest which Joshua had given ; because Canaan had long been in actual possession. There must still, therefore, be a rest into which believers enter; and that rest is the rest of the everlasting inheritance.

The only further difficulty attending this simple view of the passage, is also of a verbal kind. The sixth verse evidently states the ground of some sequence, which the reader, of course, expects to follow:—" Seeing, therefore, it remaineth that some must enter therein, and they to whom it was first preached entered not in, because of unbelief"—what follows? The difficulty of answering this seemingly simple question has been felt, and has been variously solved. In our English Bibles, verses 7—10, are generally included in a parenthesis, and the sequence is thus found in verse 11, " Let us labour, therefore, to enter into that rest, lest any man fall after the same example of unbelief." But this is worse than a cutting of the knot; it is tying another. It is nullifying the parenthetic verses, throwing them entirely out of connexion with the apostle's argument, and depriving them of any explicit sense of their own. Other critics, fancying the meaning incomplete, have supplied the conclusion from what precedes, as if the writer had thought it unnecessary formally to express it:—" Seeing, therefore, it remaineth that some must enter therein, and they to whom it was first preached entered not in, because of unbelief"—[we who have believed do enter into it.] * But this is, by no means, like the explicitness of a reasoner such as Paul.†

* Such is the filling up of the supposed ellipsis, adopted by Dr. Moses Stuart, of Andover, Mass. U. S., in his able Critical Commentary on the Epistle.

† The evidence of the apostle of the Gentiles having been the writer of this epistle, is so satisfactory, that I have thus ventured to assume it.

There is in fact no difficulty. The apostle, in the which verse, states with precision the length to which the preceding promises had conducted him. This "work that remaineth" have reference not to the time of his speaking, but to the point at which he had advanced in his engagement. And then he proceeds to add another link, to complete the chain, and establish his position. He testifies that when God sware, "they shall not enter into my rest," he could not mean the creation rest;—and, they to whom the good tidings of the rest of the promised land were first preached "not having entered in because of unbelief"—the question returns, Since "some must enter therein," no promise of God being in vain, was the fulfilment of the promise of rest completed by the actual possession of Canaan, at the end of the forty years of penal continuation in the wilderness? This is the point which his reference to David is intended to settle. By that inference connected with the eighth verse, in which he applies it, he completes his chain of proof, making it evident that there must have been more in the promise than the earthly Canaan; else, after that rest had been attained, there could have been no subsequent possibility of coming short of the promise; on which possibility, however, David's admonitions are founded.

From the point thus proved, I have said, the text is an inference, or corollary:—These things being so, it follows, as a consequence, that "there remaineth a sabbatism to the people of God."—What, then, is the ground of the inference? It appears to me to lie in this:—The two former rests, the creation rest and the Canaan rest, the completion of the work of creation, and the entr ment of his people, by a series of wonders, in the land of ...,—were both *commemorated by the keeping of a* sabbath. The seventh day was sacred to the remembrance, contemplation, and worship, of that Almighty Being who "created all things by the word of his power," and who redeemed his people from the bondage of Egypt, and brought them to the rest which he had promised to their fathers. The finishing of the work of creation was the original or primary reason for the celebration of the sabbath; and on this ground it was enjoined on the Israelites, Exod. xx. 8—11. The redemption from Egypt was, at the same time, as we formerly saw, superadded as a further reason for the observance of it, in association with the previously existing ground, Deut. v. 12—15. In the sabbatical rest, therefore, the people of God under the old dispensation were to unite the remembrance of his power and goodness, both as displayed in creation, and as displayed in their deliverance from Egypt and their settlement in Canaan.—From this consideration the inference drawn in the text appears very naturally to arise. If these two manifestations of God were commemorated by a day sacred to the recollection and celebration of them; if Jehovah rested and called his people to rest with him, in the completion of creation, and in taking possession, by a "strong hand and stretched-out arm," of that "good land," where he was to place his name, to fix his habitation, to display his glory, and to receive the homage of his chosen worshippers:—shall not a work and a rest incomparably more excellent and glorious than either have its day of grateful and joyful commemoration? shall there be no stated celebration of the great redemption finished by the Son of God, and of the Redeemer's rest after it, as the anticipation and pledge of that everlasting rest into which those who believe his gospel enter by faith? Shall the people of God not be called upon to rest with him in that all-perfect work of righteousness and mercy, in which his holy justice has rested with the fulness of satisfaction, and on which his love reposes with infinite delight?— The work of Redemption is transcendently the greatest of all the doings of the Lord. It was the theme and the sum of all ancient type, and promise, and prophecy; it was the object of the joyous anticipations and hopes of all generations of God's people from the fall, till the fulness of time; it was the guiding star of the whole course of the providential administration of Jehovah from the first promise onwards to the same glorious hour, and has been to the present day; the deliverance from Egypt and the settlement in Canaan were but two of the subservient and preparatory steps to its accomplishment; and to the very world which occupied the six days of creation, it has given its highest glory, as the chosen theatre of its wonderful transactions. It is a work, pregnant with the most illustrious honour to God, and the richest benefit to man,— a work, celebrated by the acclamations of angels, and filling heaven, through eternity, with wonder, love, and praise! Shall this greatest and best of God's works,—this work of combined holiness, and justice, and truth, and power, and mercy, by which all other works are eclipsed and thrown into shade, " having no glory by reason of the glory that excelleth,"—shall *this* work not have its due share of commemorative celebration? shall it have no part in the hallowed remembrances of the day of sacred rest? Shall

that day be abolished, at the very time when the sublimest and most interesting subject of commemoration, and
the most animating and delightful theme of praise, has just
been introduced?—the memorial of the divine works be
set aside, when the worthiest of remembrance has just
been done?—No, says the apostle. This great work shall
not want its memorial. It shall not only have a part in
the celebrations of the sabbath—but by the change of the
day it shall have the precedence and preeminence assigned to it amongst the subjects of commemoration and
praise:—" There remaineth, therefore, a sabbatism to
the people of God: for he that is entered into his rest he
also hath ceased from his own works, as God did from
his."

In support of this view, let the following considerations be carefully attended to:—

1. The *change of the word* in this verse, formerly adverted to. A different word is used for " rest" in the
verses preceding, and resumed in those which follow.—
Was there no design in this change? no design in using
this particular word here, whilst another is used both
before and after?—It is very true that good writers often
change their words, for the sake of variety: but good
reasoners will be cautious how they introduce different
terms into their conclusion from those which they have
used in their premises;* and especially terms, which,

* It will be recollected, that I am speaking here of the views of
those who consider the ninth verse as the conclusion come to from the
preceding reasoning, understanding the " rest which remaineth for
the people of God" as meaning the heavenly rest, and so identifying
the proposition with that in the third verse, " We who have believed do
enter into rest."

although they may be used synonimously, are susceptible also of a different meaning. In the present instance, the word in our text is more than susceptible of such a meaning. Its proper import, according to the only usage by which it can be ascertained, (that of the Septuagint version) is the *keeping of a sabbath.* Being regularly formed from the verb used in that version for the observance of the sabbatical rest, the Hebrews would most naturally so understand it.

It is, moreover, an admitted rule of interpretation, that words ought to be understood in their proper sense, in preference to that which is figurative, in every instance in which the latter is not required by the obvious necessity of the case. The heavenly rest may, in a figurative sense, be called a sabbatism. This we do not deny. But if an equally natural and consistent interpretation of the passage can be given, taking the word in its more proper and literal acceptation, it is entitled to the preference. It is surely in itself a somewhat singular thing, that in this verse alone the word for the keeping of a sabbath should have been introduced, and not at all in any of those which precede or follow; in which, if it had indeed the same meaning with the other that is used, it would of course have suited equally well.

2. It appears to be natural and reasonable, in such an epistle as this to the Hebrews, to expect, *a priori,* or previously to our actual knowledge of its contents, that some notice should be taken of such a change as that from the seventh to the first day of the week, as the day of sabbatical rest. Not because the Sabbath was a merely Jewish institution, a part of the Sinaitic ceremonial. We have

already seen that it was not. But one of the reasons enforcing its observance was peculiar to Israel; and the celebration of the seventh day all their fathers had received and adhered to, as a part of the will of the God of Abraham, and Isaac, and Jacob.—I employ the present argument, however, with a full impression of the caution requisite in judging a priori of what we might reasonably expect to find in any part of the divine communications. All that I say is this,—and surely it will not be denied me,—that if the words otherwise admit, without any undue straining, the sense I am putting upon them, the consideration of its being natural to look for such an intimation in such an epistle,—of its occurring in quite a suitable and appropriate place and connexion,—gives a previous presumptive probability to the interpretation.—There is no direct and pointed testimony to the change of the sabbath to be found in the New Testament, unless it be there. Not (it is necessary for me to repeat) that the train of reasoning pursued in former discourses is at all unsound or unsatisfactory:—but still, notwithstanding the legitimacy and conclusiveness of the argument from matter of fact for the alteration of the day, a positive intimation, on a subject so interesting, and so materially affecting the practice of the whole church of God, will by all be admitted to be desirable.

I do not, in this, assume the divine authority for the change, and, having founded upon this assumption the reasonableness of expecting to find some notice taken of it, found again upon this reasonableness an evidence of the authority;—which would be reasoning in a circle. I only assume the unquestionable matter of fact, of the cessation,

in the Christian church of the seventh day, and the substitu-
tion of the first:—and, if this was *not* the divine intention,
the reasonableness of expecting some notice of the subject is
as well founded on this negative supposition as on the contrary; inasmuch as such notice was necessary, for preventing a change which was inconsistent with the divine will.

3. According to the ordinary interpretation of the passage, the tenth verse refers to *the believer in Christ* entering into the heavenly rest at death, and thus ceasing and
reposing from his works and his trials.—Now, that heaven
is represented as such a rest, I have already granted—
" Blessed are the dead that die in the Lord from hence-
forth: yea, saith the Spirit, that they may *rest from their
labours*, and their works do follow them," Rev. xiv. 13.—
But two objections to this interpretation suggest themselves, which appear of no small weight.—The first, is that it
seems to be a sufficiently bold comparison, to liken a believer
ceasing from his toils and sorrows on earth, and from his
" work of faith and labour of love," to the Almighty and
infinite God ceasing from the stupendous and peculiarly
divine work of the creation of the universe. Jesus, indeed,
so compares himself—"My Father worketh hitherto, and I
work:"—but, when applied to a feeble mortal, ending his
employments and sufferings here below, I cannot but feel
(though it may be a false refinement) as if the comparison
savoured of presumption. I grant, that if an inspired
writer has actually used it, it cannot be liable to any such
charge; the presumption would be in venturing to censure
it. But perhaps (for in this I would speak with diffi-
dence) the circumstance of its apparent boldness may be
admitted as a collateral and subsidiary proof that this is

not its meaning.—Secondly: In the ordinary view of the
tenth verse, it neither assigns a reason, nor adduces a
proof, of what is affirmed in the ninth. Yet the particle
" *For*," with which the verse commences, evidently pre-
sents it in such a connexion. According to the interpretation in question, the tenth verse only describes the nature
of the heavenly rest, and affirms the believer's entering
into it :—but this can neither be a *reason why* it remaineth, nor an *evidence* that it *does* remain. Nay, it is
not even a direct affirmation of the believer's entering into
the rest ; but only an affirmation that, in entering into it,
he ceases from his works : " for he that is entered into his
rest, he also hath ceased from his own works, as God did
from his." The "*for*," the particle of causation, evidently
connects here, not with the " entering into his rest," but
with the " ceasing from his works." It is this *cessation
from the works*, then, mentioned in the tenth verse, that
forms the principal reason why there "remaineth a rest
for the people of God." But the believer's cessation from
his works, on entering the heavenly rest, I surely need
not say, is no reason why that rest remaineth for him !
What kind of argument is imputed to the inspired writer,
when he is made to say—There remaineth, therefore, the
heavenly rest to the people of God ; for the believer who
enters into that rest, ceases from his own works, as God
did from his ! Certainly this is neither a reason nor a
proof. Examine the connexion of the two verses ; and
I am persuaded that the more closely you do so, the conviction will strengthen, that, according to the ordinary
exposition, the tenth, although beginning with the particle

of cessation, contains neither reason nor proof of the ninth. This leads me to observe—

4. On the other hand, suppose the tenth verse to refer not to the believer, but to the believer's Lord;—all is, then, consistent, and full of beauty and force. The relative particle has its clear and obvious meaning. It assigns an appropriate and adequate reason for *a new sabbatism*; for a change corresponding to the circumstances of the New Testament dispensation,—a change, which should give the finished work of the divine Redeemer the first place among the subjects of joyful and holy celebration. It points out an interesting and striking analogy between the reason of the seventh-day sabbath, and the reason of the first; the former being a commemoration of the finished work of creation, the latter of the finished work of redemption.—This, too, gives the allusion in the phrase, " *as God did from his*," its full amount of meaning. The analogy thus stated, is evidently designed to give force to the preceding conclusion. It leads to a farther analogy. It intimates, that, as there is a correspondence between God's ceasing from his work at creation, and " he that is entered into his rest ceasing from his," there is a correspondence also in the consequence. This comes out in its full force from the connexion of the verses for which we plead :—as when God ceased from his work of creation, the day of his resting was hallowed as a sabbatism, or day of commemorative rest to his people ; so, when Jesus finished the work of redemption, and rested from it in his resurrection and his reception to the right hand of God, that blessed day was to be in, all time com-

ing, the day of sabbatical rest and celebration.—In the ordinary interpretation, the spirit of this allusion, and of the analogy suggested by it, is entirely lost. But when considered as part of the reason for a New Testament sabbatism, we see how forcibly it tells on the conclusion: "There remaineth, therefore, the keeping of a sabbath to the people of God; for he that is entered into his rest, he also hath ceased from his own works, AS GOD DID FROM HIS." The language of Gen. ii. 1—3, might, in the full spirit of it, be accommodated to the work of Jesus, when he rose from the dead, and to the consequent sanctification of the first day of the week:—Thus the work of salvation was finished, and all its glorious ends secured. And on the first day of the week, Jesus rose from the grave, and finally rested from the work which he had done:— therefore the ascended Lord blessed the FIRST DAY, and hallowed it.

This view of the first-day Sabbath, *accords precisely with the fact*, as to the proper nature of the day. For what is this Sabbath? Is it not exactly what this explanation of the text intimates—a commemoration of the finished work of Jesus?—a solemn and delightful remembrance and celebration of it?—a rest of the believing soul in the completed redemption, from the assurance of Jehovah's perfect and eternal satisfaction with it?—a day of joy in God's salvation, because he has "smelled a savour of rest" in the accepted offering of his Son?—a day of personal and social jubilee, of spiritual peace, and gladness, and thanksgiving, in memory of Him who "finished the work that was given him to do," who was "delivered for our offences, and raised again for our justification?"

G 2

"The stone which the builders refused, is become the head-stone of the corner. This is the Lord's doing; it is marvellous in our eyes. THIS IS THE DAY which the Lord hath made; we will rejoice and be glad in it!" Psal. cxviii. 22—24. Thus, in prophetic language, was the sabbatical rest of the Messiah and his people appropriately and beautifully announced.

6. I am quite aware of an objection which has been urged against this view of the text, drawn from the verse which follows: verse 11, "Let us labour, therefore, to enter into that rest, lest any man fall after the same example of unbelief." How, it has been asked, can believers be exhorted to labour to enter into the keeping of a Sabbath? Certainly they cannot; and, were the only reference of the rest in verse 11th, into which believers are exhorted to labour that they may enter, to the sabbatism in verse 9th, this would be fatal to the interpretation. But it is not so. The objection proceeds on a misapprehension. The admonition to "labour to enter into that rest" has reference, not to the sabbatism in the 9th verse, but to the rest in the 10th,—the rest into which "he who has ceased from his work" has entered, which his people are all destined to share with him, and of which our Sabbaths on earth, in commemoration of his work, are at once the prelibation and the pledge. We commemorate Christ's rest, and anticipate our own.

I have said, that in the commemorative celebrations of the New Testament Sabbath, although redemption has the lead, creation is not excluded. So far from it, that there is between the one and the other an interesting and

most pleasing association. When we contemplate and celebrate the wonders of creation, we are charmed with the remembrance that all the omnipotence of the Creator pertains
to Him who is the God of our salvation. This association is finely brought out in some passages of the prophets,
to establish the faith, and animate the hopes of Old Testament saints, in anticipating the fulfilment of divine
engagements. As a specimen, look to Isa. xlii. 5—9,
and Isa. xliv. 23, 24, " Thus saith God the Lord, he that
created the heavens, and stretched them out; he that
spread forth the earth, and that which cometh out of it;
he that giveth breath unto the people upon it, and spirit
to them that walk therein : I the Lord have called thee
in righteousness, and will hold thine hand, and will keep
thee, and give thee for a covenant of the people, for a
light of the Gentiles; to open the blind eyes, to bring
out the prisoners from the prison, and them that sit
in darkness out of the prison-house. I am the Lord;
that is my name : and my glory will I not give to another,
neither my praise to graven images. Behold, the former
things are come to pass, and new things do I declare :
before they spring forth I tell you of them."—" Sing, O
ye heavens; for the Lord hath done it : shout, ye lower
parts of the earth; break forth into singing, ye mountains,
O forest, and every tree therein : for the Lord hath redeemed Jacob, and glorified himself in Israel. Thus
saith the Lord, thy Redeemer, and he that formed thee
from the womb, I am the Lord that maketh all things;
that stretcheth forth the heavens alone; that spreadeth
abroad the earth by myself.' Thus, when we contemplate
Deity in his works, we transfer the lesson and the im-

pression to his relation to sinners, as the "God and Father of our Lord Jesus Christ;" and assure ourselves of final safety, through the might and wisdom of the Creator, pledged for our support, and guidance, and victory. We look at the displays of that might and wisdom around and above us, and say—"This God is our God for ever and ever: he will be our guide even unto death." When we have found a friend, we delight to dwell on his qualifications and resources for doing us good. The might and the wisdom belong to our blessed Redeemer himself, even to Him who, having "finished his work," "entered into his rest." By Him were all things created, which are in heaven and which are on earth;—all things were created BY him, and FOR him; and he is BEFORE all things; and BY him all things CONSIST." And the Spirit, whose province it is to renew and reduce to order the human heart, is the very Spirit that "moved" of old, with life-giving energy, "on the face of the waters." Thus the omnipotence of the God of creation is pledged by the God of redemption, to fulfil all the purposes of his grace:—and the omnipotence, too, that by mighty signs and wonders conducted Israel through the waste and howling wilderness, and subdued their enemies before them, and gave them possession of the land of promise, is engaged to guide and guard the spiritual Israel through all the trials and temptations, the duties and the difficulties of their journey to the Canaan above; to bruise Satan with all his hosts under their feet; and to give them a settlement with himself in the inheritance that is "incorruptible, undefiled, and that fadeth not away." While, on the Christian Sabbath, therefore, we especially cele-

bates the glories of redeeming mercy, and express our
united obligations to the God of grace! in songs of adoring
praise, it is not to the exclusion either of the work of
creation, or of the deliverance from Egypt. We associate
all the three. We see the same God in them all. The
God who made the world is the God of salvation; the
God of Abraham, Isaac, and Jacob, is the God and Father
of our Lord Jesus Christ !*

---

* On the subject of the change of the day of sabbatical rest, I have
taken no notice of the calculations of those who allege, and, with no
little sagenatdy, at least, endeavour to make it out, that at the departure of the Israelites from Egypt, a day was lost, and the Sabbath consequently shifted a day back; that this was confirmed at the time of the
manna and the giving of the law, and continued to be the case till the
period of our Lord's resurrection; that at that time, through circumstances of a similar kind, there was the gain or advance of a day; and
that by this means the original Sabbath was restored, the first day of
our week really corresponding to what was the seventh day of the
creation week.—Although I admit the ingenuity, I am by no means
convinced of the conclusiveness of the calculations by which these alle-
gations are supported. Had there been an *intentional* change of the day
at the Exodus, to answer any divine purpose, it is reasonable to suppose
that the fact, with its design, would have been recorded. The idea of
the *accidental* loss of a day, by which the Sabbath fell out of its original
and long-established course, without any specific reason for the change,
and of this having stood merely as a curious fact, to be detected in after
ages, by the ingenuity of antiquarian research into biblical times and
seasons,—is a supposition which, on many accounts, I am unwilling to
admit. But I think it unnecessary to spend time on a speculation, respecting which such an authority as Horsley has said—" It has been
imagined, that a change was made of the original day by Moses,—that
the Sabbath was transferred by him from the day on which it had been
originally kept in the patriarchal ages, to that on which the Israelites
left Egypt. The conjecture is not unnatural; but it is, in my judgment, a mere conjecture, of which the sacred history affords neither
proof nor confutation."—Serm. xxiii. vol. ii.

I have referred to Dr. Whately, as denying the permanent obligation of the Decalogue; but I have taken no notice of the strange ground on which he rests the obligation to observe the first day of the week as the Christian Sabbath. He sets aside all idea of direct divine sanction, and resolves the obligation into the authority of the church! " The first day of the week," he says, " is set apart by all Christian churches, as a religious festival in celebration of Christ's resurrection, agreeably to the practice of the apostles and other early Christians. The custom of the primitive church would not, indeed, *alone* make this an imperative duty; since the love-feasts, and some other ancient practices, are now, by the rightful authority of the church, disused; but their early custom gives *additional* solemnity to an observance that *has* the sanction of the church:—a sanction which would, even of itself, be sufficient. For, when our Lord 'appointed to his Apostles a kingdom,' and declared that 'whatsoever they should bind on earth, should be bound in heaven,' promising to be 'with them even unto the end of the world,' He must surely have conferred on his church a permanent 'power to ordain rites and ceremonies,' and to institute and abrogate religious festivals, 'provided nothing be done contrary to God's word;' and must have given the ratification of his authority to what should be thus ordained. For if his expressions have not this extent, what *do* they mean?" (Essay vi. pages 167, 168, Note.)—It is upon the principle thus laid down, that Dr. Whately identifies, in point of authority, " the Lord's-day, Christmas-day, Good-Friday, Holy-Thursday, and others," as alike institutions of the church!—My respect for the talents of such a writer as Dr. Whately will not allow me to put down one word that might be deemed contemptuous; and yet I hardly know how to treat such statements with seriousness. They serve to show how thoroughly versant a man may be in the principles and rules of " LOGIC," and yet how egregiously he may at times fail in the application of them. For, according to the statements of the paragraph just cited, what follows? 1. " The practice of the apostles and other early Christians" does not give divine sanction to the corresponding practice of the church in after ages; but, on the contrary, the " rightful authority of the church" in after ages may legitimately set aside " the practice of the apostles and early Christians!" 2. All that " early custom" does, (the custom, that is, of the apostles and first Christians,) is, to give " *additional* solemnity to what *has* the sanction of the church;" from which it would appear, that the apostles and early Christians are not to be regarded as even a part of that "church" from which the sanction of authority is given to the observance of the Lord's-day! Their practice does not even add authority; it only adds solemnity. So that the only difference between the Good-Fridays and Holy-Thursdays, which were *not* observed by the apostles, and the Lord's-day, which *was* observed by them, is, that, while all have the same authority,—the authority, namely, of the church, the "early custom" adds solemnity to the latter. Would that even this were true in point of fact! 3. The authority (is it infallible?) of "the church," as a Dictatrix, in the name of God, of the institutions to be observed by Christians, is assumed, while we are left sadly in the dark as to what "the church" signifies,—where it is, after all, that the authority is lodged. Is it the church of Rome, the church of England, the Greek church, the Lutheran church, or one or all of the dissenting churches? The observances of all these, respectively, are different. With which lies the authority? The authority of the church is an imposing sound; but unless it can be definitively settled what the church is to whose authority we are to bow, it is sound only. It means nothing. 4. The authority of this imaginary church appears, in the statement, as *identified* with the authority of the apostles, as the same with theirs, by virtue of succession;—for it was in " appointing *to the apostles* a kingdom," in " declaring, that whatsoever they should bind on earth should be bound in heaven," and at the same time " promising to be with them always even to the end of the world," that he is conceived to have certainly conferred *on the church* the power to ordain rites and ceremonies, and to institute and abrogate religious festivals: —and yet, identified as the authority of the church is with that of the apostles, the *practice* of the apostles may be altered and set aside by the authority of the church; from which it seems a natural sequence, that the practice of the apostles, to whom the kingdom was appointed, and from whom the supposed authority of the church descended, was a practice which had not the sanction of *their own* authority. The authority of the apostles, it should seem, is not to be deduced from their practice, nor is that practice to be regarded as sanctioning the church's observance; but that very practice derives its sanction from the subsequent authority of the church! and yet the authority of the church is the same with that of the apostles! 5. The authority with which the apostles were invested, when Christ said to them, " I appoint unto you a kingdom," and " Whatsoever ye shall bind on earth shall be bound in heaven," was an universal authority to dictate the laws of the kingdom, to arrange and settle the entire economy of the Christian church, to bind the whole will of Christ on the consciences of the subjects? Have they, or have they not, fulfilled this commission? Have they fulfilled it, by leaving in the hands of the church itself, to write it was their divinely appointed province to reveal truth, and to dictate duty, "authority in matters of faith," and the power of ordaining rites and ceremonies," and of " instituting and abrogating religious festivals?" Instead of settling the laws of the kingdom, have they left it to the subjects of the kingdom, to enact these laws for themselves? But, 6. There is a *salvo* for this question :—It is in these words—" provided nothing be done contrary to God's word." And is it, then, of no consequence how many or how great *additions* be made to the word of God, in the form of rites and ceremonies, provided there be nothing " contrary " to that word? How far such a sentiment is in harmony with the express declarations o. the sacred volume, both in the Old Testament and in the New, let the reader judge. Deut. xii. 32. Prov. xxx. 6. Rev. xxii. 18, 19. And are we to understand Dr. W. as giving the church a power to *take from* God's word, as well as to *add to* it, when he asserts her authority to "*abrogate*," as well as to institute, religious festivals!—The truth is, there can neither be an addition to God's word, nor a deduction from it, that is not "contrary" to it. Every addition is a denial of its sufficiency, and a marring of its beautiful simplicity; and every deduction, an impeachment of the wisdom which does nothing in vain.

Dr. Whately is greatly puzzled to make any thing of our Lord's commission to his apostles, if the words conveying it have not the meaning he assigns to them :—" if his expressions have not this extent, what *do* they mean? And yet, where lies their difficulty? Was the authority of the apostles to cease with their lives? Does it not continue in their writings? And is not the simple business of every church, and of every member of every church, to look for the dictates of their authority there? It is in THE WORD, not in THE CHURCH, that the apostolic authority now resides. To the authority with which they were invested, as the inspired ambassadors of the King of Zion, there were no successors. They have deposited the sum of their commission in the statute-book of the kingdom. They appointed its laws and ordinances, and they have recorded them.—When their Master promised to be " with them even unto the end of the world," I am far from denying that the promise includes his presence with his church, and with his servants generally, in all future time;—but with the one be it observed, as holding and promoting, and with the other, as teaching and publishing the word of the apostles. They "being dead, yet speak," and speak "as having authority." And in *this* view, their divine Master is "with them still. When Jesus, in his intercessory prayer, says, "Neither pray I for these alone, but for all them also who shall believe on me, *through their word*,"—does he include such only as should be brought to the knowledge of the truth by the living ministry of his apostles? This would deprive us, and deprive all believers since the time of the cessation of their labours in death, of any interest in the prayer or comfort from it. The words reach to the end of time. It has always been, it ever will be, "*by their word*," that any sinner on earth believes in Jesus. And the Lord continues to countenance his apostles, and to fulfil his promise of being "with them," when he countenances and blesses those who preach "their word." In being with *such* he is with *them*.

It is melancholy to think of the flimsiness of the ground on which an authority, so justly eminent in metaphysical science, would rest the obligation of observing the sabbath,—depriving it of all directly divine hold on the conscience. "Can you conceive," says Dr. Burder, in the excellent little work to which I have before referred,—" can you con-"ceive of any representation more calculated to undermine in the "hearts of men, the authority of the sabbath, than its association, in "the same rank, with days appointed by the authority of the Church of "Rome, and transferred into the calendar of the English hierarchy? "If such opinions are, *even at the present day*, taught in our colleges, "we can scarcely wonder at the license given by the highest authori-"ties, in the church and in the state, two centuries ago, for the direct "profanation of the sabbath." Lecture iv. pages 85, 86.

DISCOURSE V.

ISAIAH lviii. 13, 14.

" *If thou turn away thy foot from the sabbath, from doing thy pleasure*
on my holy day ; and call the sabbath a delight, the holy of the Lord,
honourable; and shalt honour him, not doing thine own ways, nor
finding thine own pleasure, nor speaking thine own words : Then
shalt thou delight thyself in the Lord ; and I will cause thee to ride
upon the high places of the earth, and feed thee with the heritage of
Jacob thy father : for the mouth of the Lord hath spoken it."

HAVING now largely discussed the *obligation* to observe
the sabbath, as a permanent divine institution, together
with the change of the day, under the New Testament
dispensation, I proceed to the more practical department
of our subject,—the *observance* of the day,—the duties included in its due celebration,—or the scriptural answer to
the question, " How is the Sabbath to be sanctified ? "

On this important question, I must begin with the
notice of a sentiment almost universally prevalent, and to
which I formerly adverted, as one which had been assumed
on insufficient grounds, and had obtained general currency
without due examination,—namely, that the divine requisition of sabbatical observance among the Jews was
characterised by a measure of rigid severity and uncom-

promising strictness, quite incompatible with the spirituality and freedom of the Christian economy.* It will be
proper for us, first of all, to examine a little the grounds
on which this sentiment has rested.

Now, in such examination, we have nothing whatever

---

* Thus Bishop Horsley :—" The spirit of the Jewish law was rigour
and severity. Rigour and severity were adapted to the rude manners
of the first ages of mankind, and were particularly suited to the refractory temper of the Jewish people. The rigour of the law itself was far
outdone by the rigour of the popular superstition and the pharisaical
hypocrisy; if indeed, superstition and hypocrisy, rather than a particular ill-will against our Lord, were the motives with the people and
their rulers, to tax him with a breach of the sabbath, when they saw
his power exerted on the sabbath-day, for the relief of the afflicted.
The Christian law is the law of liberty. We are not, therefore, to take
the measure of our obedience from the letter of the Jewish law, much
less from Jewish prejudices, and the suggestions of Jewish malignity.
In the sanctification of the Sabbath, in particular, we have our Lord's
express authority to take a pious discretion for our guide, keeping con-
stantly in view the end of the institution, and its necessary subordination to higher duties." Serm. xxiii.—In thus speaking of the rigour of
the Jewish law, and contrasting it with the " pious discretion," authorized as our guide in the observance of the Sabbath,—the Bishop is
guilty of a palpable oversight. It was not the Christian, but the Jewish Sabbath, of which our Lord himself exemplified the observance,
and of which he explained the principles. So that if, in laying down
these principles, what the Bishop calls " a pious discretion" was allowed, it was allowed in the interpretation of that very law, of which
" the spirit" is here affirmed to have been " rigour and severity." And
in this he hints, though inadvertently, at the very principle, or test, by
which we wish the Jewish law to be judged, and to which the following discussion is designed to bring it. When he assigns as one reason
for the rigour and severity of the Mosaic law, " the refractory temper
of the Jewish people," perhaps Christians may not be the worse for
being reminded of the apostolic admonition—" Be not high-minded,
but fear."

to do with the traditions of the elders in ancient days, or
with the equally unwarranted, and still more foolish and
frivolous restrictions of the more modern Jews. Our
business is exclusively with the divine record. Let us
look, then, at the different laws given on the subject to
Israel, along with any inspired comments upon them, to
be found in the monitory counsels of the prophets. Exod.
xx. 8—10. " Remember the Sabbath-day, to keep it holy.
Six days shalt thou labour, and do all thy work : But the
seventh day is the sabbath of the Lord thy God : in it
thou shalt not do any work, thou, nor thy son, nor thy
daughter, thy man-servant, nor thy maid-servant, nor thy
cattle, nor thy stranger that is within thy gates." Exod.
xxxv. 2, 3. " Six days shall work be done, but on the
seventh day there shall be to you an holy day, a sabbath
of rest to the Lord : whosoever doeth work therein shall
be put to death.   Ye shall kindle no fire throughout your
habitations upon the sabbath-day." Jeremiah xvii. 19—23.
" Thus said the Lord unto me, Go and stand in the gate
of the children of the people, whereby the kings of Judah
come in, and by the which they go out, and in all the gates
of Jerusalem ; and say unto them, Hear ye the word of
the Lord, ye kings of Judah, and all Judah, and all the
inhabitants of Jerusalem, that enter in by these gates :
Thus saith the Lord, Take heed to yourselves, and bear
no burden on the Sabbath-day, nor bring it in by the gates
of Jerusalem ; neither carry forth a burden out of your
houses on the Sabbath-day, neither do ye any work, but
hallow ye the Sabbath-day, as I commanded your fathers.
But they obeyed not, neither inclined their ear, but made
their neck stiff, that they might not hear, nor receive

instruction. And it shall come to pass, if ye diligently hearken unto me, saith the Lord, to bring in no burden through the gates of this city on the Sabbath-day, but hallow the Sabbath-day, to do no work therein; then shall there enter into the gates of this city kings and princes sitting upon the throne of David, riding in chariots, and on horses, they, and their princes, the men of Judah, and the inhabitants of Jerusalem: and this city shall remain for ever." Connect with these passages the words of the text, Isaiah lviii. 13, 14: "If thou turn away thy foot from the Sabbath, from doing thy pleasure on my holy day; and call the Sabbath a delight, the holy of the Lord, honourable; and shalt honour him, not doing thine own ways, nor finding thine own pleasure, nor speaking thine own words; Then shalt thou delight thyself in the Lord; and I will cause thee to ride upon the high places of the earth, and feed thee with the heritage of Jacob thy father: for the mouth of the Lord hath spoken it."

Having read the laws, let our next inquiry be, whether there is to be found any general principle of interpretation, by which we may be safely guided in defining the import of the terms in which they are couched. This is, in many instances, of first-rate consequence, in precluding controversial discussion respecting the precise amount of meaning in which words and phrases are intended to be understood, which, in themselves, are susceptible of various degrees of latitude, or of restrictedness, in their application. In vain shall we search for such a principle in the glosses and comments of Jewish rabbis,—expositors who, by their interpretations, studiously made void some parts of the law, while they loaded others with accompaniments and inventions of their own.—Where, then, shall we find it? I answer at once, IN THE CONDUCT AND THE TEACHING OF JESUS CHRIST, DURING HIS PUBLIC MINISTRY ON EARTH. When he appeared in our world, he was "made under the law." The law of Moses, both moral and ceremonial, was then in full force. And we are surely warranted in assuming, that he neither exemplified the violation of any part of it in his own conduct, nor commanded any thing to be done by others, that involved such violation; nor justified, or sanctioned, directly or indirectly, any thing whatsoever, partaking in the remotest degree of the nature of trespass,—any thing inconsistent with the original and proper meaning of any divine statute. I cannot fancy to myself ground more fair and unexceptionable. For even if any should conceive (erroneously without doubt) that *his own* conduct must not be subjected to the measure of this rule,—that for himself he takes, and was entitled to take, higher ground;—yet surely it is not for one moment to be surmised, that he either enjoined others to do, or vindicated them in doing, what was in any degree at variance with the existing law of God,—and especially with one of the laws of the tables of the covenant, the ten commandments.

Assuming, then, the correctness of this ground, or principle of interpretation, let us look to a few passages in the record of his life, which bear immediately on our present subject, and may assist us in forming accurate conceptions respecting it.

1. Math. xii. 1—8. " At that time Jesus went on the Sabbath-day through the corn; and his disciples were an hungered, and began to pluck the ears of corn, and to eat

But when the Pharisees saw it, they said unto him, Behold, thy disciples do that which is not lawful to do upon the Sabbath-day. But he said unto them, Have ye not read what David did, when he was an-hungered, and they that were with him; how he entered into the house of God, and did eat the shew-bread, which was not lawful for him to eat, neither for them which were with him, but only for the priests? Or have ye not read in the law, how that on the sabbath-days the priests in the temple profane the Sabbath, and are blameless? But I say unto you, That in this place is one greater than the temple. But if ye had known what this meaneth, I will have mercy, and not sacrifice, ye would not have condemned the guiltless. For the Son of man is Lord even of the Sabbath-day."

In this passage, we see the manner in which the Scribes and Pharisees interpreted the prohibitory restrictions of the law. But we see, at the same time, that their interpretation was wrong. We are not to conceive our blessed Master, when he says, " The Son of Man is Lord even of the Sabbath-day," as admitting that the act. of the disciples was indeed a trespass, but that He, as sustaining the authority claimed in the designation, had a peculiar right to disregard the law himself, and to give to others a dispensation from its observance. No. His words MAY, indeed, be justly considered as asserting a right to introduce such changes (like that, for example, in the particular day of the week to be hallowed) as were in full harmony with the divine intention in the law :—but to interpret them as setting aside, in the particular instance, the obligation of an existing precept, is altogether inadmissible. Jesus takes the law in its true sense,—the sense of the Divine Legislator:—and what the Scribes and Pharisees condemned, he vindicates. And he vindicates it upon a *general principle;* which he charges them with not having adverted to, or understood,—a principle laid down by Jehovah himself, the giver of the law, a due consideration of which would have prevented their bringing against his disciples, for what they had done, the accusation of trespass,—" If ye had known, what this meaneth, ' I will have mercy and not sacrifice,' ye would not have condemned the guiltless." Are we not warranted, therefore, in affirming, that every interpretation put upon the law of the Sabbath, inconsistent with the great general principle thus laid down, must be regarded, not merely as being now, but as having then been, erroneous ; as a human imposition, at variance with the purpose of the merciful Legislator ?

. Let us apply, then, the principle with which Jesus himself thus furnishes us, to the terms of the law in Exod. xxxv. 3, " Ye shall kindle no fire throughout your habitations on the Sabbath-day." You will at once perceive that the spirit of this precept is the prohibition of *servile work ;*—and that, since it is as really servile work to mend and keep up a fire by supplying it with fuel, as to kindle it, the injunction, taken strictly, must be considered prohibitory of the one as well as of the other. Let us suppose to ourselves, then, a case of sickness, such as in any way, whether for the production of extra warmth, or for the preparation of medical applications, required the use of fire:—or let us suppose a Jew settled in a cold climate, where fire was indispensable, amidst the frosts and damps.

of winter, not to comfort only, but to health:—or, indeed, we need not go beyond the winters of Judea itself. Has not Jesus given us a principle, applicable, in the full spirit of it, to all such cases? Has he not here taught us, that the prohibitory injunction was not, and never could be, intended for literal, universal, exceptionless application? —that it did not warrant the condemnation of either kindling or keeping up a fire on the Sabbath in all possible circumstances, any more than the injunction, " In it thou shalt not do ANY WORK," warranted the reprehension of the disciples by the Scribes and Pharisees on the existing occasion? It is true, there were certain laws given to Israel, which tried their faith in God, by whom they were assured that they should not suffer from their obedience, and that the evil consequences which they might naturally apprehend should be averted from them by his own supernatural interposition; preventing their enemies from desiring their land, for example, during the absence of the male population (the defence of the country in ordinary cases) when attending on the instituted feasts at Jerusalem; and guarantying the extraordinary productiveness of their soil, to make up for the want of the seventh year's crop, in which year the fields were not to be sown, nor the vineyards dressed, but which was to be " a Sabbath of rest unto the land." But we have not the slightest ground for thinking that the case before us was of this description,—that there was any guarantee of miraculous warmth, wherever, and on whatever occasion, fire should require to be kindled or mended on the Sabbath-day. The connexion of the third verse with the second, in Exod. xxxv., appears to intimate, that the fires prohibited were fires *for the purposes of work*;—including, without doubt, all *unnecessary* preparation of food. That this was included in the prohibition is confirmed by the orders given respecting the manna: "To-morrow is the rest of the holy Sabbath unto the Lord: bake that which ye will bake to-day, and seethe that ye will seethe; and that which remaineth over lay up for you, to be kept until the morning." Exod. xvi. 23.

The principle which our Lord lays down, and which he uses in vindication of his disciples, he illustrates by two Old Testament cases,—that of David making use of the show-bread, and that of the priests performing on the Sabbath, in the temple, all the menial work connected with the preparation and offering of the prescribed sacrifices. The former case relates not to the Sabbath; but it serves so much the better for explanation of the principle. There is one point only of David's conduct on the occasion referred to that is vindicated, namely, his making use, for himself and his attendants, of the hallowed bread:—from which we are taught that, by the will of Him who saith, "I will have mercy and not sacrifice," the claims of an external rite must give way before the imperative demands of humanity, and of nature's necessities. The law prescribed that the bread should be eaten by the priests alone; but the law is set aside by the urgent exigencies of hunger, and the absence, at the time, of all other supplies. The other case shows, that the prohibition of work on the Sabbath did not forbid what was required in the instituted service of Jehovah; else all that was done by the priests would have been a profanation of the day of rest. What the disciples had done might come under both examples: it was a necessary satisfying, in the simplest way, of the cravings of hunger; and it was done in the service of God, to sustain them in the execution of his spiritual work. The general principle, thus settled by the highest authority, is one which, like every other of a similar kind, is liable to perversion and abuse, by extension beyond its legitimate limits;—but it is a most important one,—and it is one which had full application to the law of the Sabbath among the Jews of old, as it has among Christians now.

2. John v. 5—10. "And a certain man was there" (at the pool of Bethesda) "who had an infirmity thirty and eight years. When Jesus saw him lie, and knew that he had been now a long time in that case, he saith unto him, Wilt thou be made whole? The impotent man answered him, Sir, I have no man, when the water is troubled, to put me into the pool: but, while I am coming, another steppeth down before me. Jesus saith unto him, Rise, take up thy bed, and walk. And immediately the man was made whole, and took up his bed, and walked. And on the same day was the Sabbath. The Jews therefore said unto him that was cured, It is the Sabbath-day; it is not lawful for thee to carry thy bed."

On this occasion, it seems to have been the law respecting the bearing of burdens on the Sabbath, which I have read to you from the prophecies of Jeremiah, which the Jews conceived to have been violated. Now we are not to imagine, that what Jesus commanded to be done was really a transgression of that law; that he enjoined a breach of a divine precept. This is quite inadmissible. Even, as I have before hinted, should we suppose him-

self, on the high ground which he subsequently takes up in vindicating his conduct from the imputations of Jewish bigotry and malice, to have been free from the obligation of the law; yet certainly we are not to suppose, that he gave an order *to another* such as involved a trespass against an explicit precept of God. But the case was one, to which the general principle laid down in the preceding passage, as the rule by which the law is to be interpreted, was obviously and directly applicable, and to which our benign Master did in fact apply it. The history shows us (verse 7) that the man was friendless and destitute. After an impotence of thirty-eight years, he had been made whole by an act of mercy. But the mercy that had healed him was consistent with itself. It followed up one act of kindness with another. How could the poor man go home without his little mattress? Where was he to repose his weary limbs at night? The same compassion, therefore, which had healed him, commanded him to use his recovered strength in carrying home his bed. It was the only way in which it could be done. The poor man, doubtless, thought, and thought justly, that the order of one who had done such a deed was quite sufficient warrant for his compliance. His words imply this:—" He that made me whole, the same said unto me, Take up thy bed and walk." But on the same principle on which Jesus gave the order,—(the principle, namely, of which we have been speaking—" I will have mercy and not sacrifice,")—I am persuaded, that if the destitute invalid had been cured by the waters of the pool, and had afterwards carried home his couch as an act of necessity, he would have been divinely vindicated from the charge of breaking the law;—that it did not require the express injunction or permission of Christ to do what he did;—but that, however severely he might have been censured by the human interpreters of the law, he would have been fully justified by the merciful Law-giver himself.

The law, indeed, in Jeremiah, respecting the carrying of burdens, has evidently reference to the business and traffic of life:—"Thus saith the Lord, Take heed to yourselves, and bear no burden on the Sabbath-day, nor *bring it in by the gates* of Jerusalem; neither *carry forth* a burden out of your houses on the Sabbath-day, neither do ye *any work;* but hallow ye the Sabbath-day, as I com-manded your fathers." Of this law, therefore, the case before us would have been no violation; there being no work done for any secular or worldly purpose, and none that could have been as well done on another day. The law, as given by Jeremiah, is illustrated by the case recorded, subsequently to the restoration from Babylon, under the governorship of Nehemiah. It stands in the following terms, and from the connexion of the bearing of burdens with other transactions of trafficking, shows clearly the nature and extent of the law of prohibition. Neh. xiii. 15—19, " In those days saw I in Judah some treading wine-presses on the Sabbath, and bringing in sheaves, and lading asses; as also, wine, grapes, and figs, and all man-ner of burdens, which they brought into Jerusalem on the Sabbath-day: and I testified against them in the day wherein they sold victuals. There dwelt men of Tyre also therein, which brought fish, and all manner of ware, and sold on the Sabbath unto the children of Judah, and in Jerusalem. Then I contended with the nobles of Judah, and said unto them, What evil thing is this that ye do, and profane the Sabbath-day? Did not your fathers thus, and did not our God bring all this evil upon us, and upon this city? yet ye bring more wrath upon Israel, by profaning the Sabbath. And it came to pass, that, when the gates of Jerusalem began to be dark before the Sabbath, I commanded that the gates should be shut, and charged that they should not be opened till after the Sabbath; and some of my servants set I at the gates, that there should no burden be brought in on the Sabbath-day."

3. In further illustration of the same topic, see Luke xiii. 10—17, and Luke xiv. 1—6. " And he was teaching in one of the synagogues on the Sabbath. And, behold, there was a woman which had a spirit of infirmity eighteen years, and was bowed together, and could in no wise lift up herself. And when Jesus saw her, he called her to him, and said unto her, Woman, thou art loosed from thine infirmity. And he laid his hands on her: and immediately she was made straight, and glorified God. And the ruler of the synagogue answered with indignation, because that Jesus had healed on the Sabbath-day, and said unto the people, There are six days in which men ought to work: in them therefore come and be healed, and not on the Sabbath-day. The Lord then answered him, and said, Thou hypocrite, doth not each one of you on the Sabbath loose his ox or his ass from the stall, and lead him away to watering? And ought not this woman, being a daughter of Abraham, whom Satan hath bound, lo, these eighteen years, to be loosed from this bond on the

Sabbath-day? And when he had said these things, all his adversaries were ashamed : and all the people rejoiced for all the glorious things that were done by him."— "And it came to pass, as he went into the house of one of the chief Pharisees to eat bread on the Sabbath-day, that they watched him. And, behold, there was a certain man before him which had the dropsy. And Jesus answering, spake unto the lawyers and Pharisees, saying, Is it lawful to heal on the Sabbath-day? And they held their peace. And he took him, and healed him, and let him go; and answered them, saying, Which of you shall have an ass or an ox fallen into a pit, and will not straightway pull him out on the Sabbath-day? And they could not answer him again to these things."

It cannot be questioned, that in both the cases—cases of every-day life, adduced by our Lord in vindication of his own conduct—both the "loosing the ox or the ass from the stall, and leading him away to watering," and the "pulling him out of a pit" into which he had accidentally fallen, the action is, by direct implication, justified, as involving no breach of the divine law,—as not only harmless indeed, but, on the principles of benevolence to the brute creation, an incumbent duty. Yet in either case, the action is a description of work,—of servile work, —no manner of which, according to the strictly interpreted letter of the law, was permitted to be done. The principle on which the justification rests is precisely the same with that before adduced by him—"If ye had known what this meaneth, 'I will have mercy and not sacrifice,' ye would not have condemned the guiltless." Jesus, therefore, does not merely vindicate himself in the particular

instances in which he was charged with conduct inconsistent with the sanctity of the Sabbath; he still maintains
the general principle:—and on another occasion, of a
similar kind, he deduces from the principle a maxim of
conduct, capable of very extensive application. Matth.
xii. 9—13, " And when he was departed thence, he went
into their synagogue: and, behold, there was a man which
had his hand withered. And they asked him, saying, Is
it lawful to heal on the Sabbath-days? that they might
accuse him. And he said unto them, What man shall
there be among you that shall have one sheep, and if it
fall into a pit on the Sabbath-day, will he not lay hold
on it, and lift it out? How much, then, is a man better
than a sheep? Wherefore it is lawful to do well on the
Sabbath-days. Then saith he to the man, Stretch forth
thine hand. And he stretched it forth; and it was restored
whole, like as the other." The maxim is, (and the
connexion shows that it has reference to acts of kindness
and compassion, whether to man or brute,) " Wherefore
IT IS LAWFUL TO DO WELL ON THE SABBATH-DAYS."
On this highest authority, then, (as we Christians esteem
it,) the Jews needed to feel no scruple, nor need we feel
any, in doing on the Sabbath whatever the comfort or
benefit of our fellow-creatures, placed by providence
within the reach of our beneficent influence, requires to
be done. I say, *requires* to be done. For if we occupy
in acts of mercy, such as might, with equal advantage
to the objects of our care, be done on other days, those
portions of the Sabbath which ought to be devoted to
what is more directly spiritual,—and this, with the view,
perhaps, of our having more time during the rest of the

week for our secular engagements,—we are then taking advantage of a good principle to cover one that is worldly and evil: we are doing a right enough thing, but in a wrong state of mind.

In connexion with these parts of our Saviour's history and instructions, it will not be out of place to mention, that one of the reasons assigned by the God of mercy for the appointment of the Sabbath of old, was the rest of the brute creation from their toils in the service of man: "Six days shalt thou do thy work; and on the seventh day thou shalt rest; that thine ox and thine ass may rest, and the son of thy handmaid, and thy stranger, may be refreshed." Exod. xxiii. 12. On the duties arising from this, on the part of the owners and employers of these and other creatures, which God has subjected to man, and which the sin of man has " made subject to vanity," causing them to " groan and travail together in pain" until now, we may speak hereafter. My remark at present is, that, under a new dispensation, of which the very genius is mercy, it cannot surely be, that this kind and gracious provision should be entirely done away; and that the law should be more benignant than the gospel. They who conceive the Sabbath to have been a merely Jewish institution, and who consider all days, under the gospel dispensation, to be alike, except so far as the inclination of men may make a difference, must regard the divine provision of a weekly rest to the animal creation as now set aside:—for where there is no authoritative enactment, but all is left optional, and subjected to the discretionary influence of general feeling, there is properly no duty. A provision more in harmony with the benevolence of the divine character, it is not easy to imagine; nor any thing more out of harmony with the nature and spirit of the evangelical system, than the abolition of such a provision. Certainly there was no preceding dispensation, with whose principles it was more in accordance than it is with those of the gospel. The rest of the seventh day we regard as a *right* of the brute creation, conferred upon them from the beginning by the God of love,—not a special right of Jewish beasts of burden, but a common right of the whole;—of which to suppose them deprived under the benign government of the Prince of peace, is inconsistent with every view given us in the scriptures of his character and of the principles of his reign. It is under this reign, that the groans of creation are in due season to have an end ;—and we cannot well conceive that these groans are, in the meantime, to be deepened and aggravated by the withdrawment of privileges formerly enjoyed, and so eminently fitted to mitigate the pressure of its woes. It will not do to compliment the new state of things by alleging that, under it, all is now left to the operation of general principles. These principles we admit to be, like their divine author, of perfect excellence, and we grant that much is left to their powerful and habitual influence: —but still, a definite privilege like the present, which cannot be invaded without a violation of divine authority, is a much more regular and efficient security, than if all were left to an influence which, however good in itself, operates, in different bosoms, in such various degrees, and is exposed to temptations so numberless, from all the suggestions of self-interest and worldly-mindedness. Had the brute creation a voice, it would plead with all the power and pathos of eloquence, for the Sabbath.

The example of the Saviour might be more largely illustrated. But my object is merely to draw from it an evidence that the Jewish Sabbath, when the law was rightly understood, was not the harsh and rigid observance which it is generally supposed to have been; but that, judging from the practical commentary of our Lord's own conduct, and from his commands and instructions to others, it was regulated by principles the very same with those which characterize his own administration. If further proof of this were required, I should have recourse to the text. There can be no question that it contains an inspired description of the duties of a Jewish Sabbath, and of the state of mind and heart in which they were to be discharged. And yet, were we setting ourselves to attempt it, would it be in our power to invent language more appropriate to describe the celebration of the Sabbath of the gospel—its nature, its duties, and its suitable frame of spirit?—This we shall have occasion to show, when we come to illustrate its different parts in detail.

The answers, then, which are given in the Assembly's Catechism to the two questions, What is required in the fourth commandment? and, How is the Sabbath to be sanctified? I conceive to be most correct in sentiment, and appropriate in expression. "The fourth commandment requireth the keeping holy to God such set times as he hath appointed in his word; expressly one whole day in seven, to be a holy Sabbath to himself;"— and " The Sabbath is to be sanctified by a holy resting all that day, even from such worldly employments and recreations as are lawful on other days; and spending the whole time in the public and private exercises of God's worship; except so much as to be taken up in the works of necessity and mercy."

The principal source of the impression, as to the difference in strictness between the Jewish and the Christian Sabbath, has, I presume, been the penalty annexed to the breach of the Sabbatical law under the former dispensation, accompanied with the remarkable instance of its infliction recorded in the Mosaic history—Num. xv. 32—36. " And, while the children of Israel were in the wilderness, they found a man that gathered sticks upon the Sabbath-day. And they that found him gathering sticks brought him unto Moses and Aaron, and unto all the congregation. And they put him in ward, because it was not declared what should be done to him. And the Lord said unto Moses, The man shall be surely put to death: all the congregation shall stone him with stones without the camp. And all the congregation brought him without the camp, and stoned him with stones, and he died; as the Lord commanded Moses." It is needless for us to speculate about the nature and amount of this man's trespass. He was gathering wood,—whether for domestic use, or as an article of merchandise, we are not told. We might frame, according to our disposition, an aggravated or an attenuated view of his offence, by introducing various suppositions, both as to what he was doing, and the end for which it was done. But conjecture is needless. The simple fact of the sentence of death being executed, should be enough to satisfy us that the case was not one to which the principle, "I will have mercy and not sacrifice" was at all applicable. The sentence was from God, to whom, by Moses, the determination of it had been directly referred; and, believing this, we must, by necessary consequence, believe that it was just.—And with regard to the penalty itself, I have, in a former discourse, shown the fallacy of the sentiment, that we cannot be bound by a precept enjoining a duty, without being bound also by the prescription of the special penalty attached to it under a particular dispensation.—So far as the nature of the trespass is concerned, it might have been a violation of the law of the Sabbath under the Christian as well as under the Jewish economy. So that, if we can only divest our minds of the association of the offence with the penalty, it requires no more rigid construction of the law to bring it under the condemning sentence of judaism than under that of Christianity.

When we speak of the law of the Sabbath as having been incorporated amongst the national institutes of the Jewish people, a question of some importance and difficulty suggests itself, respecting the extent to which the same thing may be done in other communities; whether there be any principle on which the Sabbath may still be nationally instituted and observed, and how far this principle legitimately reaches. To enter largely into such inquiries, would involve us in the general discussion respecting civil establishments of religion: and perhaps it may be admitted, that there are few topics from which considerations of greater plausibility may be derived in behalf of such establishments. than the law of the Sabbath.

To this one topic I must confine myself, and discuss it with brevity.

The situation of the Jews, as a people, was altogether peculiar. No nation, before or since, has ever been in the same. The direct interposition of Jehovah placed them in it, for special ends. As the people whom he had chosen, that he might place among them his name and his worship, they were the visible and professing church of God,—a national church, in special covenant with Him. Their laws and institutions were divine, and had, in them all the force of religious as well as of civil obligation. Every violation of them was cognizable, not only as a crime against the state, but as a sin against God; for, in truth, God was their King. The peculiar ends of their separation, and of the institution of the theocracy, or reign of Jehovah over them, as their resident and miraculously accredited monarch, can never occur again; nor can any such national relation to God ever again exist, unless by a new and equally direct and well authenticated interposition of heaven in behalf of some other favoured people. So that nothing can be more unwarrantable, nothing more strangely presumptuous, than for any other people to think of emulating what was thus divinely peculiar. The church of God is otherwise constituted now. It is not national, but composed of a selection from all nations. It does not admit of nationality, without its very nature being essentially changed,—without a reverting to the comparative worldliness and corruption of a preparatory and abolished economy. The nationalizing of the church now is just as much a going back to that which is abolished, as a resumption of the " weak and beggarly elements" of the ancient ceremonial would be; there being quite as abundant intimation, both prophetical and apostolic, of a purposed change in the constitution of the church, in correspondence with the more spiritual dispensation of the Messiah, as there is of a passing from the shadow to the substance, from the earthly to the heavenly; from the type to the typified; from the temporary to the permanent. A vast accumulation of illegitimate and inconclusive reasoning has been occasioned by a confounding of the peculiar state of Israel with the ordinary condition of the nations of the earth, and by applying to the latter the language and representations of Scripture relative to the former. While the laws of Israel had in them, as such, the authority of God, he himself being their national lawgiver; the laws of no other people can ever have in them, as such, any more than human authority. They may, and they ought to be in harmony with the moral precepts of God's law; but it is not as the laws of any particular community, that they have aught in them of divine sanction.

May the law of the Sabbath, then, be legitimately incorporated with the code of any other community, and be enforced by human authority? The answer which I am disposed to return to this question is, that in one respect it cannot, while in another it may and ought.—It is obvious, that the sabbatical rest is of a twofold description, and embraces two descriptions of ends. In its observances, and in its objects, it is at once of a secular and of a moral and spiritual character. It is a day of rest and refreshment, to man and beast, from the toils of the six preceding days,—of man, especially when subject to his fellow-man,

and of beast, as placed under the dominion of this lord of
the lower creation;—and it is, at the same time, a day to
be "kept holy," sacred to the worship of God, and the
cultivation of spiritual principles and affections. Now, it
appears to me, that in the latter of these views, the observance of it cannot be the subject of human legislation;
while in the former it may. Human laws cannot authoritatively command any one to worship God,—to worship
Him in any prescribed mode,—or even to worship Him
at all; religion being entirely a matter between each individual of accountable creatures, and Him who is the object
of its services:—far less can human laws enjoin that which
no human agency, or authority, or influence, can in any
case accomplish, the "worshipping of Him who is a
Spirit in spirit and in truth." This is what God himself,
the searcher of hearts, can alone require; and what He
alone, by his promised Spirit, can enable sinners to render.—But the temporal or secular ends of the Sabbath
come fully within the competency and the scope of human
legislation. It must be perfectly competent to the
legislature of any country, contemplating the manifold and
important benefits arising, to both man and beast, from
the hebdomadal cessation of labour, to incorporate this
part of the law of the Sabbath with the enactments of its
statute-book; and to say, respecting one day in seven, to
every member of the community, "In it thou shalt not
do any work." Certainly, by the general concurrence of
any people, this may be made a law of the land. And
under this aspect of it, it might legitimately be enforced
by civil pains and penalties. Nothing that is spiritual,—
nothing pertaining to religious observance, to the inter-

course of man with his Maker; can, consistently with its nature, admit of such coercion.' Every human law enforcing religion by threatened penalties is a statute of persecution; and, in addition to its injustice and cruelty, involves the folly of forcing what cannot exist but as voluntary, and so operates as nothing better than a bounty on hypocrisy. But human laws, I repeat, may institute the sabbatical rest, for the sake of its many secular advantages; and they may thus too accord so far with the higher ends of the divine statute, as to secure to all who, from whatever inward principle, are disposed to observe the acts of outward worship, the liberty, and convenience, and privilege, of doing so without molestation or disturbance. It were going too far to ask, how it would be possible for Christians to observe the Sabbath at all, if it were not made a part of the law of the land:—for, unless we were to deny that there was any Sabbath kept by the church of Christ for three centuries, it is matter of fact that it *was* observed in various countries, notwithstanding its being at variance with all existing institutions. But still, it is well when there *is* such a happy coincidence between the spiritual requirements of God and the legislative enactments of civil society; and they, I apprehend, have thought and reasoned very inconsiderately, and very recklessly of consequences, who, because only genuine Christians, spiritual men, renewed sinners, believing dependants on the mercy of God through Christ, can *rightly* and *acceptably* observe the Lord's day, have hazarded the wish that all such enactments were done away, and that the day were assimilated to other days, and, by all in the community excepting true believers, given up to the ordinary secular pursuits and amusements of life. I am not disposed to question, that advantages might arise from such an arrangement; especially in the more marked separation of the people of God from the world, and the mitigation of the wide-working delusion of a national and nominal Christianity, which operates with such a "latitude of ruin" to the souls of men. Yet, on the other hand, there are such unspeakable conveniencies and comforts, and such advantages too for the promotion of the cause of God, attendant upon the state of things as ordered by providence amongst us, that I cannot but number it, (in as far as regards the authoritative cessation from labour, which is all that is necessary, and the only legitimate subject of human enactment, and which, I need not say, has nothing in it of the nature of a religious establishment,) among our many national grounds of thanksgiving. These benefits I cannot enumerate at present. Some of them may be noticed when we come to speak of the benefits of the Sabbath, and the mischiefs arising from its prevalent neglect and profanation.

We may, I think, advance a step further. It does not seem enough to say, that it is merely competent to human legislatures to enact the cessation from labour on the seventh day;—the law of God, we apprehend, makes it incumbent upon them to do so. The law of the Sabbath, we have seen, was an original law of the Creator, —a law for mankind,—known from the beginning, and indicated by universal, though, in most cases, very obscure tradition. In conformity with such tradition, it comes out afresh in divine revelation, by which the primary institute was re-enacted. By this institute,

there are allotted to men six days of labour, and one of
rest, in regular alternation. This day of rest, then,
belongs to every man, by the law of God. It is property,—property to which there is a divinely guarantied
title. No one man has a right to demand it of another.
To exact labour on the day of rest, is as felonious a
trespass against the law of God, as the abstraction,
whether furtive or violent, of another man's worldly
substance. The fourth commandment secures property in time, as really as the eighth commandment
secures property in money or lands. The rest of the
seventh day is the birth-right possession of every human
being. God has given it; and man may not take it
away. When masters of servants, and owners of slaves,
speak of *allowing* their servants and their slaves the
Sunday to themselves, they speak the language of presumption. They cannot allow what they have no title
to withhold. That time is not theirs. It belongs, by
divine, and therefore inalienable prescription, to their
dependants.—It is very true, that the time thus appropriated to man, each individual is, by the same law that
appropriates it, bound to keep holy to God, using it, in
accordance with the divine intention, for the purposes of
devout commemoration of his doings, and the ascription
of homage to his name. But this is the individual's own
concern. He sins against God, and wrongs his own soul,
when he fails so to employ it, or alienates it to other occupations; but for this he is responsible, not to fellow-
creatures, but to his Creator. His not using the day
aright no more entitles another to exact his labour on it,
than a man's not "honouring the Lord with his sub-

stance and with the first-fruits of all his increase," warrants another to rob him of his property. We must answer to God for the use of our substance; but still it is our own:—we must answer to God for the use of our sabbatical time; but it is equally our own. Every man who knows that the Most High God has given such a law, has a right to claim this time; and no other man can exact it of him without felony against the statutes of heaven.—If these things be so,—if there be a parity between the law which invests a man with property in his rightfully acquired substance, and the law which invests him with property in this proportion of his time, —does it not become more than competent to human legislators,—does it not become their incumbent and imperative duty, to guard from spoliation the one description of property as well as the other?—by statute and penalty to hinder the exaction of time, as well as the abstraction of goods?—to protect their subjects in the enjoyment and use of every one of their divinely guaranteed rights?—And, since the sabbatical law is dictated, on the part of Deity, by mercy to the brute creation as well as to men, ought not human enactments, in the same spirit of mercy, to provide, as far as possible, for the security of *their* rights also? Ought they not to maintain and enforce a law, so eminently beneficial to those dumb creatures of God, which he has subjected to the service of man, but which he has thus, at the same time, compassionately protected, by statute, from oppression and waste?*

* These views of the political obligation of the Sabbath, which I have long held, I was glad to find in harmony with those of my friend,

The distinction thus made between the different ends of the Sabbath, the secular and the spiritual, defines, with some degree of clearness, the boundaries of the province of human legislation. The laws of men can neither command nor enforce what is spiritual: that lies between the

Mr. Wm. Macgavin, to whose intelligent and active mind both the church and the community have been so deeply indebted:—" We are thankful," says he, " for the protection which the law of the land gives us in this respect; and we can be so, without conceding to the civil power the right of interference in matters of religion. It is the duty of the civil Magistrate to enforce obedience to the law of God, not in relation to religious worship, but in all matters which relate to right and property between man and man. Some define the Magistrate's power to relate to the second table of the law only; but this is not quite correct. There is one command of the second table, namely, the tenth, which he cannot enforce, because it relates to the thoughts of the heart;—and there is a part of the first table which he can, and ought to enforce, because it relates to a matter of property and right between man and man. The eighth commandment gives to every man a right to his own property; and the fourth commandment gives to every man, especially to servants, and even to labouring cattle, a right to one day in seven, to rest from the service of their masters;—and it is as much the duty of the civil power to protect them in this right which can be done only by an authoritative suspension of worldly business on that day, as to protect the property and lives of the subjects generally. On this ground, and this only, I consider the rest of the Sabbath a proper subject of human legislation." Church Establishments considered, in a series of Letters to a Covenanter. Letter vii. pages 77, 78.

There is an able Article in the Ecclectic Review for June 1830, in which the principles maintained are also, substantially the same. This article, which, from some forgotten cause, had not been read by me at the time of its appearance, fell in my way since this discourse was delivered, while I was looking back in the Review for something else. And I presume I may consider the sentiments contained in it as corresponding with those of a work, from the pen of the enlightened Editor, which I have not yet had the pleasure of perusing—" The Law of the Sabbath, religious and political, by Josiah Conder."

conscience and God. But they can regulate what is secular. They can adopt the divine statute, for the sake of its temporal benefits:—nay, the rights which that statute bestows, it is their proper business to protect. And so closely are the two descriptions of ends associated, that, in providing for the secular, they take the most effectual means of securing, to all whose inclination disposes them to follow out the spiritual, the undisturbed opportunity of enjoying their desire. The association itself is beautiful; and, if my mind be not deceived by the power of habit, there seems to be something natural and congruous in it. The general repose of the toiled creation harmonizes well with the contemplative recognition, and the peaceful and solemn worship, of the great Being, by whom all was made, and on whom all depends. What mind, alive to the principles and sensibilities of piety, has not felt the stillness of the Sabbath-morn, when the hum of the busy city, or even the less noisy indications of rural labour, are hushed, delightfully congenial with the feelings of devotion?—the rest of surrounding nature, in pleasing concord with the rest of the soul?—the cessation of earthly toils and worldly pleasures, helpful to the establishment of holy sentiments, and the elevation of heavenly desires?—But on these topics I cannot at present enlarge. The text will lead us, under the different particulars of which it consists, to the illustration of the various duties, both positive and negative, which the day demands,—that is, of the things we should do, and the things we should not do, in order to the full accomplishment of the divine purposes in its institution; and also of the various modes, direct and indirect, of its profanation; and of the advantages, temporal and spiritual, personal and social, arising from its due observance.—There is one topic, of essential importance in itself, and, from its nature, calculated to supersede many minute questions of moral casuistry, as to the practical observance of the day—I mean the *right principle* of its celebration; or the *state of mind and heart* necessary to the due and acceptable keeping of the Sabbath, as deduced from a scriptural consideration of its nature and object. To this subject I shall direct your attention in next discourse,—pointing out, at the same time, some of those false principles by which the outwardly respectful observance of the day may sometimes be dictated.

DISCOURSE VI.

ISAIAH lviii, 13, 14.

If thou turn away thy foot from the Sabbath, from doing thy pleasure
on my holy day; and call the Sabbath a delight, the holy of the
Lord, honourable; and shalt honour him, not doing thine own ways,
nor finding thine own pleasure, nor speaking thine own words: then
shalt thou delight thyself in the Lord; and I will cause thee to ride
upon the high places of the earth and feed thee with the heritage of
Jacob thy father: for the mouth of the Lord hath spoken it.

AGREEABLY to intimation in the close of last discourse,
I am now to draw your attention to a topic which I then
stated to be " of essential importance in itself, and calculated to supersede many minute questions of moral
casuistry, as to the practical observance of the Sabbath,
namely, the right principle of its celebration, or the state
of mind and heart necessary to the due and acceptable
keeping of it, as deduced from a scriptural consideration
of its nature and object."

You will at once be sensible, that of these (the nature
and object of the day) there must necessarily be a right
understanding, in order to its being truly and rationally

observed; nor will it be less obvious to you, that, along with a rightly informed mind, there must be a decided sentiment of approbation, and a state of appropriate and favourable feeling, in regard to the great ends of the institution. Without these, not only can no commemorative day be duly observed, but no institution whatever, human or divine. The original Sabbath was a commemoration, as we have repeatedly had occasion to notice, of the work of creation; and to the people, of Israel it was, at the same time, by special divine injunction, to be commemorative of their deliverance from Egyptian bondage. On their part, therefore, the right celebration of that Sabbath, required the knowledge and acknowledgment of these facts,—of God's having created the world in six days and rested on the seventh,—and of his having, by a "high hand and an outstretched arm," wrought the redemption of his people;—and, along with this, the devout affections of veneration and gratitude, which these displays of his power and goodness were fitted to inspire. Such, too, is the case with regard to the Christian Sabbath. Without excluding, as formerly observed, the previous grounds of celebration, it is more especially sacred to the memory of the FINISHED WORK OF JESUS. This is its grand characteristic feature. "There remaineth a sabbatism to the people of God; for he that is entered into his rest, he also hath ceased from his own works, as God did from his." It is the celebration of a victory; of the Saviour's triumph over sin, and death, and hell; of his "spoiling principalities and powers, and making a show of them openly, triumphing over them in his cross,"—of his "ascending on high, leading captivity captive,"—and "sitting down on the right hand of the throne of the Majesty in the heavens." It is "THE LORD'S-DAY." It follows, that it can be duly celebrated, —celebrated, in the true spirit of it,—by those only, who rightly understand the design of the work which Jesus finished on the cross, and of his resurrection as the evidence of that design having been effected. The mere belief of the facts, that Jesus died and rose again, is not the faith of the gospel: that faith including also the belief of the true end or purpose of the facts. Neither, therefore, is the celebration of the Sabbath appropriate and acceptable, when it is a celebration of the facts alone, without a scriptural intelligence and appreciation of their import and design. It is not enough that there be an external adherence, even ever so rigid, to Christian institutions; the question remains, in what spirit they are attended to. Unless we celebrate the Lord's day as guilty sinners, indebted for their salvation to the finished work of Immanuel; trusting and rejoicing in Him in whom Jehovah is well-pleased; praising the glories of his person, character, and work; presenting our supplications and thanksgivings to God, in his name; and, with humble joy, anticipating the everlasting repose of heaven, through him who, having finished his work, entered into his rest —unless we *thus* observe it, the *spirit* of the day is gone: all is formal, cold, and dead; or, if there be fire, it is spurious, unhallowed fire, such as has not been kindled from the altar on which "the Lamb of God took away the sins of the world." The weekly return of the day reminds the people of Christ both of the cross and of the crown. It humbles, and it animates,—humbles, by bringing sin to their remembrance,—animates, by assuring them that it is "and atoned." It leads them back to the past, and forward to the future,—back to Calvary, and forward to Heaven. It points to the open and empty sepulchre, and proclaims—"The Lord is risen indeed" "Come see the place where they laid him." And while, with the voice of triumph, they sing—

> " Christ is risen from the dead,
> High ascended as our head,
> Enter'd heaven with his blood,
> Seated on the throne of God !".

they hear in spirit, at the close of their song, the divine monition; "If ye, then, be risen with Christ, seek those things which are above, where Christ sitteth on the right hand of God. Set your affection on things above, not on things in the earth. For ye are dead; and your life is hid with Christ in God. When Christ, who is our life, shall appear, then shall ye also appear with him in glory." Col. iii. 1—4.

Such is the true spirit of the day. External worship, in all its parts, may be regularly and punctiliously performed, while no portion of this spirit characterises it. There is no true sabbatism, unless there be the resting of the believing worshipper in the finished work of the Son of God. All the services of the day must be performed in his name, and with exclusive reliance on his mediation, —on his blood, and righteousness, and intercession; else the true spirit of the institution is essentially violated, and all bereft of what alone can render it acceptable to God. God is not "honoured" (to use the word of our text) if the worship of *a sinner* be offered in any other spirit than that of dependance on the merits of the Mediator, and a full acquiescence of heart in the gracious provisions of the gospel. We formerly noticed, that from the time of the first promise, God was worshipped by man as the God of salvation; that creation was associated with redemption in the theme of his sabbatical commemoration and praise. So it is now. It will not do for a sinner to keep a Sabbath to God, simply as creator, but a kind of deistical Sabbath to the God of nature, without any acknowledgment of the God of grace. This would be a repetition of the sin of Cain, who brought his offering to the God of providence, but withheld that sacrifice which was prescribed to man as a fallen creature, the presenting of which would have implied the confession of his guilt, of the righteousness of his condemnation, and of his dependance on mercy through the promised atonement.

I feel the necessity of insisting a little more at large on this important subject; because it lies at the foundation of the right performance of all the duties of the day; and because there is so great a variety of motives by which men may be induced to maintain its external observance, and that, too, with no small measure of rigid scrupulosity, while, from the absence of the right principle, all is vanity, and self-delusion. Allow me to particularise a few of these, as grounds of self-inquiry.

1. The Sabbath may be observed, in regard to its outward requirements, *from principles of self-righteousness.* All manner of worldly occupation may be abstained from, with a superstitious apprehensiveness,—with a jealousy of encroachment that narrows the limit of divine restriction, and says touch not, taste not, handle not—even as to what

God has left free; and all the instituted forms of outward observance may be gone about, from week to week, with an undeviating regularity, as if departure in one jot from established usage, would nullify the whole; and fill the mind with anxious disquietude:—so that, as duly as by a law of nature, the man shall be in his place, at his time, and with the exactness of an automaton shall he go through all the customary evolutions of religious exercise;—while all is done in the spirit of a self-righteous dependance on the scrupulous exactitude of their fulfilment. There may be a great deal of seeming devotion and earnestness; nay the earnestness may even be real and deep, according to the worshipper's own understanding of the terms on which his homage is given. But the spirit of the whole is at utter variance with the gospel, and consequently with the real nature and ends of the day. If the Sabbath be observed in such a temper of mind, it is kept in the letter, but broken in the spirit of it. It is not, when so observed "the Lord's day;", for the Lord has not the glory given him that is due unto his name. The reminiscences of the day, and the spirit of its observer, are in a state of perfect incompatibility with each other. No inconsistency can be imagined more direct and flagrant, than to commemorate the work of the Redeemer in the spirit of self-justification; to make the very services by which that work is celebrated, the ground of self-complacency and confidence towards God, when the first design of the work itself is to exclude, on the part of sinners, all dependance, and all glorying, save in the cross. No man can keep the day acceptably in any other temper of mind than that of acquiescence in the gospel scheme of mercy, of humble self-exclusion, and unconditional reliance on grace. To celebrate the work of redemption, while our minds, wittingly or unwittingly, are in a state of opposition to its true nature, and to the divine proposals founded upon it,—while we are doing what we fancy we can to redeem ourselves, instead of bowing to the sovereignty of redeeming love, is not an acceptable service, but a presumptuous insult. The day, it is true, is a day of joy, and confidence, and triumph, but not in ourselves. The spirit of every true observer of it is that of him who said, " God forbid that I should glory save in the cross of the Lord Jesus Christ, by which the world is crucified unto me, and I unto the world." And he who makes his Sabbath-keeping a part of his supposed justifying righteousness, and, at the close of what he conceives a well-spent day, feels the risings of self-complacency, and flatters himself that he has been adding to his stock of meritorious service, and recommending himself to the divine acceptance,—purchasing the Sabbath of heaven by the exemplary correctness of his Sabbaths on earth,—has been indulging a frame of mind thoroughly anti-evangelical, has been fostering his own pride in the very celebration of what is meant and fitted to humble him; has, instead of duly observing the day, been prostituting it to the dishonour of that Saviour whom it is designed to glorify. He has not kept the Sabbath; he has broken it.— I am aware how narrow-minded, illiberal, uncharitable, all this will by many be deemed. But " I cannot go beyond the word of the Lord, to say less nor more." I cannot let down the high tone of the gospel, to humour the vanity of the human heart. Of that gospel grace is the very essence; and I dare not compromise the honour of my God, to gratify the high-minded presumption of his fallen creature. If the essence of the gospel be grace, the first and most essential element in right sabbatical observances, must be the spirit of lowly and thankful reliance on grace, even the grace revealed in the work from which Jesus " ceased" when he " entered into his rest."

"2. The Sabbath may be kept, from *the influence of early education, and of consequent custom and habit.*

" There are few blessings more precious than a pious parentage, and a training from childhood " in the nurture and admonition of the Lord." But, like every other blessing, it is capable, from the perverseness of the heart, of producing evil as well as good. Not only may it, by heedless negligence, or by headstrong resistance, be converted into a curse, and, upon the principle that responsibility is in proportion to privilege, bring down upon such as have enjoyed it the heavier condemnation; but, unless, on the part of parents, there be much care and wisdom, and supplication for spiritual influence, there is in it a tendency, less apparent, but not on that account the less dangerous, to induce what we may term an *educational formality* in religion,—the form of godliness without the power,—the regularity of outward movements, without the inward vital principle. And to those who are impressed with the spiritual nature of true religion, as a matter between the heart and the heart-searching God, the danger will be far from appearing of a trivial kind.—A certain routine of external abstinences and exercises may be regularly gone through on every returning Sunday, merely from the influence of early practice,—a practice begun in deference to the example, and obedience to the will, of parents, and afterwards continued, from the same principles, and from the force of habit. There has been brought gradually into operation a kind of educational sense of duty, of such a nature that the conscience would not feel quite at ease under the charge of any flagrant omission or breach of those observances, with which the return of the day has, from childhood, been associated, and which have become a part of the habits of life.

I am far from meaning to say, that in such early regard to the will and example of parents, or in such educational association and habits, there is any thing wrong. All I intend is, that they are not enough. Some higher principle requires to be brought into exercise. In the midst of such routine, the product of education and custom, the great designs of the institution may never have been examined, understood, believed, and felt. There may be some general association of the day with the six days of creation—though the bond even of that association may be very slender, a filament of thought, of which the mind scarcely feels the hold:—while there may have been no self-application of the great principles of the gospel,—no personal conviction of guilt, unworthiness, danger, and need of salvation,—no faith in that finished work of righteousness and atonement of which the Sabbath is the celebration,—no true love to Him who " loved sinners and gave himself for them," and entered not into his rest till, by his agonies and blood, he had completed their salvation,—no grateful " joying in God through our Lord Jesus Christ by whom we have received the reconciliation,"—and where these are wanting, there is no true harmony of spirit with the events and remembrances of the day.

Its duties may he attendeth to; but they will be done as duties, rather than enjoyed as privileges. There may be a total absence of the genuine spirit of gospel service—the spirit of humble faith, and fervent love, and self-abasing reverence, and holy joy, and elevated hope,—by which the Sabbath of earth is rendered a blessed foretaste of the everlasting Sabbath of heaven. It may be a day of outward habits, rather than of inward experiences,—of forms, rather than of feelings,—of conformity to parental counsels and traditionary practices, rather than to divine purposes and divine injunctions,—of bodily exercise, but not of spiritual delight. Now the Sabbath is not rightly kept, unless it is, in some measure, *spiritually enjoyed;* unless the worshipper be of one mind with God, and his heart in tune to the joy that pervaded heaven, and rung out on the harps of the blessed, when Jesus, having "finished his work," "entered into his rest."

3. The Sabbath may be observed, from *respect to the law of the land.*

It must be very obvious to you, as we noticed in a former discourse, that human laws can go no farther in their injunctions than to that which is external. They can take no cognizance of the mind and heart,—of the secret thoughts of the one, and the unexpressed feelings and desires of the other. Over these they can exercise no control. I do not mean that, when a criminal act has been performed, the law pays no regard, in any case, to the intention of the agent,—the *animus,* as it has technically been termed, by which he was at the time actuated. It does; and it estimates the amount of turpitude and of evil tendency in the action, by that animus or intention, as far as it is possible with certainty to ascertain it, or even to render it circumstantially probable. This is as it ought to be; inasmuch as both the criminality of the deed, and the mischievous consequences of the example, depend, to a great degree, and in many cases entirely, on the existence of intention. There are even cases, in which the very same action may, on the one hand, be perfectly innocent and even praiseworthy; or, on the other, be stamped with the deepest moral atrocity. But, in the first place, if the outward act has not been done, the laws of men have nothing to say. The subject of an earthly government may be, in heart, an assassin, branded by the God who " tries the reins," with blood-guiltiness, condemned by that spiritual law which says, " he that hateth his brother in his heart, is a murderer,"—while human statutes can neither detect his guilt, nor, even if it were avowed, bring it to punishment. And, in the next place, if any thing which human laws enjoin be *outwardly done*, these laws can go no farther than the overt act. The inward motive may have been even so defective, the state of the heart ever so disloyal; but of that, they can take no account. It is beyond their province. It is out of their reach. It belongs to God. Human laws, indeed, regard those actions, against which they threaten punishment, as *crimes* rather than as *sins*; and they measure their enormity, and apportion their punitive award, more by the degree of harm produced by them to the civil community, than to the degree of their intrinsic moral turpitude. They cannot, in their requisitions, reach to the great principle of morality, the regard due to the authority and the glory of the universal Sovereign. In a word, they cannot command what is strictly and properly religious.

The different lights in which the Sabbath may, and may not, be the subject of human legislation, we have formerly considered. My present business is rather to admonish my hearers of the danger arising from the existing fact of the law of the Sabbath having a place in the statute-book of the country;—the danger of observing it as a civil institution, from a regard to the laws in general, and a persuasion of the salutary effects of this law in particular upon the order, and virtue, and well-being, of society. Multitudes there are, there is reason to fear, whose sabbath-keeping goes no higher in the principle of it than this. They keep the day, as subjects of the British, rather than of the Divine government. Great Britain is, in their common parlance, a Christian country; its inhabitants are Christian; its laws and institutions are Christian. On this general principle, they feel themselves bound to conform to these laws and institutions—as good, loyal, Christian subjects. They abstain, therefore, from their secular occupations and amusements, as far, at least, as public example requires:—they go to church with others, and pay what they reckon a becoming and dutiful deference to the weekly ceremonial of the Sunday. But what is there, in all this, of the spirit of obedience to God? What is there of keeping the Sabbath holy to the Lord? What is there of the mind and heart of a creature commemorating, with devout adoration, the doings of its Creator? or of a sinner, humbling himself before his offended God, in confession of sin, thanksgiving for revealed love, and supplication for mercy? What is there of religious principle, or of true and acceptable worship? It is, in truth, a mere mockery of the Most High. It is giving to himself the semblance of homage, and to his statutes the semblance of submission; while the real loyalty of the heart rises no higher than to the throne, and constitution, and laws of the British Isles. It is rendering to Cæsar the things that are God's. Like "Messiah's eulogy for Handel's sake," it is bowing at the name of the King of Zion, in honour of the king of these realms. There is nothing in it whatsoever of the "sabbatism of the people of God," which is kept by them in honour of Him who, "having ceased from his work, entered into his rest."

"Let me entreat all my hearers, to "lay to heart" the paramount importance of *right principle*. Do remember, that, in as far as you yourselves and your responsibility to God are concerned, the principle of the observance of the day may be almost, or altogether, as reprehensible in his sight as the principle of its non-observance. There may be guilt contracted in the doing, as really, and as much, as in the not doing. It is in this, as it is in every matter of external celebration,—ALL depends on the principle. There is, you are well aware, more than a possibility,—there is a possibility which has many many a time been exemplified in fact,—of praying to be seen of men, of giving alms to be seen of men, of fasting to be seen of men; and, after all, having no reward of your Father who is in heaven. Nay, more: on the authority of the same omniscient discerner and righteous judge of human conduct, there is a possibility of even "making long prayers," and receiving, in answer to them, "greater damnation." I deeply feel all the delicacy of this part of my subject. For be it, that I should presume to dissuade from doing, so any man who externally keeps the Sabbath ;—that I should think of exhorting him to desist! And yet, as I value his soul and my own, I dare not flatter him, in the delusive fancy, that, while he is uninfluenced by genuine evangelical principles, he is doing aught that the Lord of the Sabbath can be pleased with, and will accept.—On this, as on various similar points, the truth seems sufficiently simple. The duty of external observance, is incumbent on every man,—for whatever is the duty of one, is the duty of all. But then, the principle that is necessary to the right performance of the duty, is equally incumbent on every man: the obligation to any duty, indeed, necessarily involving the obligation to whatever is previously requisite to the proper discharge of it. It is the duty of all to pray ;—but the Bible teaches us, that acceptable prayer must be offered by a sinner in faith on the name of Jesus ;—whence it follows, that, on the part of all who hear the gospel, and have the word of God in their hands, the duty of prayer involves in it the previous duty of believing in Christ, and giving the heart to God through Him. In like manner, it is the duty of all to keep the Sabbath :—but this proceeds on the assumption, that it is the duty of all to believe in him whose work of salvation it commemorates ; to make that work the ground of their hopes, the source of their joys, and their sole plea for the acceptance of their persons and services ; and, under the combined influence of faith, and fear, and love, " to worship Him who is a Spirit in spirit and in truth." But are there not thousands, and tens of thousands, who keep the Sabbath from no such principles as these ? And all such we must warn anew, of the illusory nature of their dependence on outward observances, without the right state of mind. It is but as the tithing of mint, and anise, and cummin, to the neglect of the weightier matters of the law. All their noise is but "a sounding brass or a tinkling cymbal;" and of all their outward pomp and punctuality of celebration, while the high command of Jehovah, that sinners "believe on the name of his Son," is disregarded, he will say, "Who hath required this at your hands?"

This leads me to another observation of a general nature; namely, that a right principle,—a right state of disposition towards the Sabbath, and the ends of its institution,—will be the best regulator of the conduct in the outward observance of it. Where this, in any thing like due measure, exists, there will be comparatively little occasion for marking off, and defining with jealous precision, the limits of external duty. I feel it to be of the highest consequence, to aim, in the first instance, at the rectification of the inward principle; as it will preclude the necessity and save me the trouble, of many minute details, and hair-breadth distinctions, and cases of conscience, and curious questions of casuistry. It is, I apprehend, a very unfavourable symptom of the state of a man's heart, when he is prone to start these, and puzzled about their settlement; when he is incessantly on the verge of that line which separates what is spiritual from what is secular, and full of questions and hesitations respecting the side of it on which one action and another should be considered as lying; himself vacillating in casuistical doubt, and practical inconsistency; even when conscience decides in favour of the spiritual, making it manifest that his inclination is to the secular, and that he is annoyed at not being able to convince himself on that side; but more frequently finding out some plausible apology to reconcile his conscience and his wishes, and at times coming to terms of compromise, and halving the disputed ground. This is a pitiable state of mind; the course of conduct produced by it is most unhappy to the person's self, yielding neither worldly pleasure, nor religious enjoyment, without a large drawback of self-dissatisfaction; and it is no less prejudicial in its effects upon others. When the principle and disposition are right, I do not say that no questions of perplexity will ever present themselves; but they will be comparatively few, and not often of difficult decision.

The general observation is applicable to other precepts of a similar complexion. Thus, when Paul says, "Be not conformed to this world,"—he delivers a most important practical injunction. But every one must be sensible, that, where there is a disposition to be jesuitical in behalf of the world, a thousand questions may be plausibly started respecting the precise bounding lines by which the admonition should be defined; questions, of which some might present no little difficulty in the speculative solution. But the safest guide will be, having the heart under the habitually predominant influence of those principles and affections included in the counterpart of the admonition,—" but be ye transformed by the renewing of your mind." Unwarrantable conformity to the world will be most easily and satisfactorily prevented, by that *new mind* which is imparted by the renovating and transforming Spirit of God. The rectified disposition will regulate the choice, silencing the specious reasonings of corruption, and determining the conduct, more by the tact of a spiritual feeling, than by the intricacies of a perplexing casuistry.

We are naturally led by our text itself to notice the state of the mind and heart in regard to the Sabbath. It is fully expressed in these terms—" If thou count the Sabbath a delight, the holy of the Lord, honourable." The expressions imply three things :—First, sacred *pleasure* in the day; secondly, a suitable impression of *its authority, purity*, and *solemnity*; and, thirdly, a proper sense of the *dignity* of its appropriate employments.

1. There is, first, sacred pleasure in the day, with its objects and exercises :—" If thou call the Sabbath a *delight."*

This clearly includes more than mere approbation, or the conviction of propriety and duty; for there may often be such conviction, where there is little or no pleasure of heart in following it out. Delight in the appropriate engagements of the Lord's day pre-supposes a renewed heart; spirituality of affections and desires; love to the blessed object of all worship; love to Christ, in whose name, as well as *to* whom jointly with the Father and the Holy Spirit, the worship is offered; love to the saints, " the excellent of the earth," who come together on that day to unite, with " one heart and one soul," in the duties and pleasures of devotion, and in commemorating the work of their great Lord, as the ground of their personal hopes, and the bond of their social union. The " delight" must be considered as including pleasure in anticipation, pleasure in the services of the day themselves, and pleasure in subsequent reflection. This state of heart will dispose us to hail the return of the day as " the best of all the seven; because it brings before the mind, by all its sacred associations and direct engagements, events and subjects on which it delights to dwell, and invites to exercises which have a richer and sweeter relish than any earthly occupation; cheering the soul with holy joy, and elevating it to the object of its best affections, and the spring of its purest and most exquisite pleasures. If we thus "count the Sabbath a delight," instead of saying "What a weariness is it!" our wearying will be *for* it, not *of* it; we shall long for its arrival, not for its departure; we shall rejoice in its rising, not in its setting sun; we shall be "glad when it is said unto us, Let us go into the house of the Lord,"—glad of the invitation to retire from the world to God, not of the necessity of returning from God to the world; when our thoughts have found rest in heaven, they will revert with reluctance to the cares and turmoils of earth. Instead of wishing the Sabbath cancelled, our only regret will be, that we cannot protract its holy enjoyments; and our chief desire, that the redolence of its sweets may diffuse itself over our whole course during the other days of the week.

2. There is, secondly, a suitable impression of the *authority, purity*, and *solemnity* of the day and its engagements.—All these are included in the epithetical phrase, "*the holy of the Lord.*" The primary import of the term *holy* is, that the day is *set apart*. It is set apart to the Lord, and by his authority. It was He who originally "blessed the Sabbath-day, and *sanctified* it." It is "the Lord's day." It is called by him "My Sabbath." He set the original example of its rest; and he has authorita-

tively consecrated it to his own worship and service. It is holy of the Lord, and holy to the Lord.—But its being thus holy, sanctified, set apart to God, involves also the idea of purity. This was associated, under the law, with every thing, according to its nature, that was consecrated to God. Of whatever was inanimate and irrational, there was a ceremonial purifying; and this was all of which these were susceptible.—There was a similar cleansing of human agents, when they were to be employed in the divine service; but, in their case, it was only significant of what was still more essential, the moral and spiritual cleansing of " the inner man." The Sabbath is a holy day, because it is sacred to the service of an infinitely holy Being. Its peculiar exercises are pure and spiritual: —" God is a Spirit; and they that worship Him, must worship Him in spirit and in truth." He who is holy, must be worshipped " in the beauty of holiness." Time, considered in itself, is incapable of moral character. The purity of the day is the associated purity of the Being to whom it is sacred, and of those worshippers who hallow it to his service.—And in all that is thus holy, and set apart to God, there is *solemnity*. The day is associated with " the glorious and fearful name of the Lord our God." The very phrase, " holy of the Lord," conveys to the pious soul the impression of sacredness and awe. It associates with time the same sentiment of veneration that is so repeatedly associated with place, when Jehovah says, " Put off thy shoe from thy foot, for the place where thou standest is holy ground." All that is associated with Jehovah borrows of the reverence that is due to his ser-

rible Majesty." If we have a godly fear of Jehovah himself, we can never hold in light estimation that which is "holy of the Lord."—And this leads me to notice—

3. That there is in the text, thirdly, a proper sense of the dignity of sabbatical engagements. The Sabbath must be counted "*honourable*."—The Lord has put distinction and honour upon that day, by the very fact of setting it apart, in a special manner, to his own worship. Every thing derives honour from its connexion with God. O that we, his unworthy creatures, felt this as we ought! He who has honoured the day, by separating it to himself, puts the highest honour upon us, when he allows me to engage in his worship. The condescension is his, and it is infinite; the honour is ours. And can we have a higher, than when we are admitted into his presence—when we come even to his seat—when we draw near to the throne of his grace and glory, by the "new and living way which he hath consecrated for us?" We are on the highest pinnacle of moral elevation, when we are holding communion of soul with the infinite God.—The day, moreover, is "honourable," inasmuch as it commemorates the glorious works of God. This is especially true of the Christian Sabbath, as being the commemoration of the most complete and brilliant manifestation of the divine honour,—even of that work which brought "glory to God in the highest,"—which illustrates and magnifies all his perfections,—which is the object of angelic contemplation and wonder,—the source of angelic instruction,—the theme of angelic praise. We reckon a day of human institution honourable, in proportion as we attach the sentiment of

honour to the person or the event commemorated by it. The eminence of the person, and the splendour of the event or achievement, are transferred in our minds to the day, and associated with its regular return. Thus it is with the Sabbath. Glory is inscribed on this day, in letters of light. The person celebrated is the King of glory, in the achievement, his conquest of the powers of hell; and the event, his bursting the bands of death, as the signal of his triumph, and the pledge of all that victory has gained for man. What day in our world's eventful history, shall be held in honour, if not this? They must be insensible to all that is glorious in personal excellence, to all that is illustrious in moral enterprise, to all that is stupendous in power, venerable in holiness, and attractive in love, who feel not the claims to honour possessed by this sacred day.

If such be our sentiments and feelings, our inquiry will not be, with how little of hallowed time, and with how small a portion of sacred employment, we can keep on good terms with conscience, and save our credit as professors of the Christian faith. We shall have no wish to abridge the day,—no sympathy with those who would cut short, as far as they possibly can, its peculiar exercises. The celebration of it will not be so much a matter of conscience with us, as of heartfelt privilege and pleasure. Its cheerful devotions will be the element in which our souls breathe freely, and inhale spiritual health. Feeling it "a delight,"—venerating its authority, its purity, its solemnity, the "holy of the Lord,"—and regarding it "honourable" as His own day, that brings with it all the public, domestic, and personal

brightest recollections of his glory,— we shall be solicitous suitably to fulfil its public, and domestic, and personal duties, worthily to God, and profitably to ourselves.

The appropriate exercises of the Sabbath, both public and private, are spiritual. They cannot, therefore, be rightly performed, without spirituality of mind; and when the mind is spiritual, there will be a delightful harmony between the one, and the other. Spirituality of engagement will be the spontaneous product of spirituality of mind; and spirituality of mind will give zest and relish to spirituality of engagement. Upon the principle which has been laid down, I feel as if I might be released from the necessity of entering, with minute particularity, into the discussion either of what ought or of what ought not to be done on this holy day. On the latter subject, especially, however, the field is various and extensive; and, although not so much for the sake of the decidedly spiritual, yet for the sake of those (and there are many such) who may be deceiving themselves respecting their observance of the Sabbath, flattering themselves that all is well enough, while they may be doing things which ought not to be done, and leaving undone what ought to be done, and, under various pretexts, apologizing for both; — as well as for the purpose of impressing on the minds of all, the danger arising from both personal and public transgressions of the law of the Sabbath; I feel it needful to dwell a little on the incumbent duties of the day, and to enlarge more widely on its profanations. I wish to despatch the former in what remains of the present discourse.

The duties of the day may be divided into three classes, *public*, *domestic*, and *personal*.

As prefatory to our brief notices of these, it may be proper to observe, that the previous preparation of the heart, the production of a suitable frame of mind for the due observance of the day, ought, in the first instance, to be attended to; and that every thing should, as much as possible, be avoided, that interferes with this necessary end. Of this description, surely, are late-parties, and late domestic stir and bustle, on the preceding night; and long lounging in bed, and consequent hurry and confusion, want of composure of mind, haste and distraction both in private and family devotions, and even the occasional neglect of the former altogether, on the Sabbath morning. Shun these things. Let the turmoil (if turmoil there must be) of the Saturday night be closed as early as possible. Rise betimes, and begin the day with God, in your closets, and around your family altars;—that, by the reading of his word, and prayer for yourselves and your fellow-worshippers, you may be in a fit state of mind for going up to the sanctuary of God.

1. First, as to *public* duties.—The Sabbath calls you to the house of the Lord. If you do " count it a delight," you will never, for any trivial reason, absent yourselves thence. It is a day, as has been repeatedly observed, of the public celebration of events the most deeply interesting to the church of God. His people come together for this purpose. They observe the institutions of social religion; commemorating the death and resurrection, the finished work, and glorious triumph, of the Prince of life. On his death and resurrection, jointly, their hopes depend; and the remembrance and celebration of both were united in the social worship of the primitive church.

They remembered their dying Lord, in the joint partici-
pation of the symbols of his broken body, and shed blood,
while they chaunted their hymns of praise, in honour of
his triumph over death and his ascension to glory;—they
united in "prayer and supplication, with thanksgiving;"—
they received the lessons of divine instruction from the
sacred word,—and they contributed of their substance for
the poor, and for the cause of God. He counts not the
Sabbath itself a delight, who counts not these exercises a
delight; who absents himself from them on insufficient
grounds, or who attends to them with listlessness, and
longs till they come to a close. To enter here, minutely,
into the manner in which these various exercises ought to
be performed, would be tedious, and, after what has been
already said, is unnecessary.

2. Let me notice, secondly, the *domestic* duties of the
day.—There are certain spiritual functions which belong
to heads of families,—to parents and masters, which on
this day are especially incumbent;—I mean, all that is
comprehended in the spiritual superintendence, the care
and instruction, of those placed by divine providence under
their authority. I am aware, that this should, in some
respects, be an every-day occupation;—by example, by
incidental remark, by occasional admonition, by improv-
ing particular occurrences and circumstances, for imparting
useful knowledge to the mind, and drawing the heart to
God. But the Lord's day,—and especially (according
to laudable Scottish custom at least) the evening of the
day, is eminently appropriate for this important exercise.
Long has it been so devoted, in the exemplary practice
of families where God's name is recorded.

I am a decided and sincere friend to Sabbath-evening schools,—for the sake of children whom God in his providence has bereft of this natural guardians of their tender years,—for the sake of children whose parents are without the fear of the Lord, and careless about both their own souls and the souls of their offspring,—and in every case, as an occasional or stated supplement to the good efforts of Christian parents themselves, whose hearts are set upon the best interests of those who are bone of their bone, and flesh of their flesh.—I fervently wish the prosperity of such seminaries of divine tuition, for the sake of the young themselves, of the church of God, and of society;—nor can I fancy to myself a pleasanter, or more beneficial way in which the Lord's day is ruling can be spent, by those who are qualified for the work, and who have not engagements at home which claim their presence there, and their first attention,—than in the city or country, gathering such little groups around them, and teaching them, from the best of books, the best sons of heavenly wisdom, "the things that belong to their peace;"—informing their minds, persuading their wills, touching their hearts, and winning them to Christ and to the paths of life.—I earnestly recommend this employment. Some, perhaps, may now be hearing and with from a good enough motive, but, to say the least of it, with rather more than enough of selfishness (for selfishness is possible in spiritual as well as in temporal enjoyment) addict themselves to the practice of sermon-hunting on the Sabbath evenings,—I will not say with itching ears," but will even suppose the very best in their behalf, —who ought to be engaged in doing good to others, in

... the young and ... remember ... greater in the days of their youth ... which I approve and recommend as ... institutions, and ... their supplanting domestic instruction. ... is, that system of family tuition should ever be absorbed in more extended system of Sunday-school tuition; ... should I deplore seeing an end put to such pleasing domestic scenes as the tender recollections of ... bring before my own mind:—when the little groups, ... father, or mother, or both, assemble round the ... fireside,—repeat in succession their little ... ... or questions, or psalms and hymns; read from word of God, and are encouraged to inquire the meaning themselves, or stimulated to attention and understanding by queries addressed to them ... Chapter or ... with according to their years and capacities, with the ... gravity of impressive seriousness, and the kindly ... and the glistening tear of sweet affection;—when ... listen, with rivetted interest, to the pleasing and ... tales of holy writ,—of Adam in paradise; of temptation and the fall; of the wickedness of men; the patience of God, and the awful visitation of his ... vengeance in the desolating flood; of Noah, and ... ark, and the new beginning of the world; of Abraham, and Isaac, and Jacob; of Joseph and his brethren; ... in the bulrushes; of Jonah and Nineveh; of ... and the three children; and, above all, of the "holy Jesus,"—the incidents of his birth, and life, and ... by the inimitably simple and affecting narrative ... Bethlehem, and Gethsemane, and Calvary. ...

mestic scenes are the delight of every pious heart. O let not Christian parents allow them to disappear from the earth !

"3. Where these public and domestic occupations are attended to in a right frame of spirit, the *personal duties* and exercises of the day will not be neglected.—These, perhaps, are the most unequivocal tests of principle. The very publicity of the services of the sanctuary leaves room for the entrance and operation of various motives, of a mingled and doubtful character. The power of general custom, of regard to reputation, and to the wishes and expectations of others, may bring a man to the house of God, while there is little of conscientious principle, and still less of spiritual affection, in exercise. That which is public, therefore, is the least to be depended upon of the indications of godliness. It is one of those things, of which the neglect is a decisive proof of its absence, while the observance is no certain evidence of its presence.— Next to them, in this respect, stand the duties of family worship and the forms of domestic instruction. The privacy of these being greater, the proof is proportionally less equivocal. But still there is room for the influence of example, and of traditionary custom, and of other considerations, which may prompt to a pretty regular, nay, even to a scrupulously correct, observance of the duties, when there is no great measure of the spirit and life of personal piety.—The most trying question is, what is a man when by himself?—what are his employments then?—the occupations which he chooses, when no eye is upon him but that of the Lord of the Sabbath?

These are the fairest tests of principle, and of the spiritual state of the heart; there being in regard to them a far greater likelihood of purity in the motive by which the choice is dictated.—I may, a greater likelihood; for the heart being "deceitful above all things," there is, even in the most private religious exercises, a possibility of mixture. A man may, for the sake of character, court a hypocritical retirement, that he may get the credit of adding secret to domestic and public devotions. So that the question here must lie between conscience and God. The personal duties of the day are, secret prayer;—the private reading of God's word, and of such instructive books of human composure as tend to open and impress its truths and precepts, to edify the mind, and improve the heart, and draw the affections heavenward;—meditation on the contents of the word, whether read or heard, and self-examination respecting their influence upon our character and life;—and other similar exercises, for which those who "call the Sabbath a delight" will seek in earnest, as far as can possibly be accomplished, to find and to redeem time. These, I repeat, are the surest evidences of spirituality in the tastes and tendencies of the mind,—of a healthy state of soul. Try yourselves by them. I greatly fear, that, if we do so with faithfulness, we may all of us find no small amount of negligence and of sin to be acknowledged and deplored; much that has indicated a sad deficiency in our spiritual relish for spiritual things; much of precious sabbatical time that has been allowed carelessly to run to waste, or worse than unprofitably squandered.—But I cannot enter upon the ways in which this may be done, without anticipating the topics of next discourse; in which we shall consider the profanations of the Sabbath, under the three particulars enumerated in the text—" not *doing thine own ways,* nor *finding thine own pleasure,* nor *speaking thine own words.*"

DISCOURSE VII.

Isaiah lviii. 13, 14.

" *If thou shalt turn away thy foot from the Sabbath, from doing thy pleasure on my holy day, and call the Sabbath a delight, the holy of the Lord, honourable; and shalt honour him, not doing thine own ways, nor finding thine own pleasure, nor speaking thine own words: then shalt thou delight thyself in the Lord; and I will cause thee to ride upon the high places of the earth, and feed thee with the heritage of Jacob thy father : for the mouth of the Lord hath spoken it.*"

HAVING, in last discourse, dwelt at large on the *right principle* of the Christian Sabbath, or the state of mind and heart necessary to the due celebration of the first day of the week,—as well as on some of those spurious principles from which the observance of the day may be outwardly, but not acceptably, maintained ;—and having very briefly illustrated the public, domestic, and personal duties, to which the return of the day invites, and which form its appropriate and obligatory engagements :—I now proceed to call the attention of my hearers to the modes in which the day may be profaned,—arranging my observations under the three particulars specified in the text—doing our own ways—finding our own pleasure—speaking our own words.

Before entering on these, a remark or two may be proper on the phraseology of the passage. The first expression in it, descriptive of the conduct required on the Sabbath, is of a general nature—" If thou *withdraw thy foot* from the Sabbath." In order to a simple and satisfactory explanation of this somewhat singular form of speech, we ought, I should suppose, to conceive of a person as, during the preceding days of the week, following a particular course,—going forward in the prosecution of his worldly engagements,—and, when the Sabbath arrives, as stopping in his course,—desisting from his ordinary occupations,—not intruding on its hallowed hours with the footstep of earthly and secular businesses, —but waiting till it be over,—devoting it to its own proper employments and purposes,—" resting the Sabbath-day according to the commandment."

The remaining phraseology of the thirteenth verse proceeds, we are constrained to say, upon a very humbling assumption,—the assumption of a natural contrariety between man and God:—for what is the language ?—" and shalt HONOUR HIM, not doing THINE OWN ways, nor finding THINE OWN pleasure, nor speaking THINE OWN words." When man was in innocence, there was perfect unison between his mind and the mind of God There was no contrariety. His ways, his words, his pleasure, were all such as to be "well-pleasing to the Lord." There was then no inclination on the part of the creature, to alienate from the Creator the time, or any part of the time, which had, by his authority, been dedicated to his worship:—and, while the seventh day was sabbatically kept, as especially holy to Him who, on that

day, had rested from the work of his creative power, the
occupations of the intervening six days were characterized
by a habitual remembrance of God, and a devout reference of all things to Him. In that primitive period (alas!
how brief!) of man's history, there was incomparably
more of devotion in his secular employments, than there
is now in his religious exercises. His secular employments were then all imbued with the purest piety, and
were, indeed, in the spirit of them, acts of devotion:—
whereas now, his very acts of devotion are, even the best
of them, deeply tinctured with the spirit of secularity and
earthliness. Man's own ways are now contrary to the
ways of God; his own pleasure to God's pleasure; his
own words to God's words. To the spiritual mind, the
language of the text is, in this view of it, affecting and
humbling. He who "knows what is in man" knows that
the ways, the pleasures, and the words, which are appropriate to the weekly season of hallowed rest, are not
man's own; not those which he naturally chooses or pre-
fers. He likes rather the ways, and pleasures, and words,
of the other days of the week,—those things which, being
"of the earth, earthly," are in harmony with the native
dispositions and tendencies of his heart. If in the spiritual exercises of the Sabbath he has any true enjoyment,
he owes it to that new nature which is the work of the
regenerating Spirit of God in the soul, introducing new
principles of action, new objects of affection and desire,
and new sources of gratification and delight. What is
carnal and secular is his own; what is spiritual and
heavenly is God's.

We shall now take up the three branches of the text, as

they lie in seder, introducing under each those particulars of prohibition which it seems naturally to suggest. To notice every thing that might be noticed, and noticed with propriety, in all the various departments of life, would be an interminable task. From every rank, station, and profession, such questions may be expected as those which the people, the publicans, and the soldiers addressed of old to the Baptist:—" What shall we do, then? and what shall we—and what shall we do?" And it is not unlikely, that, when I have done, I may leave a hundred questions unanswered, which might be addressed to me, as cases of conscience, more important or more trivial, from different quarters of my congregation. Of one thing, however, I am very confident, that such questions would most generally be found to come from those persons, over whose minds the sacred *principles* of the sabbatical rest, which were formerly illustrated, have not a decided and settled control. And it has been on this very account, that I have felt the necessity of insisting so much on the importance of having these principles in due force and exercise,—of the heart being right,—of the Sabbath being esteemed " a delight, the holy of the Lord, honourable." The Christian, I repeat, who thus esteems it, whose heart is thus affected towards it, will not be perplexed with many casuistical difficulties about the way of spending it.

1. The first department of prohibitory restriction is, NOT DOING THINE OWN WAYS.

It is not necessary for me to prove, that this phrase does not here refer to the doing of things which are in themselves sinful. Every thing of this kind is as unlawful and inadmissible on other days, as on the Lord's day. What is in itself sinful is sinful at all times. It is perfectly true, however, that the committing of evil on that day constitutes an aggravation of its guilt. There is a cant expression, one of the world's proverbial jests, which is many a time introduced, when evil has been done on the Sabbath, to amuse the conscience and prevent it from delivering its decisions with the seriousness necessary to their being felt—" The better day, the better deed." But, according to the principles of sound ethics, the true statement is—The better day, the worse deed. We have been taught from our childhood, and the sentiment is perfectly scriptural, that "some sins in themselves, and by reason of several aggravations, are more heinous in the sight of God than others." Now, in the case before us, there is the superadded guilt of profaning that which is holy. There is an additional degree of hardihood, and of presumptuous insult to the Divine Lawgiver, in the perpetration of sin on his own day; a day, which ought to bring his character and his claims more immediately and impressively before the mind, and to awaken in the heart the sentiments of awe, and the obligations of gratitude. The superadded criminality may be likened to the superior guilt of *perjury*, when compared with that of *falsehood*, consisting in the more direct and daring affront put by the former than by the latter, upon the Majesty of Heaven,—whose name and authority are, by an oath, brought more distinctly and solemnly before the conscience.

The expression in the text comprehends in it all a man's ordinary occupations. It is illustrated by the terms of

the fourth commandment:—"Six days shalt thou labour
and do all thy work; but the seventh is the Sabbath of
the Lord thy God: in it thou shalt not do any work, thou,
nor thy son, nor thy daughter, nor thy man-servant, nor
thy maid-servant, nor thy cattle, nor thy stranger that is
within thy gates."—This, we grant is very pointed and
peremptory language. Yet, when there is a superstitious
dependance on external observances, there will generally
be found a disposition to push the laws which enjoin such
observances to an extreme of rigid interpretation even beyond the intention of the lawgiver; to refine upon them,
and to add to their requirements the "doctrines and commandments of men;" there being no length to which men
will not go in self-imposed restriction and performance,
when they are under the delusive fancy of purchasing by
what is outward and ceremonial an exemption from the
divine demands upon the heart and conscience. Thus it
was with those ostentatious religionists among the Jews
of our Lord's time, who "paid tithe of mint, and anise,
and cumin,"—with most punctilious exactitude paying
over to the sacred treasury every fraction which the law
required, while they lived in the neglect and violation of
its "weightier matters," "judgment, mercy, and the love
of God." They put a meaning on the terms of abstinence,
in relation to the Sabbath, which was beyond the intention
of the Legislator; and they scrupled, or affected to scruple, where he not only left them at liberty, but even made
that which they scrupled at their duty. On this principle it was, that they cavilled at the miracles of mercy performed by our Lord on the Sabbath. We formerly saw
the light in which his conduct was placed by himself, in

answer to their malicious cavillings,—the general principles laid down by him for our guidance,—and the decisive scriptural authority thus afforded for the exception made in the Assembly's Catechism, in behalf of works of mercy as well as of necessity. For the passages in the history of Christ's life, illustrative of this point, I must refer to a former discourse. The discussion of them cannot be resumed.—Nor is there need. The passages contain their own comment. They show us, that there is no desecration of the sacred day in the necessary care of the brute creation, which it would be a cruelty utterly repugnant to the merciful genius of the gospel to neglect; and far less in the performance of acts of kindness to the distressed of the human family, when they present themselves to our pity, and require our aid.

The principle laid down by our Lord, and acted upon by himself in that " example which he hath left us, that we should follow his steps," is obviously capable of legitimate application to a great variety of cases; and it is, at the same time, like almost every other, susceptible of abuse, by such as may be disposed to abuse it, and to extract from it a licence beyond its scriptural and reasonable limits.—For example : We have an appropriate illustration in the duties of the medical profession. These duties, on many occasions, involve in them the plea both of necessity and mercy. But there is room for abuse. The principle ought, of course, to be applied only to such cases as do absolutely require immediate or regular attendance. That physician would exceed its legitimate licence, and constitute himself a transgressor of the law, who should so far take advantage of the admission made in favour of his profession, as, on the credit of it, to convert the Sabbath into a day of business, going his rounds, as on other days, amongst his patients, to the neglect of its own sacred engagements, when there existed no plea of necessity, and when the omission of his visits would violate no claim of mercy, when, without detriment, or the risk of detriment, they could either be a day anticipated, or a day deferred.—I select this case, only as an exemplification of many more of a similar description.

"Those actions, I would further observe, are evidently to be exempted from condemnation, which are indispensable to the proper fulfilment of the duties of the day; such actions being evidently comprehended in the requisition of the duties. Such, as formerly noticed, was the ground taken by our Lord, in regard to the priests under the law, who, in the temple, in preparing and offering the victims, in purifying the sanctuary, and in other required functions, performed work, such as in ordinary circumstances, would have been a profanation of the Sabbath, and yet were blameless. Matth. xii. 5. The same thing clearly holds, with regard to all such official services as are requisite to the due observance of the public ordinances of New Testament worship. These, it is clear, are so few and so simple, as, in this respect, hardly to admit of comparison with the rites of the ancient ceremonial:—but still, as far as they go, the principle involves their vindication. I must, at the same time, be understood here as speaking, not of all the multiplied ceremonies which superstition, or fondness for outward show may have added to the "simplicity that is in Christ," but of such only as have the sanction of apostolical precept or example.

I have formerly, with a restrictive clause in behalf of domestic tuition, avowed my attachment to the system of Sabbath schools. It is, however, supremely desirable that these weekly seminaries should be exclusively appropriated to the communication of instruction strictly religious. And this, I am happy to think, is, with but few exceptions, the case throughout Scotland. Yet here, too, there are supposable cases, in which the maxim "I will have mercy and not sacrifice", may be legitimately applicable; cases in which the teaching, on the Lord's day, of the mechanical process of reading, may be not only allowable, but even an imperative duty. I refer, as you will at once perceive, to the cases of poor and friendless children, for whom no opportunity can be found, on the other days of the week, for imparting to them this essential qualification for the acquisition of knowledge. Surely, in such cases, when the alternative is between a child's remaining incapable of reading the book of God, and his being taught on the Lord's day to read it, there can be no room for hesitation. The art of reading is so inestimably valuable, not only in a general point of view, but as introductory to the perusal of the divine word, and to the consequent knowledge of its contents, and as eminently conducive both to the facility, and the permanence of oral instructions,—and is thus so intimately connected with those spiritual interests, which it is the peculiar object of the Lord's day to provide for, and to promote;—that to hesitate between the two sides of such an alternative, would be unworthy of any mind capable of taking a sound and liberal view of the principle authorized by so high a sanction. But let not the term *liberal* be misapprehended. Jealous of the sanctity of the day,—I trust with something of a "godly jealousy,"—I wish to be understood as limiting the allowance to cases of real necessity;—to cases, that is, which are not only excluded from the attainment of the benefit by any means already existing,—but for which, even by the ingenuity and the generosity of Christian benevolence, no other means can be provided. It is in such cases that we grant it to be a duty.—And when the duty is done, the same principle requires that it be done simply with a religious view, as an essential step towards the attainment of that kind of knowledge which it ought ever to be regarded as the exclusive province of Sabbath schools to impart.

With regard, indeed, to cases of exception from the general law, it may be observed, universally, that the things, respecting which it is granted that they may be consistently done, ought to be done in as little time, and with as little labour, as possible. All unnecessary expenditure of the one or of the other,—every thing beyond the absolute exigencies of the case,—must be regarded as an infraction of the law.

With such exceptions, then, founded on the legitimate application of the principle so often adverted to, *all worldly business* is, by the law of the Sabbath, prohibited. There is to be no "buying and selling, and getting gain." The pursuits of earth are to be suspended. The day is to be sacred to God. He who says, "Six days shalt thou labour and do all thy work,"—giving us this large proper-tion of our time for the engagements connected with our various secular situations, says, with the same authority, "The seventh is the Sabbath of the Lord thy God: in it thou shalt not do any work." He claims the day to himself,—not, indeed, for any advantage to Him,—for He is infinitely independent of the services and of the very existence of all his creatures,—but for our own sakes. "The Sabbath was made for man:" and, whatever profanity may think of it, there is the most infatuated and ungrateful requital of the divine goodness in the perversion and prostitution of the day to other ends than those for which it was mercifully instituted,—in secularising it, and devoting it to the comparatively worthless interests of a world, of which "the fashion" so quickly "passeth away." Multitudes, alas! there are, who have no ideas of "profit and loss," except in regard to the possessions and emoluments of this perishing world. Such characters naturally fret at the command which enjoins them to desist from those pursuits on which their hearts are set. They count the day lost, unless something be done upon it for the augmentation of their earthly gains. They say, "when will the Sabbath be gone, that we may sell corn, and set forth wheat?" and they spend, some a part and some the whole of the sacred day, in bringing up the arrears of business for the past week, or in making preparation for the week to come.

Of the *open* profanation of the Sabbath by the transactions of worldly business, there is less, perhaps, in Scotland than in any other country. There is less than in England; less in England than in Ireland; and less in Ireland than in many parts of the Continent of Europe.

Even in Scotland, however, (we have not a little of the more secret and stealthy violation of God's law—with our back-door entrances, our half-open counting-house windows, our Sunday writing chambers at home. It is so far well, that the evil is not done in the face of the world,—it shews that public opinion is still against it, and has not entirely lost its restraining influence, and by the comparative privacy, the mischief is avoided, which might result from example. But let the secret Sabbath-breaker bear in mind, that "God is not mocked." He "seeth in secret." He knows well the purposes for which men enter into their closets, and shut their doors about them,—whether for devotion, or for business,—whether to hallow his day, or to profane it. And, on this subject, let me remind all, that "the law is spiritual." It is not enough that you abstain from the active prosecution of your secular affairs—you transgress the law when you give the world your thoughts,—when your minds are planning, although your hands may not be acting,—when, although you come before God as his people, and sit before him as his people, and with your mouths shew much love, your hearts are going after their covetousness. The unseen activity of the mind is sufficient proof that, but for shame, or custom, or regard of some kind, to man, you would have little scruple in openly setting at defiance the authority of God.

Observe, further, the extension of the prohibition of work to our cattle and our servants, as well as to our sons and our daughters.—The latter should be early trained on Bible principles, to hold the Lord's day sacred, cheerfully associating with it the "reverence and godly fair, which belong to the Divine name, and at the same time the sober, but lively joy which these events commemorate and are fitted to inspire. There is in everything a danger of extremes. Young persons, naturally buoyant, are prone to a lightness and frivolity, which ought to be firmly, though kindly, repressed; but there is, on the other hand, a risk of making the Sabbath, both by precept and practice, so gloomy, austere, and superstitious as to render religion irksome, and to associate it with impressions of dislike and melancholy, and with impatient longings for freedom from its galling restraints. Either extreme ought carefully to be shunned, and the lesson taught, both preceptively and by example, that religion is at an equal distance from levity and moroseness.

With regard, again, to our cattle. It is one of the merciful intentions, although a subordinate one, of the institution of the Sabbath, that the brute creation should enjoy repose from their labour in the service of man. Thus said the Lord to Israel, and thus he saith to us—"Six days shalt thou do thy work, and on the seventh day thou shalt rest, that thine ox and thine ass may rest, and the son of thine hand-maid, and the stranger may be refreshed." Our cattle, then, are not to be used in work; that is, in the work from which we ourselves are commanded to rest. But we have seen that to the law which prohibits work, there are limitations and exceptions in regard to man. It is not, surely, extravagant to conclude, that the spirit of such limitations and exceptions is applicable to such animals as are employed in the service of man. If, for example, it be lawful for a man, and even his duty, to engage in an act of mercy to his own or his neighbour's beast,—leading it to watering, or extricating it from a pit, into which it may have fallen, on the Sabbath-day:—on what principles can it possibly be imagined unlawful, to avail ourselves of the aid of the same beast, for effecting a purpose of kindness, to one of our fellow-men?—If, again, it be no violation of the prohibitory precept, to do ourselves the menial work that is necessary to the observance of the public ordinances of God's sanctuary; how can it be construed into a breach of that precept, to employ, when necessary, our horses, or other animals, for conveying us to the sanctuary, in order to our observing his sacred ordinances? The prohibition to use them "in work," manifestly relates to the secular businesses of the week. It is from these that both man and beast are to rest:—and the interdiction is perfectly consistent with the easy, unfatiguing, uninjurious use of them, for purposes connected with the great moral and religious ends of the day.

The same general principles should regulate our conduct as to our "man-servant and our maid-servant." They are not to be required to do the ordinary work of week-days; nor is any labour to be exacted of them, beyond what is indispensable:—in order that they may have it in their power to spend the day agreeably to its own peculiar designs. It is one of Jehovah's express stipulations, Deut. v. 14, "that thy man-servant and thy maid-servant may rest as well as thou."—The occupations of the field are to be suspended. The workshop is to be closed. The work of the household is, as far as possible, to be anticipated and put over on the preceding day, so as to leave nothing to be done but what is absolutely unavoidable.—

nothing that would needlessly intrude on the peaceful serenity of the Lord's-day morning,—nothing that would, without necessity, interfere with the regular attendance of domestics, as well as other members of the household, on the means of spiritual benefit, or prevent the other duties of the day of sacred rest.

With regard to servants in business,—it has sometimes,—not unfrequently, I fear,—been a matter of tacit agreement, and even of express and positive stipulation, that a portion at least of the Sunday shall be regularly or occasionally spent in the counting-house, or in doing the work of the counting-house at home. Oh! there is something inexpressibly fearful in the idea of one fellow-creature entering into contract with another fellow-creature, to break the laws of the Most High! It is bad to yield to temptation when it comes in the way:—but what are we to say of the man who makes transgression a matter of deliberate contemplation, and stipulates for it as a sine quâ non, in his bargains and contracts? Allow me, affectionately and earnestly, to warn such young men as wish to regulate their conduct by Christian principles, to beware of giving way to any importunity, or to any inducement, however tempting, to such unhallowed and heaven-defying engagements. Let them be firm. Let them say, with mildness, but with unshrinking and principled decision, "We ought to obey God rather than men." They may, in providence, be called to sacrifice, for adherence to their principles, a desirable situation,—desirable, I mean, in as far as temporal emolument and respectability are concerned,—if they decline complying with the wishes and requirements of an ungodly employer.

Let them not yield. A good conscience is more valuable than a good berth:—and if you prefer the latter to the former, and disobey God for the sake of any earthly gain, —how can you ever look up to Him with confidence? Sanctified trials are incomparably preferable to accursed blessings.—By yielding, moreover, when the thing required is known to be against your principles, you will incur secret contempt:—while you gain the flattery of the lips, you will lose the esteem of the heart. Be assured, that, even as to this world, upright and steady consistency will prove ultimate advantage. The very man who, by his cajoling, tries to ensnare you, will, in spite of him, secretly admire, even while he frets and frowns, and affects to treat your silly scruples, and nursery prejudices, with derision. He may decline employing you; but when he sees you resolute in making the sacrifice to conscience, instead of his confidence in you being impaired, he will only feel his disappointment the more, that he must forego the services of a youth of principle. There are not wanting recorded instances, in which providence, by most unanticipated turns of affairs, has opened better prospects, and provided better situations, for youths who have thus maintained their integrity by the sacrifice of their interest,—giving a present and practical commentary on the promise, "Him that honoureth me I will honour." It would be wrong to flatter you with the assurance, in all cases, of such interference:—but, whatever be the immediate issue, He will ultimately smile upon your self-denying fidelity, and will "make darkness light before you, and crooked things straight."—But I must hasten forward to our next particular.

II. "NOT FINDING THINE OWN PLEASURE."—Alas! that men's pleasure should, in general, be so little in accordance with the demands and exercises of God's holy day! If it be counted by us "a delight," we shall find our own pleasure in its appropriate engagements:—but the expression suggests, as a just ground of divine complaint, that we are naturally prone, and that in a mournful degree, to seek our pleasure from other sources.

There are some, who "find their own pleasure" on the day of God, in prolonged sleep and indolent repose. They doze in bed; they loll at the fireside; they while away their time in listless and drowsy idleness. And such persons will sometimes attempt to cover their conduct from the censure which it merits, by a pitiful and profane jest upon the purpose of the day. "It is a day of *rest*," they remind you—putting on as arch a look as laziness will allow—"and they choose to keep it literally; they *do no work*—and nobody has any title to find fault with them." Some of them, it is very possible, may even be a little more serious, and profess to be thankful for a day of rest, as an exceedingly good and necessary thing. But, although such persons do not work, and thus negatively keep the commandment, they are only, after all, taking their own way of "finding their own pleasure." Their behaviour makes it abundantly manifest, that they are utter strangers to the spiritual enjoyments, which the day, in its weekly return, brings round to the hearts of those who "call the Sabbath a delight;"—that they know nothing, either of the rest of the soul in the work of Christ, or of the believing anticipation of that everlasting rest, into which He who finished his work himself entered; and which all his faithful followers are successively to share. The sabbatism of heaven will, indeed, be a rest; but not one of indolent repose,—of lethargic inactivity; not a drowsy cessation of all the corporeal and mental energies, of all the passions and sensibilities of the soul;—not a mere luxurious quiescence of the spirit amidst the sweetness of heavenly blandishments. "His servants shall serve Him"—shall "serve him day and night in his temple."

There are many who feel no scruple at spending the day, occasionally and even frequently, in jaunting and travelling; "finding their own pleasure" in this way.— There is a threefold evil in the practice. They misspend the day themselves :—as far as their influence goes, they prevent others from spending it as they ought, make them partakers in their own delinquency; and contribute to the ignorance, and carelessness, and ruin of a class of men whom the system of Sunday travelling and jaunting deprives, from week to week, of all opportunities of spiritual instruction and benefit:—and they hinder their cattle, or the cattle of others (than which too there is hardly a description of creatures that need it more) from enjoying the advantage of this kind and merciful appointment.

There is a travelling in the way of business, which is also lamentably prevalent. I have myself many a time been shocked, to hear men, with so much light-hearted self-complacency, talk of their so planning their arrangements, in different places, when on their business tours, as to save a day, by getting on so many stages on the Sunday. As that is a day when no business can be done, they contrive to get their transactions, where they happen to be, pushed through on the Saturday, so that they may have the idle day for getting forward, and being all in readiness to commence active operations, in their next station, on the Monday morning. This is what they boastingly call economizing time; and they plume themselves, amongst their fellow-travellers, on their ingenuity and alertness in the practice of this economy. So thoroughly and so unceremoniously, is the authority of the God of Heaven left out of their reckoning. They save time!—the sole end for which they live being (as it should seem) the successful prosecution of their secular interests,—the "buying and selling and getting gain;" their only solicitude, how they may get on in the world; how quickly and how largely they can amass its wealth; what fortune they can realize before they die. All time they regard as saved, which they can by any means render subservient to these ends. Instead of considering time as gained, when they can contrive to redeem any portion of it from secular, and apply it to spiritual purposes, they fret over every moment as lost, which they cannot directly employ in bettering their circumstances; its value being estimated solely by its relation to this paramount and worthy object of living.

It may be permitted to observe here, that the system prevalent throughout the south of our island, of running stage-coaches on the Sabbath as on other days, and of publicly allowing and countenancing other modes of travelling on that day, is the occasion of its desecration there to an incalculable amount;—an amount, not to be estimated by the mere number of Sunday travellers, but by a great variety, direct and indirect, of collateral circumstances:

and of these not the least is the general impression of secularity produced upon the public mind. This is always important. It is comparatively an easy matter, to ascertain, by a process of calculation, the amount of business carried on, and the number of hands actually employed; —but the secularizing influence of the whole system upon the minds of the people, the worldly associations which it produces, its tendency to obliterate the distinction between the Lord's day and the other days of the week, are sources of moral and practical evil, of which the results are far from being so easily estimated. I rejoice in the continued freedom of Scotland from the pernicious system of Sunday travelling, whether on land or on water,—and in the steady resolution of ministers, and magistrates, and Christians generally, to prevent its introduction; and I trust, it will be many a day before the decencies of a Scottish Sabbath, however much disposed many may be to sneer at them for their puritanical precision, and to fret at them for their mercantile inconvenience, shall in this respect be violated.*—These decencies,

* On the subject of Sunday travelling, the reader may be gratified with the following graphic sketch of its rise and progress, as well as of the amount of secularity and annoyance produced by it in the days of Bishop Horsley; and since that recent date, no one will fancy the amount to have diminished.

" It appears from what has been said," says the Bishop, " that the practice which has become so common in this country, among all ranks of men, of making long journeys on the Sabbath without any urgent necessity, is one of the highest breaches of this holy institution. It breaks in upon the principal business of the day, laying some under a necessity, and furnishing others with a pretence, for withdrawing from the public assemblies: and it defeats the ordinance in its subordinate ends, depriving servants and cattle of that temporary exemption

alas! have already experienced too many melancholy en-
croachments. I am not one of those who forget the
admonition of Solomon—" Say not thou of the former
days, they were better than these; for thou dost not
inquire wisely concerning this." I am conscious of no
tendency to croak over multiplying evils, so as to over-
look or to underrate the progress of good; to load heavily
the scale of woes, and omit to put in the counterpoise of
blessings; to turn my back to the light, and gaze, in
brooding sullenness, upon the gloom. But, in the present
case, whatever may have been the causes (we cannot now
from fatigue, which it was intended both should enjoy. This, like
other evils, hath arisen from small beginnings; and by an unperceived,
but a natural and a gradual growth, hath attained at last an alarming height. Persons of the higher ranks, whether from a certain
vanity of appearing great, by assuming a privilege of doing what was
generally forbidden, or for the convenience of travelling when the roads
were the most empty, began within our own memory to make their
journeys on a Sunday. In a commercial country, the great fortunes
which are acquired by trade have a natural tendency to level all distinctions but what arise from affluence. Wealth supplies the place of
nobility; birth retains only the privilege of setting the first example.
The city presently catches the manners of the court; and the vices of
the high-born peer are faithfully copied in the life of the opulent mer-
chant and the thriving tradesman. Accordingly, in a few years, the
Sunday became the travelling day of all who travel in their own
carriages. But why should the humbler citizen, whose scantier means
oblige him to commit his person to the crammed stage-coach, more than
his wealthier neighbour, be exposed to the hardship of travelling on the
working days, when the multitude of heavy carts and waggons, mov-
ing to and fro in all directions, renders the roads unpleasant and unsafe
to all carriages of a slighter fabric; especially, when the only real inconvenience, the danger of such obstructions, is infinitely increased to
him, by the greater difficulty with which the vehicle in which he makes
his uncomfortable journey crosses out of the way, in deep and miry
roads, to avoid the fatal jostle? The force of these principles was soon

stop to investigate them); facts numerous and glaring will not allow me to deny, that, in regard at least to the outward gravity and decorum of sabbatical observance, there has been amongst us a grievous declension.

Some there are, who enjoy themselves, on the sacred day, in feasting. "They find their own pleasures" at the social board, "eating and drinking, and making merry," giving the wings of festive hilarity, to hours which would otherwise pass heavily and drearily, loaded with the dulness of ennui.—For the provisions of that feast which God has spread for sinners in the gospel, they have

perceived; and, in open defiance of the law, stage-coaches have for several years, travelled on the Sundays. The waggoner soon understand that the road is as free for him as for the coachman,—that if the magistrate examines at the one, he cannot enforce the law against the other; and the Sunday traveller now breaks the law, without any advantage gained in the safety or pleasure of his journey. It may seem, that the evil, grown to this height, would become its own remedy. But this is not the case. The temptation indeed to the crime among the higher ranks of the people exists no longer; but the taste for the day among all orders is extinguished, and there is a return to the mere habit of profaneness. In the country, the roads are crowded on the Sunday, as on any other day, with travellers of every sort. The devotion of the villages is interrupted by the noise of carriages passing through, or stopping at the inn for refreshment. In the metropolis, instead of that solemn stillness of the vacant streets in the hours of public service, which might suit, as in our fathers' days, with the sanctity of the day, and be a reproof to every one who should stir abroad but upon the business of devotion, the mingled racket of worldly business and pleasure is going on with little abatement; and in the churches and chapels which adjoin the public streets, the sharp rattle of the whirling phaeton, and the graver rumble of the loaded waggon, mixed with the oaths and imprecations of the brawling drivers, disturb the congregation, and stun the voice of the preacher."—Sermons, vol. ii. pages 234—237.

relish, no taste for the spiritual food which, on the day of sacred rest and joy, is distributed to his people. This is not what they like. They feed their bodies with the "meat that perisheth," but care not for "that meat which endureth unto everlasting life."—They are fond of the circle of social festivity—and having, it may be, paid their respects to the religion of their country by their presence at church in the morning,—they get into their element in the afternoon and evening, and shew with how much heartedness gust they enjoy the pleasures of the table and of the convivial party.

Let Christians beware of *giving in*, by any undue conformity, to this fashion of Sunday dining-parties. There are many evils in it. There is the dissipation of the mind—the worse than useless consumption of time, in a way as far as possible from being conducive to the appropriate ends of the day; the neglect of domestic instruction, and the effectual counteraction of its influence; the employment of servants in need-less and superfluous work; and the pernicious example of worldliness and secularity both to servants and to children, from whose minds, by such conduct, the sacred associations of the day are in danger of being obliterated. Let Christians beware of such conformity, even under the pretext that their parties are religious. The example to the world, who will sneer, with a meaning shrug, at these convivial coteries of the saints, is manifestly injurious; and all such parties, where the corporeal and the spiritual appetites are alike consulted, and Christian conversation requires the prelude of a dinner, are in imminent danger of degenerating into worldliness, or into what is perhaps still worse, religious gossip; in which all the persons, and topics, and novelties of the day come under desultory review, calling forth, too frequently, tempers and remarks that are not much in unison with the spirit of Christ, and far from conducive to " godly edifying which is in faith," while the conscience, pleasing itself with a name, calls it spiritual conversation, and all look forward, with perfect self-complacency, to the next delightful party !—Away with such unseemly anomalies: which are too like a compromise with the world, a hankering after its indulgences under the covert of piety, an incongruous coalition of the carnal and the spiritual.   Let the culinary fare of the Sabbath be simple and moderate,—such as requires the least possible trouble in the preparation; so that servants may not, unnecessarily, be kept from attendance on the house of God, or from availing themselves of private opportunities of reading his word. Let not their souls be famished, for the cooking of a dinner and the pampering of the lowest of the appetites:—or, if they *will* themselves famish them, let not the responsibility rest with you.

Walking is another very common way,—one of the most common of all,—in which persons " find their own pleasure" on the day of God.   I am aware of the hazard incurred by venturing to speak of exceptions;—of the eagerness with which many may be disposed to catch at them, and to bring under their covert a great deal more than is intended or expressed. Yet exceptions, in the present case, there certainly are; and, in specifying them, I have only to request of my hearers, that they understand me as meaning no more than what I actually say. When the state of a man's health, then, is such as, by medical prescription, to require the open air, for checking disease, or for promoting convalescence, or even for temporary relief and comfort, I cannot fancy HIM prohibiting it who said, "If ye had known what this meaneth, 'I will have mercy, and not sacrifice,' ye would not have condemned the guiltless":—I cannot fancy HIM who vindicated the leading of the ox or the ass to watering, and who pleaded for the loosing of the daughter of Abraham from her bond, on the Sabbath-day, condemning any one of his disciples for giving the support of his arm to an exhausted and emaciated invalid, whose debilitated frame required the refreshment and bracing of the summer air. If any shall perversely take advantage of this allowance, and shall either pretend sickness, or find a plea for indulgence in every trivial ailment, and get the sanction, direct or indirect, of any medical practitioner, of inferior grade, or of easy conscience, for their practice,—the responsibility is theirs, not mine. I mean only what I say. I speak of cases of real need. The responsibility, I say, is theirs:— it is so, just as much as if they were to pervert the simple fact, that "Jesus and his disciples went through the corn fields on the Sabbath-day," into a general licence to Sunday-walking; or the other fact, recorded with equal simplicity, that "Jesus went into the house of one of the chief Pharisees, to eat bread," (that is, to dine,) "on the Sabbath-day," into a similar licence to Sunday-dining parties. —Again: I can perceive no trespass against the law of the Sabbath, in a retired walk in the country, alone or with a pious friend, when the object is secret meditation, or private social converse on the things of God, when the spirits are devoutly cheered by the sights and sounds of nature, and the heart is softened, and elevated to Him, "...whose riches the earth is full." And here too, is it necessary to put in a caution? Be it remembered, then, by such as are on the watch for a salve to their consciences, that, by a retired walk in the country, I do not mean a walk from the town into the country, a walk which requires passing through crowds before it can be enjoyed; nor do I mean a walk in the country, where others are walking, and walking idly, or improperly. I mean no walk by which an example is set that may be injurious. I refer to the case of such Christians as, residing permanently, or occasionally, in the seclusion of the country, have the opportunity of stepping abroad into the open air, either by themselves, or with a bosom-friend, unseen possibly by any eye, but that of God, or, if seen by any fellow-creature, by those only who know their character so well as to be quite aware of the manner in which their time is spent, and in no danger of drawing from it any evil surmise, or any improper licence. Even this liberty, however allowable in itself, should not be taken by any Christian, if even to his soul there is a likelihood, or a risk, of the example proving disastrous. There being, to the pious mind, no comparison whatsoever between the sacrifice of the gratification, and the leading of a soul astray.—There may be other things, for which the excuse might, perhaps, be fairly pleaded that they are in themselves harmless;—but, with regard to these, whatever they be, let this great general principle be duly minded—that a true child of God, under the control of a tender conscience, will infinitely rather forego the pleasure or the benefit, than either offend the least and weakest member

of the spiritual family, be ... a stumbling-block in the
way of the world. And ... a single lip against his profession and his Lord. But all idlers walking, or riding for
mere pleasure, to while away the time, and to
be seen, to talk of worldly things, must come under the
divine interdiction—"not finding thine own pleasure."
And of this there is a melancholy superabundance ...
around our own city, on the evenings of the Sabbath;
multitudes of idle saunterers, and strolling parties of
laughing, and talking, and gossipping companions of ex-
hibitors of their Sunday clothes on public promenades;
of vagrant and mischief-working youth, who have no one
at home to care for their souls. To such an extent do-
... does this evil prevail in the outskirts of the city, that
one is afraid to be seen passing along its various ap-
proaches, even in the necessary discharge of duty, lest he
should be classed with the herd of Sunday walkers, and
furnish them with the plea of his alleged example. This
growing sin should, by every possible means, be discoun-
tenanced and checked.

Shall I mention public amusements?—On the continent
of Europe, it is fearful to think of the flagrant defiance
of all principle, and of all decency, that in many places
prevails. The theatres, and other resorts of public amusement and profligacy, are open and openly frequented; and
the best—that is, the most popular, entertainments are
reserved for the Sunday evenings. There is comparatively
little occasion for saying any thing on such a subject here:
less than there might be even in the south of our own
island. Long may a gracious Providence preserve our
country from the invasion of such practices, and from the

deadly infection of the principles from which they spring.

Alas! there is little occasion for so perilous a spirit, to give, under the pretext of acquisition, the relaxation, and enlargement of public authority to the desecration of the holy day. ... ...

... ... men may ... ... their ... ... on the day of God, by making it a season of literary recreation, and scientific experiment and research. The recreation may in itself be innocent, and the experiment and the research may be honourable and useful. But they are foreign to the great ends of the day; and, however innocent, and however excellent in themselves, are a sinful desecration of it. The reading of this day, so befitting harmony with its nature and end, should be the reading of the divine word, or of such uninspired works as are fitted to open its truths, to impress its principles, to imbue the ... with the spirit of love and purity which persuasively draw the heart to God, and to guide the feet in the ways of his testimonies —— the experiments of this day should be the careful application to our own Christian profession of the tests of its genuineness with which the word of God furnishes us, —— the subjecting of our souls to the rigid process of self-examination, —— and its researches the investigation of the divine character, of his discoveries of himself to us, especially in those wonders of his redeeming love, into which "angels desire to look," —— exploring the mine of "the unsearchable riches of Christ," —— examining into those divine things, and into the amount and influence of our acquaintance with them, —— "searching and trying our ways," that we may the more heartily and unreservedly turn unto the Lord. Whatever tends to sanctify the Lord God

ing our hearts, to the comfort of our faith and our hope, ...
ly the spiritual joys to animate our zeal, to inflame our ...
here, to quicken our diligence in duty; and, in general,
to promote our holiness, and to prepare us for the Sabbath of everlasting rest above:—whatever, I say, tends
to such results, is fit employment for the Sabbath. On
earth ... with which God continues to favour ...
... and scientific experiment and re-search. The recrea-

... The ... article of prohibition ... the text ...
"... THINE own words." ...
... The same general observation holds good here, which
was made respecting our own ways. The expression is
not to be understood merely of sinful words; ... corrupt
communications," ... proud, passionate, profane, impure,
and otherwise evil words. These are wrong, and to be
avoided, with constant vigilance, at all times, and in all
circumstances. Yet here too, as in the former case, the
sacredness of the day does give additional aggravation to the
guilt. Let me press this principle a little farther on your
attention. Inhumanity is always evil ... but the atrocity
of it is deeply enhanced, when expressions of light-hearted
merriment are uttered in the very midst of a scene of
heart-rending woe. So profanity is always criminal ...
but what shall we think of the profanity, that gives utterance to its mirth and its blasphemous buffooneries, in the
very ... contemplation ... of the sublimest and
most overpowering displays of the divine majesty? You
can readily conceive what an addition is made to the guilt
of a sentence of profane scoffing, when it is supposed to
have come from the lips of an Israelite, in the very view
of the ... "blackness, and darkness, and tempest," the thun-

to its very theory, and far more

down of the head, like a bulrush," and ... and ... ... which ... for a moment ... into a ... which ... religion with an ... ... and ... seems incapable of understanding how ... can ... be ... In this serious ... and cheerfulness are ... features incompatible. [What more cheering to the sceptic ... heart, than the lovely light of the rising sun] ... the cheerfulness inspired by this liveliest and most beautiful ... scene of nature, what expression could be ... appropriate ... and ... than ... the light of the Sun of Righteousness dawning on the ... is inexpressibly cheering—but it is a serious ... fulness, a calm and lively delight, a delight, however, which by mutual communication, by reciprocal inter change among the children of God, may often rise to all the liveliness ... of spiritual joy. And who that has experienced that joy, will envy the "laughter of the fool," so aptly likened by the wise man to the crackling of thorns under a pot"—a sprightly blaze, but quickly dying away, and leaving nothing behind it but ... Let me remind Christian parents, however, and other guardians of youth, of what was on a former occasion suggested, that the perpetual investiture of religion in the garb of gloom, sitting in sackcloth, and ... "face foul with weeping, and on her eyelids the shadow of death,"—is apt to have a most prejudicial influence on the youthful mind. Religion should be made to appear, according to its real nature, as a fountain of joy,—like its divine author and object, "light without any darkness at all." Every thing different from this is a slander upon its true character. Yet beware. There is an opposite

DISCOURSE VIII.

ISAIAH lviii. 13, 14.

"*If thou turn away thy foot from the Sabbath, from doing thy pleasure on my holy day; and call the Sabbath a delight, the holy of the Lord, honourable; and shalt honour him, not doing thine own ways, nor finding thine own pleasure, nor speaking thine own words; then shalt thou delight thyself in the Lord; and I will cause thee to ride upon the high places of the earth, and feed thee with the heritage of Jacob thy father: for the mouth of the Lord hath spoken it.*"

In last discourse, I endeavoured to point out and illustrate the various descriptions of Sabbath-profanation, which might be considered as included under the three particulars in this text—"not doing thine own ways, nor finding thine own pleasure, nor speaking thine own words."—There now come before us, as I then, in conclusion, announced, some of the benefits resulting from the due observance of the Sabbath, and some of the evil effects of its neglect and profanation. The two will be most easily, as well as with most advantage, considered together, as, under the different departments of illustration, they naturally present themselves in contrast.

In proportion as the Sabbath, with its objects and duties, is viewed more or less spiritually, shall we find a greater or a smaller number of persons ready to give their assent to the observations I am about to make. There are views which may be taken of the day, and views too not without their relative importance, such as have in them nothing whatever of spirituality, to which many will at once subscribe, who are destitute of all relish for its appropriate exercises and most important ends. Not a few of those to whom I allude will even profess to admire the wisdom and the goodness of Deity, as apparent in those purposes of humanity and mercy which they acknowledge the Sabbath to answer, while they are strangers to the slightest movement of genuine spiritual feeling, and disregard the proper requirements of the day without scruple or remorse.—Let me illustrate my meaning.

One of the subordinate ends answered by this divine institution is, as we have before repeatedly noticed, the rest of that part of the brute creation which is subjected to the service of man. Now, the spirit of humanity is pleased with this. To the feelings of a benevolent mind there is something very interesting in that expression of the law—"that thine ox and thine ass may rest;"—and, when considered as indicative of the character of that Being whose "tender mercies are over all his works," it is not less interesting to the spirit of piety than to that of benevolence. It would be unreasonable to refuse this a place among the divine intentions, when it stands before us so expressly specified; and every man, who feels a compassionate concern about the comfort and enjoyment of the inferior creation, must experience a conscious satis-

faction in contemplating this design of the day? "Are
not two sparrows sold for a farthing? and one of them
shall not fall to the ground without your Father." The
Almighty Creator has made nothing which, after having
made it, he overlooks as unworthy of his card. When
Paul puts the question—1 Cor. ix. 9, "Doth God take
care for oxen?" it would be a miserable misinterpretation
of his words, dishonouring to God, and at variance with
the entire tenor of his own oracles, to explain them as
conveying the sentiment that such creatures were beneath
his notice, and had no part in his providential superintendence. The spirit of the question is simply this—
Whether, in the precept of the Mosaic law, "Thou shalt
not muzzle the ox that treadeth out the corn," the design
of the injunction be exhausted in its literal import;
whether it regarded oxen alone; or whether it did not
involve a PRINCIPLE, capable, without departure from the
divine intention in the precept, of direct and authoritative
application to the subject under his discussion (the temporal maintenance of ministers of the gospel),—the principle, namely, that "the labourer is worthy of his meat."
God *does* "take care for oxen:"—and, although the highest interests of his intelligent and immortal offspring are
the primary object of his concern in the institution of the
Sabbath, and in all its sacred ordinances, he mercifully
unites this object with the comfort and well-being of
those brute tribes which he has placed under man's control, by which means, the day becomes, in every view of
it, an illustration of his own character. It is delightful
to reflect, amid the stillness and the peacefulness of a
Sabbath morning, how these creatures are enjoying their

repose from the toils of the preceding week; and the reflection derives peculiar interest from the remembrance of the fearful abuse of this law of subjection by the depravity of man; an abuse, to which, amongst other views of the sufferings of creation, the apostle refers, when he says, Rom. viii. 20—22, " The creation was made subject to vanity, not willingly, but by reason of him who hath subjected the same " and " we know that the whole creation groaneth and travaileth in pain together until now." Alas! that this subjection to vanity, this groaning of the subject creatures, should so frequently and so affectingly be seen, in the very denial of the rest which the law of the Sabbath prescribes, and, by the very promise with, entitles them to enjoy. It is one of their divinely chartered rights, which is too often presumptuously withheld from them by the selfishness and cupidity of man,

But, whilst the humane and the pious mind cannot but be pleased with this collateral end of the day, there is not seldom to be found a specious sentimentalism, which affects to be wonderfully charmed with the repose of the overwrought and worn-out victims of human cruelty and avarice, and which is apt to mistake for piety the admiration it is so forward to express of the kindness apparent in this provision of the benevolent Deity; whilst it discovers no symptom of pleasure in the principal design of the day, and never dreams of any thing like a personal consecration of it to God. This is only one of the many delusions practised upon itself by a heart which He who best knows it has pronounced deceitful above all things, and desperately wicked; a delusion by which it soothes

founds natural sensibility with devotion,—substituting compassion for the brutes in the room of piety to God, secretly pluming itself on the tenderness of its feelings, and, on the credit of them, maintaining a comfortable self-complacency, in the absence of every thing that can deserve the appellation of religion.

On a similar principle, there are many who approve and admire the Sabbath, as a day of refreshing rest from toil to the labouring classes of the community. And this too is a topic on which much might be said, and said with truth, of what is gratifying to the kindly feelings of the heart. "That thy man-servant and thy maid-servant may rest as well as thou," says the law;—and, although, without doubt, the principal meaning of this is, that they should enjoy the full benefit of the spiritual rest of the Sabbath, as well as their masters; yet their repose from labour is, with equally little doubt, to be included; the latter, indeed, being necessary, in order to the former. The return of that sacred day is full of interest in this view, as a period of respite, a breathing time, to the toil-worn labourer and artisan: in which he reposes from the fatigues of the week:—a time which, as far as man is concerned, he can call his own,—over which no fellow-creature is entitled to issue his commands.

Perhaps we do not sufficiently think of the extent of temporal comfort and benefit resulting from this divine arrangement. Of a single Sabbath spent in labour without any great inconvenience or suffering, we can readily enough conceive; but we can have little idea of the degree in which uninterrupted, unrelaxing toil, going on from week to week, and from year to year, would be injurious and destructive to the health, and comfort, and life, of multitudes of our fellow-creatures. In this way, a benignant God combines the temporal and the spiritual interests of mankind. The Sabbath, amongst fallen creatures, operates as a kind of alleviation of the sentence, "In the sweat of thy face shalt thou eat bread," at the same time that, in the higher view of it, it is a divine means of bringing men back to God, to spiritual blessing, and to eternal life, through Him whose finished work of righteousness and atonement is the chief subject of commemorative celebration.

The extent, I should apprehend, is incalculable, in which the health, the decency, the order, the personal and social enjoyment, of the peasantry of our favoured land, are secured, and promoted by the weekly return of the sacred day of rest; and as incalculable, the sacrifice which would be made of these by the annihilation of its observance. In proportion as it should come to be disregarded, and the decencies of its external celebration to be done away, might we confidently look, for the accompaniments of poverty, and filth, and disorder, and general discomfort and wretchedness. There is no estimating, in Scotland, the amount of counteracting influence exerted by the Sabbath in the prevention of such evils; the regularity and constancy of its return calling for the equally regular recurrence of cleanliness, and tidiness, and decorum, and leaving no interval sufficient for the formation of contrary habits.*

---

* The following language of Judge Blackstone, though framed, of course, upon the principle of Christianity being the established religion, and, as such, a part of the law of the land, expresses briefly and forcibly,

Some there may be, who are ever disposed to regard it as so much time lost,—as a certain number of hours deducted weekly from the acquisition of secular gain. But, with whatever truth it may be so regarded in particular cases, the simplest principles of political economy and of common sense should satisfy any man, that this view of it has no truth in its general application. Not only would unrelaxing labour wear out the energies of the workman, and so lessen his gains by the most lamentable of all causes—the lessening of his ability; but even if his energies were unimpaired, and his ability increasing, what after all, in a mercantile view, would be the result of adding a seventh part more to the working time of all the artisans in the country? What but an augmentation of the quantity of produce, and a consequent reduction of the price? And a reduction in the price of the article produced necessarily

along with the moral advantages, those secular benefits of the Sabbath for which we here plead :—" Besides the notorious indecency and scandal, of permitting any secular business to be publicly transacted on that day, in a country professing Christianity, and the corruption of morals which usually follows its profanation, the keeping of one day in seven holy, as a time of relaxation and refreshment as well as for public worship, is of admirable service to a state, considered merely as a civil institution. It humanizes, by the help of conversation and society, the manners of the lower classes; which would otherwise degenerate into a savage ferocity, and sordid selfishness of spirit :—it enables the industrious workman to pursue his occupation in the ensuing week, with health and cheerfulness :—it imprints on the minds of the people that sense of their duty to God, so necessary to make them good citizens; but which yet would be worn out, and defaced by an unremitted continuance of labour, without any stated times of recalling them to the worship of their Maker." Commentaries on the Laws of England, vol. iv. page 63.   1811.

involves in it a corresponding reduction in the wages of the labour that produces it. There would thus be no ultimate advantage,—and especially to the labourer himself; while the personal, domestic, and public deterioration and loss, even in many temporal and secular respects, would be such as nothing supposable, as the result of the cessation of the weekly rest, could possibly countervail.

But oh! let peasantry, let artisans, let all, beware of overlooking the great and special purposes of the day, which have been formerly pointed out. Let them beware of fancying that its ends are fulfilled, that its benefits are exhausted, when, even in the highest measure, its secular advantages have been realized. The purposes of the day, I must not cease to remind you, are chiefly spiritual; and such also, of course, are the benefits to be derived from its due observance.

If, therefore, we would fairly appreciate these benefits, we must suppose the day to be observed rightly,—according to its proper nature, and the divine intention in its institution,—in accordance with the principles of its celebration which have now been more than once adverted to. It is very plain, that of no institution can the advantages be correctly estimated, unless the institution be observed in consistency with its true nature and design. To do justice in this respect, for example, to such ordinances as the passover and the feast of tabernacles among the Israelites, it would be necessary, not only to suppose every outward prescription in the divine ceremonial accurately followed out—that were comparatively little—the chief thing requisite to a fair estimate is the intelligent association, in the minds of the celebrators, of the

commemorated events with the commemorative rites. It
was in connexion with the events that the rites were
instituted; and it is in the remembrance and impression
of this that all their virtue lies; it is from this that their
moral influence must be appraised. The same is the case
with the Lord's supper; and, indeed, from the nature of
the thing, with every institution whether civil or sacred.
On this principle, then, we must form our estimate of
the benefits of the Sabbath. We should deal unfairly
with it otherwise; taking our standard of its utility not
from what is, if not strictly adventitious, yet subordinate, and not
from what is primary and essential. And to all, surely, who
have, in any measure, been taught of God to observe the
day aright, understanding its principle and entering into
its spirit,—keeping it holy to Him in the closet, in the
family, and in the sanctuary, I may with confidence
appeal, whether they have not found it, and that in an
eminent degree, the source of both pleasure and profit.

Spiritual pleasure presupposes a spiritual mind, a
heart rendered capable, by the renewing power of the
Spirit, of the enjoyment of spiritual things,—imbued
with spiritual sensibilities and desires. This is obviously
indispensable to the appropriate exercises of the Lord's
day being at all relished. The unrenewed may like the
day well enough, as a day of bodily rest, or of exhibition
at church, or of seeing their friends, or of any of the varieties of animal and mental recreation. But in regard to
its true nature, they may well say, "What a weariness
is it!" Unless the mind be spiritually disposed, there
can be no pleasure in spiritual occupations;—and, where
there is no pleasure,—where, if engaged in at all, it is

not from the heart's choice,—where they are gone through as a necessary drudgery, rather than welcomed as a delight,—there cannot be supposed any real profit. A day for spiritual observance must be a day for spiritual men. There must be a correspondence between the nature of the ordinance and the character of the worshipper; else it cannot be duly celebrated, nor yield its proper and precious results.—Again, then, I make my appeal to spiritual men,—to all who have "tasted that the Lord is gracious," whose "hearts God has touched," and turned to himself,—whether this day has not been, and is not now, one of the most efficient means, through the promised blessing of the God of grace, of confirming and advancing in their souls the principles of godliness,—the vital spirit of piety; of enlarging their knowledge; of establishing their faith; of invigorating their hope; of inflaming their love to God, to Christ, to Christians, to mankind; of quickening their joy; of giving life and energy to their zeal and diligence; and, in general, of forwarding their progress in that holiness "without which no man shall see the Lord."

You will deeply feel, my fellow Christians, the secularising tendency of your worldly engagements during the week; the incessant proneness of your deceitful hearts to forget God and spiritual things, and to take their impression from the world, and the things of the world. You feel this, and you bewail it. But, oh! what an amount of additional influence would be given to the world over your affections, were the counteraction of the holy Sabbath entirely taken away! How fearfully enhanced would be your peril, if, instead of the regular and frequent return of a time sacred by God's own appointment, to the exercises of devotion; you were to be laid in the very midst of universal and unintermitting secularity; to catch at opportunities and moments of leisure, for the cultivation of your souls! How could it be, but that the mind and heart should become thoroughly ——— to the world," and gradually divested of every ——— of spirituality?—that the living spirit of godliness should become sickly, and die away?—that the fire of religious feeling should expire for want of fuel, or be quenched by the deluge of worldly cares?—Ask yourselves, I pray you, and answer from maturity of reflection,—how much of your stability and growth in faith and holiness you owe to the Lord's day,—to its private reading and meditation, to its domestic exercises of instruction and devotion, and to its public meetings in the sanctuary, for hearing the word, celebrating the ordinances, and joining in the worship of the Lord. We may safely affirm it as a fact, assured by recorded experience, and such as it is natural and reasonable to expect,—that all who have been eminent in godliness, have been eminent for their conscientious and devoted observance of this sacred day. The two descriptions of eminence, indeed, operate reciprocally as cause and effect,—each producing and promoting the other.

The exercises of God's sanctuary have, in all ages, been the delight of his people. Even in ancient days, amid the comparative twilight of Judaism, how fervent were their expressions of attachment to God's house, and to the place where his honour dwelt!"—expressions, such as may well put to shame the listless apathy of many a New

Testament worshipper, though enjoying the fulness of evangelical light and privilege. "How amiable are thy tabernacles, O Lord of Hosts! My soul longeth, yea even fainteth for the courts of the Lord:—my heart and my flesh crieth out for the living God. Yea the sparrow hath found out a house, and the swallow a nest for herself, where she may lay her young; even thine altars, O Lord of hosts, my King and my God. Blessed are they that dwell in thy House; they will be still praising thee." "O God, thou art my God; early will I seek thee: my soul thirsteth for thee, my flesh longeth for thee, in a dry and thirsty land, where no water is; to see thy power and thy glory, so as I have seen thee in the sanctuary!" —"One thing have I desired of the Lord, that will I seek after, that I may dwell in the house of the Lord all the days of my life, to behold the beauty of the Lord, and to inquire in his Temple."*——When there is such pleasure as this in public devotion, we may be well assured there will be a corresponding pleasure in its more private duties. The day, throughout, will be a holy festival, from whose rich and varied provision the soul will derive equal delight and nourishment; and, " taking the cup of salvation, and calling on the name of the Lord," will renew, with a cheerful alacrity, the consecration of its powers to his service. I repeat an observation formerly made, that there cannot be a more unfavourable symptom of the state of religion in the soul of a professed child of God, than when he begins to abridge the Sabbath,—to think he has discovered reasons himself, or force in the reasons of others, by which the obligation of devoting it entirely to God is

Psal. lxxxiv. 1—4. lxiii. 1, 2. xxvii. 4.

M

brought into question :—when he begins to think six days too little for the world, and one too much for God. Of every right-hearted believer in Christ, it will be the sincere and bitter regret, that his spiritual principles and affections should not have vitality and vigour enough to maintain the vivacity of his religious exercises for the space of one day. But how any Christian can bring himself to wish to be rid of any part of the day, and to argue himself out of the obligation to keep it all sacred, unless from a previous inward declension in the spiritual life,—I must again avow myself incapable of comprehending.

The preceding observations relate chiefly to the influence of the Sabbath on INDIVIDUALS. Let me now advert for a little to its influence on FAMILIES.—After what was said in a former discourse on the domestic uses of the Sabbath, it will not be necessary to dwell long upon this. O what spiritual desolation,—the desolation of ignorance, irreligion, and vice,—would speedily extend itself over families, even over those where God's name is recorded, were the Lord's day expunged from amongst the days of the week;—were that day assimilated to the rest;—were there no public assemblings for the worship of God, and for the reading and preaching of his word, to keep alive, in the youthful mind, the impression of the divine existence, and character, and claims!—and were those precious seasons of domestic instruction to be universally discontinued,—when the children gather around the family hearth, or kneel around the family altar,—when they are taught, by precept and example, by the communication of knowledge, and by the exercises of domestic devotion, that "a fear of the Lord, which is the beginning of wisdom?"—were there nothing before the view of the rising generation, with all its susceptibilities of early and of earthly impression, but one interminable scene of secularity,—one universal, entire, and perpetual absorption of mind and body, of time and toil, in the interests of the present world!

The evenings of the Lord's day are the seasons most naturally devoted to such domestic scenes as have just been adverted to, and were formerly more particularly described;—and when suitably redeemed for these exercises, they are inestimably precious. Without them, how many would be left entirely destitute of religious instruction, who now happily enjoy it; and of those who might continue to receive it, how much more desultory, irregular, and imperfect would the instruction necessarily be; and, wanting, moreover, those accompaniments of sacredness with which it is now surrounded, how comparatively light and transient would be its impression upon the mind,—how much more in danger of resembling the seed which fell from the sower's hand among the thorns, or that which dropped by the way-side, and was picked up by the fowls of heaven,—of being choked by the cares and pleasures of this life, or of being immediately caught away by the malignant and ever-watchful enemy of souls!

In regard to the influence of such domestic exercises, it may be further observed, that it is not merely their effect in the communication of divine instruction to each member of the family individually that is valuable; but their general uniting and spiritualizing influence upon the whole collectively. When all the young members of the

domestic circle are brought together, when they are sat
down together at the feet of the same earthly and the
same heavenly instructer,—if they are not treated with
partiality; and their respective tasks, by injudicious com-
mendation and ill-administered reproof, made the occasion
of mutual jealousy,—they will be made to feel a new
bond of attachment; they will cling, with a common feeling of grateful fondness, to father and mother, as their
kind and affectionate teachers; and their hearts will warm
to one another, as fellow-learners, needing and receiving
the same instructions. The bond of piety will thus be
superinduced on that of natural affection; and it will be
felt by themselves, and seen by others, " how good and
how pleasant a thing it is for brethren to dwell together
in unity." Such Sabbath-evening scenes will have the
happiest tendency to charm away the little quarrels (if
such there may have been) of the preceding week, to settle concord, and to imbue the heart with the meekness
and gentleness of Christ." They will, in this manner,
not merely impart saving instruction to individual children, but exert a sweet and powerful influence on domestic union and social joy.

There is already enough of spiritual ignorance among
the young. O let us not, by desecrating any portion of
the Sabbath, and taking off the obligation of its universal
sacredness, increase to an indefinite degree the evil we
deplore.

I have associated with the domestic instructions of the
Sabbath its domestic devotions. Let me not in this be
misconceived. Let none imagine, that, because I have
spoken of the domestic devotions of the Lord's day, I am

look with indulgence on the practice of those heads of families, who confine to that day either the devotions or the instructions of their household.—With regard to religious instructions, I would lay it down as a maxim, that every day should have its lesson in religion, as regularly as in any other branch of knowledge.—If parents were duly attentive to this,—if along with the daily reading of the Scriptures by their children, they would accustom them to commit to memory two or three verses of the Bible, a few lines of a hymn, or a single question or two of a catechism, accompanying the little tasks with an occasional affectionate and simple comment, and revising the whole on the Sabbath as a part of its weekly exercises,—it is wonderful how rapidly an acquaintance with divine truth would thus accumulate, and how beneficial would be the general influence upon the mind.—When religious instruction is confined to the Sabbath, there is a risk of producing in the minds of children one of the most unfortunate and pernicious of all impressions,—the impression, that religion belongs to the Sunday; of which the consequence is, that, instead of cultivating it as a principle, or set of principles, of every-day and habitual influence, they never think of it but amongst the forms of a weekly ritual, and feel as if from Monday till Saturday they had to do only with the world; and as if religion would be as much out of place on any of the other days of the week, as the world and its businesses would be out of place on the Sabbath.

This danger is still more imminent in the case of those who confine to the first day of the week the exercises of family devotion. In doing so, they live in the criminal neglect of a daily and important duty,—and a duty which ought to bring with it a daily delight;—and besides this, they counteract, by their negligent and irreligious example, the beneficial influence of all the instructions which on the Sabbath they make a form of imparting. They thus far do what lies in their power to shut God out of the minds of their children and servants from the one Sabbath to the other, and thus to secularise their spirits, and reduce devotion to a Sunday form.

The third light in which we would contemplate the benefits of the Lord's day, and the evils of its neglect, relates to CHURCHES. By churches, taking the word in its simple New Testament meaning, I understand associations of believers in Christ, with their respective office-bearers, united by faith and love, for the observance of his ordinances, with a view to his glory, to their own spiritual benefit, and to the good of the world. Of such associations it must be obvious to you, stated religious meetings are essential to the very existence. I see not how a church could possibly have a being without them. He who " knows what is in man,"—who made him, and who has made him with a nature in which social dispositions are deeply inherent, has appointed the association of his people in churches, and appointed ordinances for them in their associated capacity. Had he seen that the interests of the spiritual life in their souls would be equally well provided for, by the private meditations, and the insulated personal devotions, of individuals,—we should, in all probability, never have heard of social institutions; for the infinitely wise does nothing in vain. But he knew our nature better. He knew how animating and invigorating the joint recognition of the paramount claims of religion; how confirming to its principles, and enlivening to its affections, the combined exercises of devotion. When believers come together into one place, and mutually recognise each other there, the very sight conveys to each heart all the power and persuasion of reciprocal encouragement. They assemble, to remember and to celebrate the same events,—events in which they have all one interest, as being the common ground of their hopes, and the common source of their joys; and love and gladness circulate from soul to soul, and speak from eye to eye. They are strengthened in temptation; they are soothed in sorrow; they are animated in danger; they are encouraged in difficulty; they are braced and nerved for duty. Like comrades in arms, they cheer each other on in the "good fight of faith," pointing to the great captain of their salvation, recounting his excellencies and his conquests, and anticipating victory and triumph under his banners.

The powerful influence of association is every day experienced amongst men. A common feeling of interest in one object never operates so mightily, as when they who are the subjects of it come together, to witness, in company, that by which it is excited.—Would the recent coronation of the Sovereign of these realms, think you, have produced any thing like the same effect on the spirit of the people, had it been possible for each individual of them to have witnessed it alone? Suppose every one, in solitary succession, to have seen the splendid and interesting spectacle,—would this successive view have left upon the public mind any thing approaching to the same impression?" I need not answer the question. The native feeling of every bosom has already answered it. The charm lay, not merely, nor chiefly, nor, comparatively, almost at all, in the spectacle itself, however gorgeous, and however imposing:—it lay in the congregated multitudes of the subjects of the same prince witnessing it in company. That man's mind must be singularly constituted, who can be one in such a multitude, without sharing the kindred emotion, without catching the universal impulse, without yielding to the irresistible current of the common enthusiasm; when every glistening eye turns, in the ardour of expectation, to a common object of interest; when every arm is waved in the shout of joyous acclamation; when every voice gives utterance to one sentiment of gratulation and patriotic loyalty;—when thousands, and tens of thousands, meet together, and look on together, and shout together,—every one in the full assurance, that the feelings of his own bosom have the sympathy of all the bosoms around him:—it is then, and it is thus, that the power of excitement is felt, that party differences are lost for the time in the one dominant emotion of British patriotism; and that the King is enthroned in the hearts of an attached and united people.* -

" Similar ought to be the effects of the meetings of the subjects of Jesus, to celebrate the past, and anticipate the future triumphs of their exalted Prince,—even of Him who "hath on his vesture and on his thigh a name written, KING OF KINGS, AND LORD OF LORDS." They commemorate with joy his finished work; his resurrection

* The discourse was delivered on the Sabbath se'ennight, after the *coronation* of his present Majesty, William IV.

from the dead; his exaltation to universal dominion; and all his divine qualifications for government;—and they anticipate the time when He shall come again, revealed in his glory,—when, "the Lord himself shall descend with a shout, with the voice of the archangel, and with the trump of God, and the dead in Christ shall rise, and they who are alive, and remain shall be caught up together with them in the clouds, to meet the Lord in the air, and so shall be ever with the Lord." Oh! what will the acclamations be, with which the King of Zion shall then be greeted by his joyful subjects,—"loud as from numbers without number, sweet as from blest voices, uttering joy!" In their reflections on the past, and their anticipations of the future, his people feel the animation of social delight: their bosoms beat high with the lively impulses of loyalty to their King, and of attachment to one another. They admire, they adore, they love, they hope, and they rejoice together.

"I was glad," said a royal saint of old time, "I was glad when they said unto me, Let us go into the house of the Lord;"—and the assemblies of the first Christians at Jerusalem, were meetings of cordial union, and exulting joy. So it is, or so it ought to be, still. The assembled Saints of God, when, on the hallowed morn of the day of rest, they unite their voices in the hymn of triumphant praise to their exalted and glorified Lord,—

"Yes, the Redeemer rose,
The Saviour left the dead,
And o'er our hellish foes,
High-raised his conqu'ring head;"—

when they listen to his word, the source of their loftiest joys, the charter of their spiritual liberties, the foundation of their dearest hopes;—when they sit at his table, and partake together the commemorative symbols of his dying love;—have the life of their souls renewed.—They feel themselves "all one in Christ Jesus"—"one body," animated by "one Spirit," "called in one hope of their calling," having "one Lord, one faith, one baptism, one God and Father of all; who is above all, and through all, and in them all."—And then, their public meetings have an influence on their private devotions. They carry from them the spirit of the communion of saints; and even to their most secret and solitary exercises of fellowship with God, this imparts animation and vigour. They think of their brethren. They have them on their hearts. They have present to their minds the delightful assurance, that there are multitudes of one heart and one soul with themselves, who, though separate and even distant in place, are uniting with them in spirit at the footstool of the divine throne. So that, even when they "enter into their closets, and shut their doors about them, and pray to their Father who is in secret," they can retain with delight the social form of address:—the very appellation "Father" reminds them in their solitude of the family, of which Jehovah, the God of salvation, is the Head, and of which they are but individual members; and thus, feeling themselves one with the whole "household of faith," they say, in terms of his own direction, "OUR Father who art in heaven!"

The last topic on which I wish to say a few words, before drawing this discourse to a close, is that influence of the Sabbath in regard to CIVIL COMMUNITIES.

I endeavored, in a former discourse, to define, on both subjects, the province of human laws. They have neither the right to enjoin, nor the power to enforce, any thing that is spiritual. This belongs exclusively to Him who alone has the knowledge and the control of the heart. The spiritual keeping of the Sabbath, therefore, is entirely beyond the sphere of human legislation. But, as we formerly showed you, there are other ends of the institution besides the spiritual. It has secular ends. There were in the view of the divine Legislator, in giving the command, benefits of an outward and temporal kind, both to man and beast. These benefits it is perfectly competent, nay, more than competent, it is imperative,—to every earthly government, to secure to all, whether human or brute, placed by providence under the protection and control of its laws. The fourth commandment in the decalogue, while it institutes the Sabbath as sacred to the service of God, secures also to every man the use of that day, as so much property in time; so that whosoever attempts to invade that time, and to exact it from others for his own ends, is as really a robber, as if he were to wrest from them their money or their lands;—and this species of property, as well as others, it is the business of legislators to secure to their subjects, and to protect from wrongful encroachment and abstraction. Human governments cannot authoritatively say to their subjects, "Remember the Sabbath-day, *to keep it holy;*" the spiritual consecration of the day being the subject of divine requision alone;—but, looking to the temporal benefits which the sabbatical law contemplates, and to the secular rights which it confers, they can say, "In it thou shalt not do any work." And, when the secular objects of the day are thus secured, and those who are disposed to devote it to its higher ends are protected in so doing, all appears to be done that human laws can legitimately effect.

These general principles were formerly laid down more at large. I have briefly repeated them, that there may be no mistake in the minds of any of my hearers, when I speak of the benefits of the Sabbath to the community. The benefits which I regard as its legitimate result, are those which arise from the due enforcement on all of its secular observance, as a day of abstinence from work, and the protection from annoyance of those who choose to observe it spiritually, as a day sacred to God. And these benefits are great and manifold. It has been already noticed, what an amount of injury would arise to the health, comfort, cleanliness, and life, of the working classes of society, from the cessation of the seventh day's intermission of labour, and the uninterrupted and unrelieved pressure of their wearing-out toils. Now, whatever operates injuriously on these is essentially prejudicial to the community; of which a healthy, vigorous, cleanly, comfortable population is the beauty, the strength, and the security.—By the suspension of labour on that day to the brute creation as well as to man himself, the lord of this lower world is, moreover, profitably reminded of his own dependance, and of the duty of cultivating the sentiments of humanity and mercy. "On the Sabbath," says

Bishop Horsley, "man is to hold a sort of edifying communion with the animals beneath him, acknowledging by a short suspension of his dominion over them, the right of the Creator in himself as well as in them, and confessing that his own right over them is derived from the grant of the superior Lord." It is thus calculated to cherish a kindly fellow-feeling with the inferior creation, and so to infuse a pervading spirit of gentleness and good-will, repressing the harsher tendencies of our nature, mellowing the national character, and diffusing over social life the softening of a general sympathy and amenity of disposition. To some, this may be no recommendation. They may rather deprecate the prevalence of a spirit of gentle and over-refined tenderness, as inconsistent with the military character of the country, the trade of a soldier not comporting well with extra delicacy of feeling; and they may even recommend cruel and ferocious sports for the sake of maintaining the national courage. But in this there is a double error. In the first place, the ordinary condition of a country is, or ought to be, a state of peace; and in attempting to mould the national character, we ought, in all reason, to have our eye especially on its ordinary condition, not on that which forms the exception, and respecting which the maxim of every friend of his country and of mankind must ever be—the less of it the better. But, since the exception may, and too often does occur, and it is indispensable that every country be provided for it when necessity requires, we have to remark further, that humanity and gentleness are not to be confounded with shrinking timidity and nerveless imbecility of character. The spirit of lofty, daring has had its residence in many a bosom along with the spirit of kindness. Manly courage and brute ferocity are not the same. As there ought to be no war but what is strictly defensive, and as all defensive war should be the result of necessity, and the dictate of duty,—it is the former, not the latter, which ought to be in requisition,—steady, principled, determined courage. And is there, then, a divorce between such courage and humanity? The very reverse. Cruelty is the more frequent associate, not of courage, but of cowardice.

There are few things of greater consequence to the peace and prosperity of a community, and to that union which is strength, than the maintaining of a good understanding between the different orders of its population,—a right state of reciprocal feeling between the high and the low, the rich and the poor. And to this few things can more effectually contribute, than their being convened before their common Creator, and reminded that "the Lord is the Maker of them all,"—reminded of their common origin, their common dependance, and their common obligations. "If ever the poor man holds up his head," says Dr. Paley, "it is at church; and if ever the rich man views him with respect it is there: and both will be better, and the public more profited, the oftener they meet in a situation, in which the consciousness of dignity in the one is tempered and mitigated, and the spirit of the other erected and confirmed."

But there are benefits from the Sabbath to the community of a higher order. The day of cessation from earthly toil is the day also of public assembling for the worship of God; when his own people meet; when they do (or rather, I fear I canot say, ought to do), all, in their power for promoting the knowledge and influence of the gospel; when multitudes are, by various motives, brought together to hear the word of God; when thousands of children are collected, to receive its salutary instructions in ways appropriate to their age and capacities; when various other means are put in operation, for enlightening ignorance, and subduing depravity, and turning sinners from "the error of their way." Apart from the present and everlasting profit thus accruing to individuals, the increase of the number of those who are savingly converted to God is the very highest of all blessings to a country. Ungodly men may scoff at the assertion; but it is not, for their scoffing, the less true, nor is the blessing the less real:—nay, even the scoffers themselves may indirectly participate in it, at the very time when they are thanklessly and profanely scorning it. "God's eye is upon the righteous; his ear is open to their cry:" and for their sakes, for the favour he bears them, and in answer to their prayers, many a national calamity may be averted, and many a public blessing bestowed. "My only solid hopes for the well-being of my country," says an eminent Christian philanthropist,* "depend, not so much on her fleets and armies, not so much on the wisdom of her rulers, or the spirit of her people, as on the persuasion that she still contains many who, in a degenerate age, love and obey the gospel of Christ; on the humble trust, that the intercessions of these may still be prevalent, and that for the sake of these Heaven may still look upon us with an eye of favour." Sodem

* Wilberforce.

of old, the sacred history informs us, would have been spared at the intercession of Abraham, could fifty, forty, thirty, twenty—nay ten righteous persons have been found there. The case is recorded, like some others, to teach us the operation of a principle,—a principle that pervades the entire administration of divine providence, although the intricacies of that administration are often too involved to admit of our discerning it,—the regard, namely, of a faithful God to them that fear him;—and it is not without sound scriptural reason, however fanatical the ungodly world may pronounce it, that the poet, in the lofty spirit of patriotism and of piety, applies the principle and the case to the metropolis of our country:—

> "O Thou, resort and mart of all the earth,
> Chequer'd with all complexions of mankind;
> And spotted with all crimes; in whom I see
> Much that I love, and more that I admire,
> And all that I abhor;——
> Ten righteous would have sav'd a city once)
> And Thou hast many righteous.—Well for thee,
> That salt preserves thee; more corrupted else,
> And therefore more obnoxious, at this hour,
> Than Sodom in her day had power to be,
> For whom God heard his Abraham plead in vain"

There is, moreover, an influence (as these lines indeed suggest)—a moral and spiritual influence, exerted on the community by these, its Christian members. There is a " virtue that goes out of them," in their respective spheres, both of higher and of lower life; there is a restraining and overawing power in their holy and consistent example; which operates favourably on the general character of the population. Now, it is chiefly by means of the

Sabbath, that the number of these "lights of the world"
is maintained and multiplied. It is by the Sabbath,
that the spirit of true religion is kept up and diffused;
that the "salt of the earth" is prevented from being
ing its savour," and so from losing its antiputrescent
virtue in checking the spread of corruption. And
it has been true from the beginning, it is true now,
and will hold true to the end, that it is "righteousness
which exalteth a nation."—Even the general outward observance of the Sabbath has a happy effect in diffusing a
moral decency among the public. It operates like a sana-
tive medicine in the political body, counteracting the moral
poison of infidelity and sin, and contributing to the pre-
servation of its health and soundness. It will be found,
in point of fact, that, by a natural reciprocation, in proportion as moral profligacy spreads, the Sabbath is disregarded and profaned,—and that the disregard and
profanation of the Sabbath may be assumed as a pretty
correct test of the prevalence of profligacy. Infidels are
aware of this. They see the value of the Sabbath, as one
of the great safeguards of Christianity; and they have
bent their energies to its abolition. Our own infidels
have set themselves, in turbulent hostility, against the
efforts of those who unite to maintain its sacredness. And
what was the introduction of *decades* by the atheistical
revolutionists of France, but one of the means by which
they sought the extinction of religion, and the disruption
of all its salutary restraints? The policy of the old ser-
pent was in the device. As an additional proof of this,
and a further incitement to Christians to promote, by all
means in their power, the due observance of the Sabbath,

may be mentioned, the confessions of our condemned crim-
inals, at every successive assize. From how large a proportion of these culprits is the acknowledgment and lamentation
to be heard, that Sabbath-breaking was the beginning of
their wicked career,—one of the first steps in that course
of vice, and profligacy, and crime, which has terminated
in the hulks, or on the scaffold !

Although no other nation can ever sustain the same
relation to Jehovah, as that in which ancient Israel stood,
yet, from his promises, and threatenings, and conduct, towards that people, the general state of the divine mind on
the subject now before us, as well as on not a few others,
may be clearly and impressively learned. Our text contains a promise :—" IF thou turn away thy foot from the
Sabbath, from doing thy pleasure on my holy day, and
call the Sabbath a delight, the holy of the Lord, honourable ; and shalt honour him, not doing thine own ways,
nor finding thine own pleasure, nor speaking thine own
words: THEN SHALT THOU DELIGHT THYSELF IN THE
LORD, AND I WILL CAUSE THEE TO RIDE UPON THE HIGH
PLACES OF THE EARTH, AND WILL FEED THEE WITH THE
HERITAGE OF JACOB THY FATHER: FOR THE MOUTH OF
THE LORD HATH SPOKEN IT. The promise, may be
regarded as pledging the divine word to Israel, that if, in
this and in other respects, they were willing and obedient,
they should enjoy the favour and blessing of the God of
their fathers ;—that he would crown them with victory
over all their enemies and oppressors, and put them in
possession, as a security against their future assaults, of the
lofty strong-holds, and "munitions of rocks," in which they
had trusted ; that he would establish them in the perma-

nant possession of the land of promise, with all its embowelled treasures, and all the luxuriance of varied produce, which the blessing of the Almighty himself could cause it to yield. And, in this temporal view of it, the promise stands in harmonious contrast with those threatenings of displeasure, and dispossession, and suffering, which are elsewhere attached by the prophets to the violation of the same precept:—" If ye will not hearken unto me, TO HALLOW THE SABBATH-DAY, and not to bear a burden, even entering in at the gates of Jerusalem on the Sabbath-day; then will I kindle a fire in the gates thereof, and it shall devour the palaces of Jerusalem, and it shall not be quenched:"—" But the house of Israel rebelled against me in the wilderness: they walked not in my statutes, and they despised my judgments, which, if a man do, he shall even live in them; and MY SABBATHS THEY GREATLY POLLUTED: then I said, I would pour out my fury upon them in the wilderness, to consume them. But I wrought for my name's sake, that it should not be polluted before the heathen, in whose sight I brought them out. Yet also I lifted up my hand unto them in the wilderness, that I would not bring them into the land which I had given them, flowing with milk and honey, which is the glory of all lands; because they despised my judgments, and walked not in my statutes, but POLLUTED MY SABBATHS: for their heart went after their idols. Nevertheless mine eye spared them from destroying them, neither did I make an end of them in the wilderness. But I said unto their children in the wilderness, Walk ye not in the statutes of your fathers, neither observe their judgments, nor defile yourselves with their idols. I am the

Lord your God; walk in my statutes, and keep my judgments, and do them; and HALLOW MY SABBATHS; and they shall be a sign between me and you, that ye may know that I am the Lord your God. Notwithstanding the children rebelled against me: they walked not in my statutes, neither kept my judgments to do them, which if a man do, he shall even live in them; they POLLUTED MY SABBATHS; then I said, I would pour out my fury upon them, to accomplish my anger against them in the wilderness. Nevertheless I withdrew mine hand, and wrought for my name's sake, that it should not be polluted in the sight of the heathen, in whose sight I brought them forth. I lifted up mine hand unto them also in the wilderness, that I would scatter them among the heathen, and disperse them through the countries; because they had not executed my judgments, but had despised my statutes, and had POLLUTED MY SABBATHS, and their eyes were after their fathers' idols." * To the realizing of such threatenings as these, Nehemiah must be considered as having had reference, when he thus contended with the Sabbath-breakers of his day, even with the "nobles of Judah"—" What evil thing is this that ye do, and profane the Sabbath-day? Did not your fathers thus, and did not our God bring all this evil upon us, and upon this city? Yet ye bring more wrath upon Israel, by profaning the Sabbath." †

It is very obvious, that communities, as such, can be the subjects of judicial visitation only in this world; and that there is a principle of national retribution, according to which—(although in a way that may many

* Jerem. xvii. 27. Ezek. xx. 13—24.   † Nehem. xiii. 17, 18.

a time, be beyond the reach of our short-sighted penetration)—the dealings of providence towards the nations of the earth are regulated, no careful reader of his Bible can question. The following language of God, by Jeremiah, relates no doubt, in the first instance, to those nations and kingdoms against which express messages of denunciation had been dictated to the prophets, to be by them communicated:—but they as evidently contain a general principle of the divine administration, of which it requires only an inspired history of the world to show us the application. "At what instant I shall speak concerning a nation, or concerning a kingdom, to pluck up, and to pull down, and to destroy it; if that nation, against whom I have pronounced, turn from their evil, I will repent of the evil that I thought to do unto them. And at what instant I shall speak concerning a nation, and concerning a kingdom, to build, and to plant it; if it do evil in my sight, that it obey not my voice, then I will repent of the good wherewith I said I would benefit them."* —"Sin, which is the only cause of the destruction of individuals, is also the sole cause of the ruin of nations. They perish not, till their iniquities are full."† —If these things be so,—and if the sins that draw down the wrath of God on communities are both the sins to be found in the public councils and acts of their governments, and at the same time the collective aggregate of the sins of individuals,—may we not, with good reason, reckon among the grounds of apprehension for our country, the lamentable amount

* Jer. xviii. 7—10.
† The Prospects of Britain, by James Douglas, Esq. of Cavers, p. 13.

amidst the enjoyment of so large a amount of privilege of
sabbath-profanation ?..
.....But the promise is one of more ample import. Although it is primarily addressed to Israel, yet it is to Israel,
we apprehend, as constituting the church of God; and under typical language, it expresses the fulness and perpetuity of spiritual blessings. He who delighted in the Sabbath
should have a larger and larger measure of the highest and
richest of all privileges—delight in the God of the Sabbath.
HE would " lift upon him the light of his countenance:"
—He would " manifest himself to him, as he doth not unto
the world :"—He would " come unto him, and make his
abode with him," and fill his soul with the joy of his salvation ; thus putting the song of gladness into his lips—
" This God is our God for ever and ever : he will be our
guide even unto death :"—He would " bruise Satan under his feet shortly," and give him a full and final victory
over all the enemies of his salvation—over " principalities and powers, and the rulers of the darkness of this
world, and spiritual wickednesses in high places :"—and
He would, in the end, give him complete and inalienable
possession of the inheritance above,—the inheritance,
couched under the promise of the earthly Canaan, and
typified by it,—the inheritance that is " incorruptible,
undefiled, and that fadeth not away."—" The mouth of
the Lord hath spoken it."

Is not the general lesson of all this to Christians, that
it is their duty to be sensitively jealous of every encroachment on the sanctity of the Sabbath,—jealous of it in them-

selves, jealous of it in others ;—and that they should leave
no legitimate and accessible means untried, for checking
the progress of its profanation, and promoting its scriptural observance ?—In one discourse more, we shall consider what these means are,—and close the entire subject
with some general improvement.

DISCOURSE IX.

MARK ii. 27.

" The Sabbath was made for man."

THESE words I had occasion formerly to quote, in evidence of the Sabbath having been instituted for mankind universally, and not for the Jews alone. But they express something more than the universality of the institution; they intimate its benevolent purpose. It was in harmony with the twofold character of God, as "light" and "love;" the dictate at once of holiness and of kindness. It was designed for the benefit of the creature, in union, of course, with the glory of the Creator. That it is eminently fitted to subserve both these ends, it has been the object of former discourses to show. In proportion, then, as our minds are impressed with the number and magnitude of the benefits resulting from the observance of the day, and of the mischiefs ensuing from its neglect and profanation, we should be solicitous, by every legitimate and accessible means, to promote the one, and to check and suppress the other.

All the commands, and all the institutions of Jehovah are the dictate of love; and those who disregard and vio-

late them " forsake their own mercies." There is, in their
disobedience, as much infatuation as there is impiety.
They injure themselves, while they dishonour God.
What, then, should be our aim on the present subject?
—what the practical problem which we should seek to
work out? Certainly, to fulfil the divine intention, in
bringing from the day as large an amount as possible of
advantage to man, and of glory to God. But alas! this
is not a problem which requires only that we maintain in
its purity, and preserve from corruption, a newly instituted ordinance ;—that we keep what is now duly observed
from falling into neglect and prostitution. It is not a
problem of prevention merely. It is, to a melancholy
extent, a problem of correction and reformation. The
evils already abound. They are great and manifold,—of
long standing, and of difficult removal. We have not
merely to preserve a sound constitution in its healthy
state; we have to deal, in the way of cure, with one that
is already a prey to virulent and deadly distempers. This
renders the case at once the more important and the
more perplexing; but, withal, the more peremptory in its
demands on the united counsels and energies of the
people of God.

The fact of most extensive, open, and daring profanation of the Lord's day, is not less sure than it is alarming.
The complaints and lamentations of the most enlightened
Christians of all denominations, in the south of our island,
are loud and deep. They represent the evil as " having
" reached a height which renders it an element not less
" of political danger than of moral corruption,"—as " out-
" raging all the sanctities of religion, all the decencies of

N

" morality, and defying all laws, civil, ecclesiastical, and
" divine." I shall enter at present into no invidious comparison of the degree to which, in south and north respectively, this outrage against the laws of God and of
our country prevails. From some of the more flagrant
evils which there call most loudly for interference and
reform, we are as yet, and let us be thankful for it, happily free. But we have enough, and far more than
enough, to deplore; and we are in danger of its increase.
Indigenous and imported abuses are, in rapid succession,
appearing amongst us; and, instead of our southern
neighbours learning from what remains of the example of
our sober sabbatical habits, there is a far greater hazard
of our catching the contagion of their augmenting profligacy, and of our becoming, mutually, corrupters of each
other. It is very true, and we rejoice to admit it, that
in our large cities and towns, the streets, at the several
hours of assembling for public worship, do still present a
spectacle highly animating and imposing; the " sound of
the church-going bell" drawing thousands, in all directions, to the house of God. The eye of strangers is captivated by this; and inferences much too favourable
(would that they were otherwise!) to the general character of our population, are drawn from it, and are made
the basis of many an eloquent eulogium, and of many a
high-flown description, with much more in it of Eutopia
than of Scotland as it is. Alas! what multitudes are far
otherwise occupied than in finding their way to the sanctuary, to hear and to worship there! By what multitudes
is the Sunday incomparably the worst-spent day in the
week! And of those who do, from various motives,

attend at church, how many are there by whom what remains of the day is miserably desecrated, in an endless multiplicity of ways; their inconsistency far more than neutralizing the effect of their church-going example! It is an appalling thought, and an indication of the tendencies of our fallen nature as affecting and humbling as it is frightful, that more crime should be perpetrated on the Sabbath than on all the other six days of the week together. What a handle this to infidelity! What an argument of practical cogency, to the man who pleads for the abolition of the day, as in experience more noxious than salutary! Deeply satisfied as we are, that the argument is unsound,—that, even setting aside divine authority, it is founded on partial and fallacious grounds, —yet how desirous should we be, by every possible means, to take it out of the lips of the caviller, by putting an end to its practical existence!

The question now before us, then, is—What are the means to be employed, for checking the profanation, and promoting the observance, of the Sabbath? They must be means which unite, as far as possible, efficiency of operation, with legitimacy of principle. Such as have, or seem to have, the former without the latter, we dare not employ; and such as have the latter without the former, we should employ to little purpose.

There is nothing which I should more strongly deprecate, than the interference of human laws in matters of religion. And I am aware, that the very mention of such a thing, in connexion with the Sabbath, will stir up, in some bosoms, all the jealousy of their dissenting principles. In the religious view of the Sabbath, I am as hostile as any man to such interference. In religious belief, and religious practice, every man's conscience should be perfectly free, these being matters that lie solely between himself and his God; nor should any civil privilege, or civil privation, be attached to the holding, or rather to the professing, of particular religious sentiments, or to the observance of particular forms of religious practice,—every thing of this kind being, in itself, alike unjust and impolitic, and operating, moreover, as a restraint to the conscience, and a bounty on hypocrisy. But I must call to your recollection the distinction formerly made, and already repeatedly adverted to, between the two classes of ends intended to be answered by the Sabbath,—namely, the secular and the spiritual; and the principle deduced from this distinction, that human laws, while they may not interfere with the latter, and never do interfere but prejudicially, may and ought to regulate and enforce the former. The department in which we plead for the legitimacy of civil enactments, and for the enforcing of such enactments by appended penalties, (for what is a law without a penalty?) is not religious; it is strictly political. There are contemplated in it the secular advantages to the community, of the hebdomadal cessation from labour. Beyond this human laws cannot legitimately go. Even in this department there are difficulties. But in what department of human legislation are there none? How full of intricacy and perplexing casuistry are many other branches of law, relative to the rights of property, and the modifications of crime? How much room is left, in innumerable cases, for special pleading, and diversity of judgment?—and how much difficulty in framing statutes, so as to embrace all the varieties of offence!—and in what one instance has this ever been done with complete success? It is not so much, however, with the difficulties that may be found in reducing principles to practice, as with the principles themselves, that I have at present to do. And upon the ground of the distinction referred to, I have no hesitation in calling for the execution of such existing laws as have reference to the regularities and political ends of the Sabbath; and for the enactment of new ones, if the old are found impracticable or inefficient. I am aware of the delicacy of my ground. I am aware how apt magistrates may be, even from good principles and well-intentioned zeal, to go beyond their limits, and out of their sphere. And the difficulties of the case have been multiplied by that intermingling of civil and sacred, of political and religious, which, on this and other subjects, has unavoidably arisen from the meretricious union of church and state. But still, our aversion, on New Testament principles, to this union, should not be allowed to blind and pervert our judgments, and carry us away to the opposite extreme. We must not allow ourselves to forget, that, although the principal ends of the Sabbath are spiritual, there are those which are subordinate and secular; that these are not to be overlooked; and that it is to the attainment of these that the statutes and penalties of human legislation should be directed. To this they are competent; to this they are obliged; but by this they ought to be limited. There must be no legal requisition, and enforcement, of a certain measure of attendance on divine worship; far less of attendance at prescribed places. The worship of God, being a purely religious service, must be entirely voluntary, the dictate of principle and of pious disposition; and is quite beyond the province of any authority beneath the Supreme.* Neither must there be any interference with the private and domestic modes of spending the day. Be they ever so inconsistent with its spiritual nature and ends,—ever so much opposed, in this respect, to the mind and will of Him by whom "the Sabbath was made for man,"—there must be no vexatious system of domiciliary visitation and inquisitorial espionage, —no harassing encroachment on the privacies of life,— no interference with any mode of passing the time, that

* By I Eliz. c. 2, it was enacted, that "all persons not having a reasonable excuse, shall resort to their parish church or chapel (or to some congregation of religious worship allowed by law) on every Sunday, on pain of punishment by the censures of the church, or of forfeiting one shilling to the poor for every such offence."—And by 3 Jam. 1. c. 4, these penalties are ordained to be "levied by the churchwardens by distress, on the warrant of one Justice."—And "he who was absent from his own parish church was to be put to prove where he did go to a place of worship." 1 Hawk. c. 10.—Dickenson's Exposition of the law, relative to the office and duties of a Justice of the Peace, Vol. iii. p. 453.

All this is *ultra vires*. It is what human laws have nothing to do with. The attempt to carry such enactments into effect would inevitably give rise to all that was ridiculous, as well as to all that was partial and irksome, in oppression. One cannot but smile to think of such an attempt being made now-a-days. Our Justices of the Peace, (coming into court with "clean hands" themselves, of course) to be judges of what constitutes a "reasonable excuse," for absence from church!—and all who could not give a good account of themselves to be amerced in one shilling a-head to the poor for each offence! If such a fine were impartially levied, we should hardly need poor's-rates.

does not disturb public peace, or trespass on public decorum. If compulsion cannot, on any right principle, be applied to the public duties of religion, still less can it to those which are personal and domestic.*

The chief difficulty, on our present subject, however, even when we have ascertained the general principle of the propriety of human legislation for securing the temporal ends of the Sabbath, is, to define the limits of *legal*

---

* In Hume's Commentaries on the Criminal Law of Scotland, a long succession of statutes is referred to on the profanation of the Sabbath. extending, at various intervals, from 1503 to 1663. Into the provisions of these multiplied statutes, whether obsolete or still in force,—or, indeed, into the law of the case, in its practical detail, either in Scotland or in England, it is not at all my purpose, or within my province, to enter. The distinct discussion of the different enactments; the inquiry respecting each, how far it is correct in principle, and within the proper sphere of human authority;—how far capable of execution; and, if so capable, how far calculated to answer the intended purpose, without a weighty counterbalance of evil; would necessarily lead into voluminous argumentation; of which the probable result would be, that some are right, and some wrong, and some mixed, both in principle, and in sound policy, and in capability of execution. " Prosecutions for mere profanation of the Sabbath," says Mr. Bell, (Diction. of the Law of Scotland, Art. Sunday,") " are now very rarely resorted to; and, when absolutely necessary, they ought to be conducted with prudence and deliberation, and not with that mistaken zeal, which frequently counteracts the object it has in view." That all such prosecutions should be conducted in the manner described, is an obvious truth. But the very making of the observation arose from the extreme difficulty of framing laws which do not mix the religious with the political, and of which the execution is not in danger of trenching on the rights of conscience. The " prudence and deliberation" are most imperiously called for in the *framing* of the laws. The more prudently and deliberately they are framed, and the less necessity, consequently, is left for the restraining influence of these virtues in prosecuting for their violation, the nearer are the laws to what all laws ought to be.

and moral means, for repressing its abuse, and promoting its observance. The main this point of difference between them, quid id minus, quia id est ... hi ... and ... in drawing the boundaries, namely, that moral means may be applied in every department of Sabbath violation, there being considerations of a moral nature, which may be urged, in behalf of both the secular and the spiritual observance of the day, and in deprecation of both its secular and its spiritual abuse—but this cannot be said of its legal means. They have their own department, beyond which, they encroach on a higher province, and cannot be employed, without a legalised, but unwarrantable, infraction of the law of God. Moral means may be used in the secular department, but legal means cannot be used in the spiritual ...

There are two points to which the laws of society, on this subject, ought to be directed. The first, of course, is the prevention of all cognizable breaches of the great general requisition, which enjoins the suspension of the ordinary occupations of buying and selling, and getting gain;—and the second is the protection, from all unnecessary interruption and annoyance, of those who choose to devote the day to its more appropriate end, the exercises of religion. With regard to the former, there may be many difficulties experienced, both in adjusting the laws, so as to embrace alike all classes of the community, and to do nothing by partiality; and, at the same time, to proportion and enforce penalties, so as effectually to enforce their observance. I have already asked, in what branch of law itself are not similar difficulties. But there are cases, and the present is one of them, in which the difficulties are much augmented by the indisposition of our legislators to apply their minds to the subject, and either to be at pains in the devising and modelling of the laws, or very solicitous about the attainment of their adequate observance. There is a disinclination to the abridgement of liberty on that day, among the high as well as among the low. The members of our legislature, as they may not themselves be free from this prevailing disinclination. Every law they frame must, trained as they are, with unrighteous partiality, they enact rigid prohibitory statutes for the poor, while they leave the rich and the noble in the enjoyment of the coveted freedom, they incur the merited hatred and scorn of the community. Were there as serious a disposition, on the part of our law-makers to meet the exigencies of this case, as at times discovers itself in other departments of legislation, the difficulties would be wonderfully diminished. Were there half as much application of mind to the understanding of the subject, and half as much pains expended upon the practical application of the knowledge thus acquired, as we see bestowed in correcting the errors, reforming the abuses, clearing away the encumbrances, abbreviating the forms of process, hastening decision, and ensuring its rectitude in the Court of Chancery,—were there one twentieth part of the zeal in this cause, that has discovered itself either for or against reform in our national representation;—I am very far from saying that no difficulties would be felt; no embarrassing obstacles present themselves;—but they would be as nothing compared with what they appear, in reality or in pretext, to the unwilling mind. The disinclination to meddle with the subject cloaks itself with some wonder

their aversion to alter the laws;—with others, under their
compassion for the labouring poor;—with others still,
under their apprehensions of all undue political interference with religion;—while, alas! there is too much reason
to fear, that there is, with a large proportion of all, the
three classes, a listless unconcern about the whole matter,
or a desire to take and to give indulgence, keeping even
existing statutes in abeyance, and acting under their convenient connivance.

It is not my business to dictate to the legislature, or to
enter into legal views of the case, and propose suitable
and efficient enactments. To this I pretend not to be
competent. My sole object is, to ascertain correct principles.

We, in the northern part of the island, are as yet happily free from the crying evils, prolific of so many others,
of public markets, and open shops, and stalls and hawkers
in our frequented streets, and Sunday travelling, by coach
and steam, and the vending of Sunday newspapers,[*]
and other sources of corruption to public morals, which
are either notorious infractions of existing statutes, or
tolerated inconsistencies with them. These evils have

---

[*] There are, if I mistake not, *thirteen* Sunday newspapers published
in London, of which upwards of 40,000 copies are openly sold, on that
day, in 300 shops! It is needless to say, that some of these papers
derive their zest to the public mind, from their containing not merely
the ordinary news of the day, but a collection of caricature and buf-
foonery, of all the varieties of sporting intelligence, from the turf, and
the ring, and the cock-pit, of anecdotes (the more laughable the better)
of high and low, of fashionable and vulgar life, mixed up, more openly
or more artfully, with the poison of infidelity and irreligion, in forms
adapted to all capacities and all characters. And this is SUNDAY
READING!

risen to an enormous amount of public annoyance, and of
moral mischief, in the south. And, alas! there is an irreligious spirit prevalent, which treats with indifference and
scorn every lamentation over the wrong, and every serious
proposal of amelioration ;—a spirit which, it is to be feared,
has, in no small degree, infected our legislative assemblies
themselves, and which gives to the offenders a disdainful
sense of security, and enables them to treat with a careless defiance, or a contemptuous leer, such as would remind
them of the laws, and intimidate them into submission.
And, indeed, with regard to not a few of the protecting
penalties, being of ancient enactment, they have, in our
times, become a mere mockery, and might as well have no
existence.

I must repeat, that the enactments, for which I plead,
are such as regard, solely, the *secular ends* of the Sabbath,
in which light alone it can be a law of man, and enforced
by human penalties. And, in this point of view, there is
perhaps quite as much, if not even more, of difficulty, in
regard to the *amusements*, than in regard to the labour and
the merchandise of the day. It was a singular anomaly
in Christian legislation (so called by a miserable mis-
nomer) when, in the century before last, the celebrated
" BOOK OF SPORTS" was published, under the high sanction of royal and episcopal recommendation and authority,
specifying and prescribing the amusements in which the
good people of England might lawfully indulge on the
Lord's day. The wisdom of the first James suggested
the scheme, and the piety of the first Charles had the
credit of reviving it. As it was dictated by aversion to
puritanism, whose " most uncourtly strictness" suited not

the royal taste, its indulgences were sufficiently liberal, including, by express mention, dancing, archery, leaping, vaulting, May-games, Whitsun-ales, and morris dances. The royal mandate was laid upon all ministers, to read this book of sports to their congregations, and so to give it their express or tacit sanction; and, if the order was disobeyed, the consequence, to the conscientious culprit, was prosecution, suspension, and imprisonment. The pretext for this plenary indulgence to the desecration of the Sabbath, (for, indeed, it was little better,) was the prevention of excess,—of excess, in the two opposite extremes of puritanical dulness, and unrestricted licentiousness. How it was likely to operate upon the public mind and character, I leave you to judge. Had it been meant to devise a method for effectually obliterating all impressions of the sacredness of the day, and for erasing the lessons designed to be communicated by the reading and preaching of the word, one better adapted to this purpose could not well be imagined. You may form to yourselves some estimate of the effect produced by it, from the following simple but graphic description, from the pen of the justly eminent Richard Baxter: "I cannot forget," says he, "that in my youth, in those late times, when we lost the labours of some of our godly teachers, for not reading publicly the Book of Sports, and dancing on the Lord's day, one of my father's own tenants was the town-piper, hired by the year, (for many years together,) and the place of the dancing assembly was not a hundred yards from our door. We could not, on the Lord's day, either read a chapter, or pray, or sing a psalm, or catechise or instruct a servant, but with the noise of the pipe and tabour, and the shoutings in the streets, continually in our ears. Even among a tractable people, we were the common scorn of all the rabble in the streets, and were called puritans, precisians, and hypocrites, because we rather chose to read the Scriptures, than to do as they did; though there was no savour of non-conformity in our family. And when the people, by the book, were allowed to play and dance out of public service-time, they could so hardly break off their sports, that many a time, the reader was fain to stay till the pipes and players would give over. Sometimes the morris-dancers would come into the church in all their linen, and scarfs, and antic dresses, with morris-bells jingling at their legs; and as soon as common prayer was read, did haste out presently to their play again."

"Greatly as the Sabbath is still neglected or profaned among us," says the late lamented Mr. Orme, from whose life of Baxter these sentences are quoted, "it ought to afford sincere satisfaction, that such scenes as the above could not now be transacted in any part of England; and still less, I rejoice to add, in any part of Scotland. What shall we say, then, of an eminent prelate, who lived a century later, when he ventures to affirm on such a subject—"The present humour of the common people leads, perhaps, more to a profanation of the festival, than to a superstitious rigour in the observance of it. But in the attempt to reform, we shall do wisely to remember, that the thanks for this are chiefly due to the base spirit of puritanical hypocrisy, which, in the last century, opposed and defeated the wise attempts of government to regulate the recreations of the day by authority, and prevent the excesses which have actually taken place by a rational indulgence!"—It is upon the very same principle that the haunts of impurity have in some countries been legalised, and licensed, and subjected to rules of police, and so, with certain prudential restrictions, taken under public patronage; and the same kind of plea has been urged in vindication of the practice.

I am not sure that any law can be framed respecting amusements on the Sabbath, except upon the general principle, that no man, in his mode of spending the day, shall be a disturbance and annoyance to others. This would lead to the interdiction and suppression of a large propor- tion, if not of all sports and pastimes of an open and pub- lic nature. With regard to what is private, it is impos- sible that laws can interfere: and, were it possible, it would be beyond their legitimate province. Even as to what is public, the principle can only be laid down gen- erally, leaving room for questions not so much of moral as of legal casuistry; and for special cases, in behalf of which pleas of exception might be put in, as being free of the charge of outward disturbance or annoyance to any one. I say, *outward* disturbance or annoyance: for I am at present speaking of *human laws;* and, were we to take into our definition of disturbance and annoyance, the offence and grief given to the moral and religious feelings of the better part of the community,—we should, I appre- hend, get beyond the limits of such legislation; inasmuch as nothing can divest the pious bosom of this offence and grief, but the true spiritual observance of the day;—which, of course, is what no law of man can enact, or, by enact- ing, produce.—On this subject, as on a number of others, there is little that can be done in the way of legal statute:

—the suppression must be the result of moral means, industriously and extensively put into operation, and of the power of consistent example on the part of those by whom they are employed.

Before proceeding to notice these moral means, I may hazard the observation, that, with regard to the external observance of the Sabbath, so far as enacted and protected by the laws of the land, it is eminently injurious to the community, (setting the law of God out of the question,) when the very enactments which enjoin and protect the sabbatical rest are openly violated in those quarters where deference to the laws ought most sacredly to be exemplified. What are we to look for, as the effect in all the descending grades of society, when, from time to time, in all the newspapers, the people read of successive cabinet councils held on the Lord's day, without even the pretext of any pressing state emergency to justify it; when they thus see the Sabbath, in the transactions of public as well as of private business, converted into a day for *saving time ;*—and what is still worse, when they read of its being chosen as the day for the festivities of ministerial dinners, by which not only do the guests set at nought the law of God, but the fundamental principle of the law of the land is infringed, by the necessary employment of hundreds of hands in the preparation and service of such entertainments; and moreover, of Sunday parties in high life, in their multiplied varieties, more select coteries, or more numerous and promiscuous companies, in the first style of fashion, and duly puffed off to the public, in defiance of all the proprieties and decencies of the day of rest;—when they read of these and of all the other ways, in which the very framers of the laws are themselves the examples of their infraction:—what, I say, are we to look for in this effect, but that this spirit thus displayed should be caught in the ranks below; that inferiors should feel themselves as well entitled to disregard the laws as their betters; till once reption should spread downwards, till the deadly infection reaches, in the political body, "from the crown of the head to the sole of the foot?"

"After all, however, even so far as regards the outward observance of the Sabbath, I should trust a great deal more to the influence of moral means, than to that of legal statutes; and, with respect to the prospect of its true spiritual keeping of the day, but dependance must of course be on these entirely. Laws can have do nothing. And, important as the secular ends of the Sabbath are, its moral and spiritual purposes are incomparably more so. These it ought to be our chief desire, and our chief endeavour, to promote. It is by the advancement of these, that we do good to the souls of individuals, and that, by the extension of moral and spiritual ends, we elevate the character of the community. The Sabbath, as we have repeatedly observed, can only be rightly kept under the influence of right principle. It follows, that the most effectual, and indeed the only effectual way of increasing the amount of its right and Scriptural celebration, is the diffusion of right principle. "Herein," then, "let us exercise ourselves." We cannot be engaged in a work more truly conducive to the good of men, and to the glory of God, than the bringing of our sinful fellow-creatures around us, under the power of those principles of true godliness, which will cause them, whenever they feel their influence, to "call the Sabbath a delight, the holy of the Lord honourable."

When we speak of moral means, however, the designation includes more than this; more than the means of promoting the spiritual celebration of the day, under the predominance of spiritual principles and feelings, and with a view to its spiritual results,—the results of holy impulse and divine blessing, which it brings to the soul. Moral means may be used also for promoting the outward observance of the day, and securing to individuals and to the community its secular advantages. We employ them, when we exhibit and impress the value of these advantages, when we shew to the individual, and shew to the member of the community, what benefits, even of a temporal kind, will arise to himself and to society, from a due attention to the weekly day of rest. We may thus exert a practical influence, through the medium both of self-love and of patriotism.—Legal enactments and moral means may be brought into operation together. I would lay it down as a general maxim, however, that the more of the latter and the less of the former, so much the better. When we succeed by moral means, we effect our object, not only much more agreeably, but much more thoroughly and durably. The difference is like that between influencing the mind of a child by argument and persuasion, and swaying and constraining it by the terror of the rod.—We may check Sabbath-profanation, for example, in a species of it that is mournfully abundant, by shutting public-houses during divine service, and after certain specified hours; and we may, through our local magistracies, try to accomplish this effectually by a constant system of threatening, and vigilance, and fine, and privation of licence, and other means of intimidating self-interest and coercing contumacy. To a certain extent we may succeed. But such means serve to bring into exercise a counter-system of watchfulness, and deception, and falsehood and perjury, and bribery and corruption, by which, in many instances, the strictest *surveillance* of magisterial duty will be evaded;—especially as it is impossible that such surveillance should be at all times equally on the alert:—and a bad feeling is, besides, engendered, by the difficulty and invidiousness of drawing the line of distinction between such houses and houses of refreshment of a somewhat higher order it may be, which are not subjected to this rigorous superintendence. While, therefore, as we conceive, the general principle of human laws on this subject perfectly warrants, in the cases in question, the interference of the magistrate; inasmuch as, no satisfactory reason can well be assigned why the sale of intoxicating liquors should be tolerated on the Lord's-day, while the sale of all other articles, save medicines, is interdicted. Yet it is, in every respect, an incomparably more desirable method of checking and doing away this kind, and this prolific source of other kinds, of Sabbath-profanation, to put down, by the use of moral means, the intemperance itself, which is the maintenance of those Sunday haunts and nurseries of profligacy,—as well as the inlet to so vast a proportion of the vice and crime, the discord and the wretchedness, with which the lower caste of society so fearfully teems. And, without discussing at present the merits and demerits of temperance societies, I must be allowed to say in their behalf, that their object is one of the most important which the mind of Christian, of patriot, or of philanthropist can contemplate; that the general principle on which they are founded,—which is, substantially, the application of combined example ·to the accomplishment of an end which individual and insulated example has utterly failed of affecting,—is capable of the simplest and most satisfactory justification;—that, whatever objections may be entertained against them, and be felt sufficient by individuals to prevent their actually joining them, I cannot imagine how any Christian, as a friend to morality, to the true interests of his country, and to the personal and social happiness of his fellow-men, can regard them with indifference, or fail to wish them God-speed;—and for this reason amongst others, that their success will contribute, in no small degree, to diminish the profanation, and to promote the sober and serious observance, of the Lord's day. For surely, the consideration is fearful, that the Sabbath should be the great tippling day,—a day of greater business and profit to the dram-drinking houses of which I have been speaking, than all the other days of the week together! Such being the melancholy fact, every step towards the suppression of intemperance is equally a step to the cure of Sabbath-profanation. They are sins that mutually produce and cherish each other.

But neither the relinquishment of intemperance, nor the sober church-going observance of the Sabbath, will save the soul. Still, therefore, let us bear in mind, that the first and most important description of moral means is the promotion of the knowledge and belief of the gospel. Every thing short of this, however useful and desirable, is yet deficient. It is something to gain men from intemperance; it is something to bring them, from spending the Sabbath in the fields or in the ale-house, to spend it in church, and at home :—but it is not enough. The heart may still be unrenewed; the sins of the life unpardoned; and the soul in jeopardy of perdition. We do too little, then, although that which we do is good,—when we confine our attention to the former objects. We must go further. Intemperance and Sabbath-breaking have a source. Like other sins, they are streams from a fountain. We must go to the fountain. Our grand aim must be to heal the waters there. We must assail the propensities to evil by that truth which is "the power of God unto salvation." If, through the blessing of God, we succeed in bringing that truth to bear upon the evil desires and passions of the heart, so as to subdue it to Christ, we have gained every thing we could wish. We ensure sobriety and Sabbath-keeping, and every other practical virtue, by introducing the principle of them all. Whereas, if we keep working merely at the motives to temperance, and to outward church-going decorum on the Sunday, the product of our successful assiduity may be no more than a self-righteous formalist, who may have gained much for the comfort of this life, but little or nothing for the life to come.—Let us seek, then, by all means in our power, to make known the truth of God,—both by persuading men to come and hear it, and by carrying it to them, and recommending it to their attention and to their believing acceptance. This is the shortest, the most direct, and the most effectual way, to the attainment of all our ends. Make men believers ; and you make them "sober, righteous, and godly."

But while this is true, I do not mean that we should not employ all other subordinate and auxiliary methods of restraining the profanation and encouraging the observance of the Sabbath.—Tracts should be profusely circulated, not only containing gospel truth; but directly setting forth the nature, the obligation, and the benefits, (spiritual and secular, private and public,) of the Sabbath, as "made for man," and containing in its institution an evidence of the divine goodness.—In our great towns, too, such institutions as the Glasgow City Mission, are of admirable utility, for suppressing the profanation, and promoting the observance of the Lord's day; the agents of such institutions, in their visits of mercy, finding their way amongst the very classes of the population where the evil most affectingly prevails, and bringing directly to bear upon them all the moral and spiritual means of its correction. That Christian who professes anxiety to promote reverence for the Sabbath, acts most inconsistently with his profession, if he withholds his countenance and support from such associations.

And O! let Christians remember, how much may be done, of evil or of good, *by their example.* I would press this, with all earnestness, upon their attention. It is of far more importance than they are generally aware. There is good reason to fear, that no small portion of the profanation of the Sabbath which Christians lament, owes its origin to laxity in the conduct of many who bear the profession of the gospel. Christians do not sufficiently consider, what advantage the world are ever prone to take of every thing in their conduct that can at all be construed into allowance of what they themselves wish to practice;—how much further the evil of their example goes than the good?—from how slight an indulgence on the part of a saint they will deduce a wide and licentious sanction. Surely, this ought to make Christians exceedingly cautious and circumspect. When they find their example even in what they may conceive to be, in itself, and as they practise it, innocent, pleaded in behalf of indulgences far beyond the harmless limit which they have set to themselves —it becomes their duty to exercise self-denial, and, although they may conceive it, and justly conceive it, a hardship, that the perverseness of others should deprive them of a liberty in which God and conscience do not condemn them, yet, since God and conscience do not require them to take the liberty, and no principle, therefore, is violated or compromised in its relinquishment, there can be no hesitation as to the path of duty. If by their walking on the brink of a precipice, the result is that others fall over it, will they, for the sake of showing their liberty, persist in keeping near the edge, and disdain the consequences?—" When I first attended seriously to religion," says Mr. Scott, the justly venerated commentator, " I used sometimes, when I had a journey to perform on the next day, to ride a stage in the evening, after the service of the Sabbath; and I trust my time on horseback was not spent unprofitably. But I soon found, that this furnished an excuse to some of my parishioners, for employing a considerable part of the Lord's day in journeys of business or convenience. I need not say, that I immediately abandoned the practice." On the same principle ought Christians ever to act, even in things of still less questionable harmlessness than the practice here specified. It is not for us to say, " If men *will* pervert and abuse our example, we cannot help it; the fault is their own, and let them take the consequences." This is not the benevolent spirit of the gospel. O! what is any little liberty of ours, however harmless, when compared with encouraging fellow-sinners in their worldly and self-destroying courses. Such sacrifices are not once to be named. Life should not be dear to us, when the stake to be won by its forfeiture is—the souls of men.

Let Christian parents inculcate upon the minds of their children, from their earliest years, reverence for the day of God, as a part of that " fear of the Lord," which is " the beginning of wisdom;" and let them carefully ex- emplify it before their families, in their own habitual practice. Let them attend to this, not only for the sake of their children, but for the sake of the benefit to others from their children's example. If, in this matter, per- sonal example is valuable, domestic example is, if possi- ble, still more so. It is in families, in an especial manner, that the reverence of the Lord's Sabbaths must be main- tained, and transmitted to future generations. If, in the families of any of God's people, there appear an undue relaxation of the holy, but kindly, discipline of the domes- tic Sabbath, other Christian families will speedily catch the infection,—the children pleading and claiming the same indulgence, and the parents gradually yielding to the claim. The domestic example, too, like the personal, will be abused by the semi-christian, and by the sober worldling, as a sanction for much more unfettered licence ; till the sacredness of the day comes to be lost, and its salutary restraints thrown entirely away. Awake, awake, my brethren, to the danger. Let not the domestic Sabbath, in any of your families, be undistinguishable from other days; but be it the resolution of every one of you, in the strength of promised grace, " As for me, and my house, we will serve the Lord!"

And let churches also do their duty. If it be a law of God, that the Sabbath be hallowed, the breach of that law should not, any more than the breach of others, be allowed to pass unnoticed and uncensured. I am aware, when I say so, of the difficulty that may sometimes be experienced, in defining the limits of the law, and determining in what cases, and to what extent, its prohibitory enactments have been violated. But the law does not, in this respect, stand alone. There are cases of nice and delicate casuistry, in regard to other laws, as well as in regard to this. But the occurrence of these cannot, in any case, affect the great general principle, that every church of Christ is bound to see to it that his laws be duly observed; and, among the rest, that his own day be becomingly sanctified in the personal and domestic conduct of its members,—that the flagrant neglect of its public ordinances, or its private duties, be not permitted, without expostulation, admonition, and, if contumaciously persisted in, even exclusion; and that, in this, as in other respects, the members should mutually and faithfully watch over one another,—not in the spirit of prying curiosity and intermeddling officiousness, but of humble and affectionate interest in each other's spiritual prosperity, and earnest solicitude for the glory of Christ, and the purity and growth of his kingdom.

This subject has been, throughout, of a nature so directly practical, that I do not feel it necessary to enlarge in the way of what is usually called *improvement.* There is one point, however, which I conceive to be of essential importance, for preventing all self-deception in any of my hearers, and so of delivering my own soul from the guilt of their blood. The point to which I advert is, the necessity of considering the observance of the Sabbath, not as a mere insulated duty, but as a TEST OF CHARACTER. I know nothing more important than this. The manner in which you spend your Sabbaths is an index to the state of your hearts towards God. It affords a fair and satisfactory criterion of the security or the danger of your present condition, and of your prospects for eternity. This is a light, indeed, in which we ought to regard every particular description of trespass. We have but done our work by halves, when we have convinced any one that he has been wrong in this particular, and have even induced him to reform. We wish every one, whose conscience tells him that he has been profaning or neglecting his Sabbaths, idling or secularizing their sacred hours, to carry his self-examination a little deeper. This is not a mere defect in his character, requiring to be remedied. It is one among many indications that his " heart is not right with God ;" that he is yet unrenewed in the spirit of his mind. —We do not call upon him, therefore, merely to set about amending this defect, and doing better for the future :—we call upon him to lay to heart the solemn words of the Saviour—" Verily, verily, I say unto thee, except a man be born again, he cannot see the kingdom of God !" There is something more necessary for sinful creatures,—crea-

o

tures who have not merely broken particular precepts, but whose nature is in a state of opposition to the very principles of the divine law,—a state of " enmity against God," —there is something more necessary for such creatures, than the mere relinquishment of this or the other evil, and the performance of this or the other duty. There must be a change of heart. The divine promise must be fulfilled, " A new heart will I give you, and a new spirit will I put within you; and I will take away the stony heart out of your flesh, and I will give you a heart of flesh." Without this, the mere external reformation of a particular fault may leave you as far from God as ever. It will be but whiting the sepulchre. It will be but giving the aspect of life to death; colouring the cheek of the corpse, while no vital pulse beats in the heart. Let a man's reputation be ever so high, for sobriety, integrity, and charity, as these virtues are understood in the world: his heart may still be under the dominion of a deep-seated ungodliness. God may not be in all his thoughts. And of the continuance of this alienation from God, there cannot be a more direct and conclusive indication than want of reverence for the Lord's day; an evil, indeed, which, from its nature, can never stand alone: it will invariably be found in union with the neglect of other duties that are properly religious, and especially of those private exercises of personal devotion, in which the renewed soul finds its chief delight. Men may think little of it. They may not class Sabbath-keeping among the virtues. They may think, and they may say, that if they give every man his due, no one has a right to interfere with the use which they make of their time. Be it so. But has not God this right? What

if He shall remind you, that the time has been *his*, not
yours?—that you have been alienating from him what
should have been spent to his glory; and, while you have
been boasting of giving every *man* his due, have been, in
this and in many other things, withholding his due from
HIM?—and what, too, if he should add to this the charge
of ingratitude, in that you have ungenerously abused his
goodness, in perverting to other purposes the time given
you by him, for attending to your best and highest interests? Say what you will of it, your neglect and profanation of his day is one of the clearest signs that your
hearts are not his; and that all your boasted virtues are
destitute of the very first principle of whatever deserves
the name. You must be "renewed in the spirit of your
mind." The "love of God must be shed abroad in your
hearts." While it is otherwise, your very virtues are
ungodly. They cannot find acceptance with him, whose
first requisition is, that the heart be given to himself.
This, and this alone, will sanctify your virtues. It will
put God into them. And you will then make it manifest
that they are fulfilled from a new principle, by associating
with your duties to men those higher duties,—which, before you left out of account in the estimate of your character, but which now you see to be entitled to the first
place,—the duties you owe to God. Then, in the private
and public exercises of devotion, you will come to Him
as your "exceeding joy." Deeply sensible that your profanation of his day has not been the mere omission of a
duty, but an awful result and indication of the alienation
of your hearts from Himself, you will bewail the precious
time you have lost, implore forgiveness through the aton-

ing blood of his Son, and seek his grace to redeem the past by the faithful improvement of the future. Then will you understand and feel the full import of the text,— " THE SABBATH WAS MADE FOR MAN." You will see the love of God in it. You will feel it a privilege and a pleasure; and you will keep it, with joy and persevering constancy, as at once a testimony for God, and a means of benefit to your own souls. Your Sabbaths on earth will give you foretastes of the everlasting Sabbath of heaven, and will make you progressively meet for its holy exercises and joys. The man who relishes not God's Sabbaths here, is deceiving himself, if ever he talks of his hope of heaven. He may call by this name some vague undefined expectation of a heaven of his own;—but the heaven of the Bible, the only existing heaven, is not the object of his hope ; for the blessings which are to constitute its felicity, are not the objects of his desire; and we can never hope for that which we regard with dislike and aversion. He who has no enjoyment in communion with God on earth, has not a heart to enjoy heaven. If to such a man the Sabbath of a day be a weariness, what would be the Sabbath of eternity ?

It is a striking thought of the poet,* that the man who has attained his seventieth year has lived *ten years of Sabbaths*. Let all my hearers remember, that in every period of life there is the same proportion. Let them seriously ask themselves, how they have been using the sabbatical time with which a long-suffering God has been favouring them ; and what account they will be able to give of it

* Graham.

to Him, in the day of final account and retribution. If hitherto you have been wasting it, O waste no more of it;—not another hour;—it is precious. Let this very day be the beginning of a change. Now, even now, let your preparation commence for the everlasting Sabbath. And how, do you ask me, is it to be begun? There is but one way:—by coming to God, as sinners conscious of guilt and impurity, feeling their helplessness, and seeking fitness for heaven, through the peace-speaking blood of the Lamb, and the renewing grace of the Spirit. You must, with entire self-renunciation, make HIM the ground of your confidence, who " finished his work, and entered into his rest;" and you must look to the fulness that is in Him, for the spiritual supplies that are needful to " stablish you, and keep you from evil," and to bring you to his heavenly kingdom.

And, Christians,—mark *your* duty. Mark the apostle's practical improvement of this subject to you. It is contained in Heb. iv. 9—11. " There remaineth, therefore, a Sabbath-keeping to the people of God; for he that is entered into his rest, he also hath ceased from his own works, as God did from his. Let us labour, therefore, to enter into that rest," (the rest into which Jesus has entered) " lest any man fall after the same example of unbelief." And what is this labour? It is " the work of faith:"—it is " the labour of love." It is the persevering effort of practical service, of which faith and love are the principles and springs. It is not the labour of proud self-confidence, as if heaven were to be won by any merits of your own; it is the labour of humble dependance on grace, through the merits of the Redeemer. Your faith worketh by love.

You "live to him who died for you, and rose again;" knowing, on the same authority, both that "by grace ye are saved," and that "without holiness no man shall see the Lord." The labour, and the final result, are both described, in animated terms, by the apostle Peter:*—"And besides this, giving all diligence, add to your faith, fortitude; and to fortitude, knowledge; and to knowledge, temperance; and to temperance, patience; and to patience, godliness; and to godliness, brotherly-kindness; and to brotherly-kindness, charity. For if these things be in you, and abound, they make you that ye shall neither be idle, nor unfruitful, in the knowledge of our Lord Jesus Christ. But he that lacketh these things is blind, and cannot see afar off, and hath forgotten that he was purged from his old sins. Wherefore the rather, brethren, give diligence to make your calling and election sure; for if ye do these things, ye shall never fall: for so an entrance shall be ministered unto you abundantly into the everlasting kingdom of our Lord and Saviour Jesus Christ." There, in that "everlasting kingdom," the preparatory Sabbaths of earth shall be exchanged for the perfect rest, and purity, and joy, of the eternal Sabbath of heaven. And the greater the difficulties, the severer the trials, the fiercer the conflicts, through which they have passed in this world, the sweeter, from the power of contrast, will be the experience of that endless rest. Rest is sweet to the labouring man after the fatigues of a toilsome day:—rest is sweet to the soldier, when peace returns, after the hardships and perils of a long and har-

* 2 Pet. i. 5—11.

assing campaign :—so will the rest of heaven be sweet to the laborious servant and faithful soldier of Jesus Christ, when, having "fought a good fight, and finished his course, and kept the faith," he "enters into peace." The remembrance of the toils and dangers, the sufferings and sorrows of time, will contribute to give an enhanced zest to the repose of eternity. "What are these which are arrayed in white robes? and whence came they?—These are they who came out of great tribulation, and have washed their robes and made them white in the blood of the Lamb. Therefore are they before the throne of God, and serve him day and night in his temple : and he that sitteth on the throne shall dwell among them. They shall hunger no more, neither thirst any more; neither shall the sun light on them, nor any heat. For the Lamb, which is in the midst of the throne, shall feed them, and shall lead them unto living fountains of waters : and God shall wipe away all tears from their eyes."*

* Rev. vii. 13—17.

FINIS.

R. Khull, Printer, 55, Virginia Street.

9 780243 889754